La Lucha for Cuba

La Lucha for Cuba

Religion and Politics
on the Streets of Miami

Miguel A. De La Torre

UNIVERSITY OF CALIFORNIA PRESS

Berkeley / Los Angeles / London

University of California Press
Berkeley and Los Angeles, California
University of California Press, Ltd.
London, England

Library of Congress Cataloging-in-Publication Data
De La Torre, Miguel A.
    La lucha for Cuba : religion and politics on the streets of Miami / Miguel
A. De La Torre.
        p.   cm.
    Includes bibliographical references and index.
    ISBN 0-520-23526-6 (alk. paper) — ISBN 0-520-23852-4 (pbk. : alk. paper)
1. Cuban Americans—Florida—Miami—Politics and government.
2. Cuban Americans—Florida—Miami—Religion.   3. Cuban Americans—
Florida—Miami—Social conditions.   4. Exiles—Florida—Miami—
Political activity.   5. Exiles—Religious life—Florida—Miami.   6. Exiles—
Florida—Miami—Social conditions.   7. Christianity and politics—
Florida—Miami.   8. Oppression (Psychology)—Political aspects—
Florida—Miami.   9. Miami (Fla.)—Politics and government.   10. Miami
(Fla.)—Religious life and customs.   I. Title.
F319.M6 D4   2003
305.868'72910759381—dc21   2002015443

Manufactured in the United States of America

11 10 09 08 07 06 05 04 03
10 9 8 7 6 5 4 3 2 1

The paper used in this publication meets the minimum requirements of
ANSI/NISO Z39.48—1992 (R 1997) (*Permanence of Paper*).♾

This book is dedicated to the memory of Pachicho from the previous generation. While we may disagree politically, his selfless courage to fight la lucha *has won my respect.*

It is also dedicated to the future generation, specifically Sophia, Lucas, and Roman. May they never forget their heritage or their lineage.

El vino, de plátano; y si sale agrio, ¡es nuestro vino!

José Martí

Contents

List of Illustrations — xi

List of Abbreviations — xiii

Preface — xv

1. An *Ajiaco* Christianity — 1

2. *La Lucha:* The Religion of Miami — 26

3. Psalm 137: Constructing Cuban Identity while in Babylon — 52

4. Machismo: Creating Structures of Oppression — 81

5. The End of the Elián Saga: The Continuation of *La Lucha* — 118

Notes — 141

References — 161

Index — 171

Illustrations

Praying for Elián	2
Elián and Jesus	6
A human cross	8
Cuba in bondage	12
Guerrilla training camps	44
Mártires de la lucha	46
Protesting Bernardo Benes	50
The 1971 Cuban airlift	63
·Cuban rafters	67
Elián's home as museum	119
Closing the Port of Miami	132
Los Van Van protest	134

Abbreviations

CANF	Cuban American National Foundation
CIA	Central Intelligence Agency
CBC	Christian Base Communities
CFC	Center for a Free Cuba
FACE	Facts about Cuban Exiles
ICCAS	Institute of Cuba and Cuban-American Studies
INS	Immigration and Naturalization Service
KKKK	Ku Klux Klan Kubano
OC	Martí, José. 1963–1973. *Obras Completas*. 27 vols. La Habana: Editorial Nacional de Cuba.
PIC	El Partido Independiente de Color (The Independent Party of Color)
SALAD	Spanish American League against Discrimination
UMAP	Military Units for Assistance to Production

Preface

The suggestion that an Exilic Cuban religious expression based on hatred exists is unsettling for many Miami Cubans, who demand absolute conformity in thought in order to present a united front against the "forces of evil." Criticism of the Miami Cuban community is interpreted as support of the Castro regime. Anyone who criticizes the community's normative attitude toward the present regime in La Habana runs the risk of being labeled a communist and ostracized. Nevertheless, influenced by the writings of the Cuban father of liberation, José Martí, who always fought against injustices, even when the abusers were his own people, I stand against all structures that perpetuate oppression, even when those structures benefit my own community. Consideration of how one's own social position masks oppressive structures is a foundational precept of any theology of liberation. Thus personal concerns for my community in Miami, and for my homeland on the island, force me to gaze intently on my people in the hope of raising unspoken issues.

My hatred for Fidel Castro has been ingrained in me since childhood. From a very young age, I have considered Castro the earthly personification of Satan. My earliest memories are of extreme poverty in New York City, where I recall my parents personally blaming Castro for our plight. My best friend's father was executed by the Castro regime, and many friends of my parents met a similar fate. My own father, arrested and awaiting execution, barely escaped with his life, fleeing Cuba with only the clothes on his back. Others whom I know and respect spent decades in Cuba's prisons. I recall a friend telling me about an *abuelita* (grand-

mother) who every morning walked through her house appearing to recite the rosary. In reality, with each bead she whispered, "God damn you
to hell, Fidel." My own grandparents died without my ever seeing them,
and I remain separated from family members I've never met. My family
has always taken pride in being among those who never supported Castro during his rise to power. For me, as for most Exilic Cubans, hating
Castro is as natural as loving our children. In fact, this hatred has taken
on religious proportions. For many Cubans in the Miami community,
everything good, holy, pure, true, and sacred is the antithesis of Castro
and his regime. Belonging is measured by the intensity of righteous indignation directed toward Castro. In fact, I propose that from these deep
emotions a religion indigenous to the Miami Cuban experience has developed.

The overall purpose of this book is to unmask the not-so-well-hidden
intra-Hispanic structures of oppression that operate within the Cuban
Exilic community of Miami, Florida. Through the lens of religion and
culture, I analyze how this once-marginalized Latina/o group rose to
power and privilege, distinguishing itself from other Hispanic communities in the United States. I examine the role religion played in this as-
cension, and how Miami Cubans have deployed a religious expression
called *la lucha* (the struggle) to justify the power and privilege they have
achieved. Within the context of *la lucha,* I pay close attention to the religious dichotomy created between the "children of light" (Exilic Cubans)
and the "children of darkness" (Resident Cubans). I close by examining
the controversial Elián González custody battle and showing how the
cultural construction of *la lucha* has become a distinctly Miami-style spirituality that makes *el exilio* (the exile) the basis for religious reflection, understanding, and practice.

Hispanics throughout the United States have been historically forced to
contend with poverty and marginality. Consequently, many U.S.
Latino/a scholars of religion construct a religious perspective from the
margins of U.S. society, that is, from the viewpoint of the disenfranchised. Yet for Exilic Cubans in Miami, living at the margins is hardly a
reality. The recent international custody battle for the five-year-old
Cuban boy Elián González showed how a once-oppressed Latino/a
group is much stronger and more influential with regard to U.S. foreign
policy initiatives than probably any other Hispanic group. Yet the
strength of the Miami Cuban community is not limited to its effects on
foreign policy. Since they form a single-issue voting bloc, it could be ar-

gued that Exilic Cubans were paramount in determining the contested 2000 presidential election. How is it that they have been able to achieve positions of power and privilege in the political, economic, and social arena of Miami? How is religion understood and deployed differently among Exilic Cubans in Miami? These two questions are related, and I intend to answer them in these pages. The Miami Exilic Cuban community serves as an example of what can occur when a minority group takes control of societal power structures without dismantling those structures.

Intra-Hispanic oppression within the Cuban community traditionally has been ignored by Latino/a religious scholars because the phenomenon contradicts their liberationist motif. In this book I examine those modes of oppression by employing an ethnographic methodology. While the text deals with issues of Christian ethics, specifically intra-Cuban race, class, and gender oppression, my approach comes from a cultural studies perspective. I will show how Miami politics create oppressive structures that are then legitimized as religious.

To set the stage, the first chapter, "An *Ajiaco* Christianity," briefly reviews the events surrounding the 1999 Elián saga. The chapter then proceeds to lay out the book's overall thesis. Additionally, in this chapter I situate myself within the overall Exilic Cuban experience, specifically my personal perspective based on research, academic training, and life experience. The next chapter, "*La Lucha:* The Religion of Miami," reviews the religious, historical, and political events that led to a large exodus of Cubans to Miami. Special attention is given to their socioeconomic position and the role their cultural capital played in their eventual capture of the city's power structures. Both a history of the development of the Exilic community and how that development influenced the establishment of religious beliefs are explored. The chapter concludes that the religious expression of the Miami Cuban community, an expression I will be calling *la lucha,* fuses and confuses religiosity with political power.

The third chapter, "Psalm 137: Constructing Cuban Identity while in Babylon," explores ethnicity as a construct designed to protect the power and privilege achieved by Exilic Cubans. By juxtaposing the biblical story of the Babylonian captivity as found in Psalm 137 with the experience of Exilic Cubans, the chapter debunks the construct of Exilic Cuban ethnicity. The religious dimensions of different political battles are explored to show the dichotomy established between the Exilics (good) and Residents/Castro (evil). I review different case studies of Miami events to show how the overall political goals of the community have become a holy war, and what happens to those deemed infidels. It is not the intention of this chapter to provide the reader with a theological perspective; rather it aims to use religious symbols existing among Cubans to elucidate how their power acquires religious proportions.

In the fourth chapter, "Machismo: Creating Structures of Oppression," I explore the intra-oppression the Exilic Cuban community tries to mask. I do so by introducing the multidimensional aspect of this oppression, maintaining that machismo fully includes sexism, heterosexism, racism, ethnocentrism, and classism. The chapter elucidates how all forms of oppression are identical in their attempt to domesticate the nonelite male Other by transferring effeminate characteristics onto him. This paradigm of machismo demonstrates how Miami structures of oppression operate. The final chapter, "The End of the Elián Saga: The Continuation of *La Lucha*," explores how the special relationship between the United States and Cuba influences how Exilic Cubans are perceived in radically different ways than are other Latino/a groups. Moreover, the chapter will explore how this perception influences the Exilic Cuban identity in what can be called the beginning of a postexilic Miami.

I would be remiss if I did not take the time to thank those who have helped me with this book. I specifically wish to thank Dr. Gastón Espinosa of the Hispanic Churches in American Public Life for the writing grant they awarded, which allowed me to research and explore the Elián saga in greater detail. I am also grateful to Reed Malcolm of the University of California Press, who worked closely with me, for what seemed like an eternity, to give shape to this project. In addition, I am grateful to Dr. Luis Leon for his advice and encouragement while this book was still in its infancy, and to Dr. Laura Pérez, who read the manuscript and provided valuable feedback. Likewise, I offer gratitude to librarian Anthony Guardado at Hope College, who provided countless hours of researching and checking academic sources. My colleagues in the religion department at Hope College also have earned my gratitude for providing suggestions and insight on portions of this manuscript. It is an honor to work with such scholars. Additionally, Jonathan Schakel, who proofread the text, deserves my appreciation for his faithfulness to the goals of this project. As always, my wife, Deborah, and children, Victoria and Vincent, deserve special thanks for their unwavering belief in my work, even when I lacked the faith to continue.

Finally, I give special thanks to those first Exilic Cubans from my family who came as adults to this country, specifically my parents, Miguel and Mirta, my uncle Pachicho, and *mi tía* Adela. They are part of a generation that faced unbearable hardships as foreigners in a strange land. And while we may differ in some of our views concerning our homeland, their *lucha* has profoundly influenced my life. But I also look to the future, to the next generation of Exilic Cubans in my family, specifically Ricky and Tortica. I hope and pray they will always be as proud as I am of our predecessors.

CHAPTER I

An *Ajiaco* Christianity

On Thanksgiving Day, 1999, while the United States feasted on the traditional turkey dinner, a small Cuban boy of five was found off the coast of Fort Lauderdale clinging to an inner tube. Within a few days, Elián González's name became nationally known, as the boy emerged at the center of a furious custody battle between the Exilic and Resident Cuban communities.[1] Surrounding Elián's new temporary Miami home, Catholics and Protestants, rich and poor, young and old gathered to pray. Signs written in blue beseeched the nation to "Pray for Elián." Exilic Cubans held hands and surrounded the house to recite the rosary. These same worshipers were prepared to unclasp their praying hands and lock arms to prevent the U.S. government from taking Elián. While the world focused on the unfolding political saga of this child, a religious subtext developed. Some worshipers claimed to have seen the Virgin Mary hovering over Elián's Miami home. Others referred to Elián as the miracle child, or Miami's Jesus. Across the street lived a santera, a believer in the African-based Cuban religion known as Santería. For her, Elián was a child of Ochún, the quasi-deity of the sea. She and other followers of Santería believed that Ochún had spared Elián's life to bear witness that she is still the mother of all Cubans.

The Elián story illustrates how religion, politics, and power merge within the Miami Exilic community. The focus of this book is not to determine what Elián's fate should have been, or to review the legal and political battles that surrounded his case. Rather, it is to explore how the powerful Exilic Cuban community in Miami formed a religious response

Praying for Elián: Supporters of Elián form a human chain around his Miami home. When rumors spread that INS officials were en route to the house, supporters locked arms to prevent their passage. Photograph © Al Diaz/*The Miami Herald*.

to the Elián story, and how that response unconsciously masks a political agenda designed to maintain and increase the power base of that community. Along the way, it attempts to understand how a community of fewer than a million Exilic Cubans amassed the power to influence the strongest government in the world, confounding for months the U.S. endeavor to return Elián to Cuba.

The Unfolding Saga

What actually occurred in the Straits of Florida before Elián's rescue at sea remains a mystery. According to the official reports, a seventeen-foot aluminum boat left Cardenas, Cuba, for the United States on November 21, 1999, at 4:30 A.M. Stories that Elián's mother was seeking freedom for her child notwithstanding, it appears she probably left Cuba to follow her boyfriend, who had planned the boat trip. On board were fourteen individuals, one of them Elián. Hours before the boy was rescued, the boat capsized off the Florida Keys. Except for Elián and two adults, all the others drowned, including his mother, Elizabeth Brotons. Two Broward County fishermen, cousins, were out on the water when they spotted an inner tube bobbing in the ocean, shortly after 9 A.M. Thanksgiving morning. When he saw a hand move from within the tube, one of the fishermen jumped into the ocean and pulled Elián out of the water. Exhausted by his ordeal, Elián was taken to the hospital for medical treatment. He was released the following day, and the Immigration and Naturalization Service (INS) gave temporary custody of the boy to Lazaro González, the child's great-uncle, who lives in Miami. This ensured that the boy would be cared for while the agency determined his immigration status. The next day, November 27, from his home in Cardenas, the boy's father, Juan Miguel González, demanded the return of his son. With that, Elián was thrust to the epicenter of a fierce political tug-of-war between the Exilic and Resident Cuban communities.

Four days after Elián was pulled from the water, on November 29, he literally became the poster child for the Exilic community. Because it was believed that Fidel Castro might attend the World Trade Organization meeting that early December in Seattle, posters and flyers were rapidly produced with a picture of Elián on a stretcher under the caption "Another Child Victim of Fidel Castro." Elián's political appeal as a symbol of opposition to the Castro regime was obvious. Yet his true value to the community became apparent only with his transformation into a religious symbol. This rapid metamorphosis was not the Machiavellian formulation of a few individuals with political power, but rather the cumulative effort of the entire Exilic Cuban community in its attempt to comprehend the will of a God who had seemed so silent during the forty years of their "captivity" in Miami.

As a sacred symbol, Elián merged the religious and political hopes of the Miami Cuban community. According to Father Francisco Santana of Our Lady of Charity Shrine, "[Exilic Cubans] were making the connection that this child was like a sign that was sent to us by God, that some-how this was connected to the end of communism in Cuba" (Bikel 2001). How could Elián have become a deific symbol? Sacred language being rooted in symbols and myths, anything secular (a river, stone, star, ani-mal, or human being) can be transformed into something sacred, a marker pointing to something greater than itself (Eliade 1963, 11). Reli-gious people, such as prophets or apostles, or religious objects, such as totems, are not the only or even the supreme representations of Divinity. Anything or anyone can reveal aspects of the Divine (Eliade 1957, 20–65). And Elián, as deific symbol, not only reflected the sacred, but he also came into being in a sacred manner.

Elián's physicians insisted that the child failed to demonstrate any physical evidence of prolonged exposure to the sea, concluding that the boy was in the water for hours, not days. Nevertheless, as the story spread, his few hours in the ocean became two and a half days, in turn raising the question, How can a child survive that long, alone, in the sea? The answer, clearly, was, Only by a miracle from God. As the battle over Elián's immigration status grew fierce, his symbolic worth increased as the Exilic community spoke of him in deeply religious terms. An uncon-firmed report, circulated widely within the community, recounted the tale of dolphins circling Elián's inner tube, protecting him from sharks. Dolphins, in the early Christian Church, symbolized salvation: not only was Elián saved, but now he had come to save. Even the Midrash (Jew-ish rabbinical commentaries) contains stories of how dolphins saved some Israelite children who lagged behind while crossing the parted Red Sea during their flight from Egyptian bondage.

"He's a miracle," said Maria Rodriguez, fifty-five, while attending the annual Three Kings Day Parade, a celebration of the three wise men bringing gifts to the baby Jesus. "The fact that he made it for two days, with dolphins circling around him—that proves he's a miracle." At his great-uncle's modest home, religious candles lined the sidewalk as the Ex-ilic community began to compare Elián to Jesus.[2] The day of the parade, January 9, *El Nuevo Herald,* the Spanish version of *The Miami Herald,* also linked Elián to the baby Jesus in its headline "The Three Magi Kings at the Feet of Elián."[3]

The Church was even more open in its comparison of Elián to Christ. During a prayer vigil held on March 29, the clergy assured the crowd that God was on the side of the Exilic Cubans. "In Cuba, some people have made Elián a symbol of the new Che [Guevara], so it is not so unusual that some people in Miami are seeing him as the new Christ," said one of the prayer vigil organizers, the Reverend Gustavo Miyares of Immaculate Conception Church. María Ester Fernández, another organizer of the multiple prayer vigils in front of Elián's house, best summed up the convictions of the Exilic community when she said, "We continue praying that Elián stays, because God wants it. . . . Just as Christ died for us and on the third day was resurrected, so will the Cuban people be resurrected."[4]

Within a short time, the community began to point out that, like Jesus, Elián arrived just weeks before Christmas, at the end of the millennium, on the day on which thanksgiving is offered to God. Even the year 2000, the sixth millennium since the supposed creation of the earth, turned Elián, like Jesus, into a symbol of hope. Along with likening Elián to Christ, the community also believed him to be protected by the Virgin Mary. As many as forty people attested to seeing the image of the Virgin on the glass door of TotalBank in Little Havana. She appeared, it was believed, to protest Elián's return to Cuba. The bank, on Twenty-seventh Avenue, quickly became a pilgrimage stop for the multitudes that came with flowers. Some rubbed their babies against the windowpane for good luck.[5] One woman reported seeing a vision of the Virgin with child surrounded by two giant dolphins.[6] These stories are reminiscent of the widespread Cuban tale of drowning fishermen being saved by la Caridad del Cobre (the Virgin of Charity), Cuba's patron saint. Even la Virgen de Guadalupe, believed to have appeared to an indigenous Mexican peasant more than four hundred years ago, made an appearance as a spot on a mirror in the bedroom where the boy slept.[7]

The Exilic community also created religious rituals to bind the sacred to the secular. On Mother's Day, May 14, 2000, dozens of women and children, *vestidos de luto* (dressed in mourning black), gathered by the seawall behind the Shrine of Our Lady of Charity to honor Elián's mother. A prayer service was held, culminating in the tossing of roses into a makeshift raft. Ana Rodriguez, thirty-five, a mother of three who participated in the event said, "It's for her and all the mothers that have died for freedom. Not only Cuban mothers."[8] Having turned Elián's mother into a martyr, the community continued to honor her memory by naming a street after her (87 Court in Hialeah Gardens) and erecting a shrine to her at the Bay of Pigs memorial on Thirteenth Avenue in Little Havana.

As the sacred and political occupied the same space, the boundaries between the two became blurred in the minds of the supporters who gathered before Elián's house to pray. Jorge Mas Santos, the chairperson of the Cuban American National Foundation (CANF), the most powerful

Elián and Jesus: Supporter Pedro Lorenzo holds an enlarged
copy of an *Ideal* magazine cover, which shows Elián cradling
the baby Jesus. The question is, Which one is the Christ? Photograph © Al Diaz/*The Miami Herald*.

Exilic Cuban political lobbying organization in the United States, helped
complete this fusion when he said, "Praying in a religious ceremony is the
best way to show our support."[9] Despite the fact that the official Catholic Church hierarchy of Miami took a position of neutrality, citing "moral
uncertainty," local priests became major players in the unfolding drama.[10]
The Reverend Francisco Santana, of the Shrine of Our Lady of Charity,

literally brought the church into Elián's Miami home. Six nights a week, he celebrated a private mass for Elián's family, and while not specifically praying for Elián to stay—so as not to contradict the Church—he led prayers asking for God to touch Elián's father, Juan Miguel, so that he could love as a father should despite any political pressure received from the Castro regime.[11] Albeit in a roundabout way, those gathered essentially prayed for Elián to stay.

As Miami's miracle child, Elián is credited with forging new ties between Catholic priests and mainline evangelical Protestant pastors, traditional rivals in both Miami and La Habana. Father Santana and fellow Catholic priests, along with Protestant ministers, made ecumenical history when they officially turned the protest for justice in front of Elián's house into a daily vigil. Santana proclaimed, "We are transforming, as of this moment, the cries demanding justice in front of Elián's house into a permanent prayer vigil, so that God can complete the miracle that He himself begun."[12] Six Catholic priests and six mainline Protestant pastors (viewed as the twelve disciples of Christ) took turns leading the nightly prayer vigil. On Fridays, they led joint prayer services. Presbyterian pastor Manuel Salabarria said it best: "We have a common ground, a common interest, and a common purpose." To maintain this alliance, the Reverend Santana put aside the devotion to Mary so as not to "offend" the Protestants.[13] During one of these massive prayer vigils, tens of thousands of Exilic Cubans marched down Calle Ocho (Eighth Street) in the shape of a cross, as both Catholic priests and Protestant ministers joined forces in proclaiming the miracle child.[14] As a sacred symbol, Elián had brought temporary healing to centuries of religious rivalry, surely a task beyond the ability of mere mortals.

Using Elián as a symbol was not limited to Catholics and Protestants. Practitioners of Santería also saw religious symbolism in the boy. One of the side stories that emerged during the Elián saga centered on a note that Lazaro González, the boy's great-uncle, wrote to Elián's grandmothers. He entrusted the note to Sister Jeanne O'Laughlin, host to the boy's grandmothers in late January 2000 during their trip to the United States. Sister O'Laughlin forgot to pass the note on, finding it in her pocket days later. The note warned that Castro wanted the child so he could make a Santería sacrifice of him. This concern was based on the most frequently repeated rumor on the streets of Little Havana: that Castro had been forewarned of a child saved by dolphins in the sea who would overthrow his regime and that he had to acquire the boy to prevent the fulfillment of the prophecy. Elián (Jesus) was being sought by Castro (Herod), who

A human cross: On the evening of March 29, 1999, tens of thousands of Exilic Cubans holding candles, flashlights, and glow sticks marched through the streets of Miami, forming a flickering human cross. Photograph © Raul Rubiera/*The Miami Herald*.

wanted to kill the messiah threatening his rule. Even Miami's auxiliary bishop, Agustin Roman, was quick to make the comparison between Castro and Herod after reading the Scriptures about Herod wanting Jesus killed to preserve his reign.[15]

According to both Resident and Exilic practitioners of Santería, Castro participates in this Afro-Cuban religion, even traveling to Africa to be initiated into its mysteries. Yet the annual oracles indicate that somehow Castro had offended Elegguá, the first and most powerful *orisha* (quasi-deity). Elegguá is depicted as a child, and some see Elián as the child whom Elegguá had chosen to overthrow Castro. This, Exilic devotees of Santería believe, is behind Castro's obsession in having Elián returned.[16]

Some believe Castro's obsession may be rooted in his own experience with his estranged wife, Mirta Diaz-Balart de Núñez, who left for the United States with their five-year-old son, Fidelito, against Castro's wishes. While Castro was imprisoned in the early 1950s for his revolutionary activities, his divorced wife, unbeknown to Castro, brought his son to Miami to be raised in the United States. Castro was incensed that his Miami relatives and political enemies, the Diaz-Balarts, would be raising his son as an Exilic Cuban. He vowed to regain his son and his honor, regardless of the consequences. Eventually, Castro convinced his estranged wife to allow him to see his son while Castro was exiled in Mexico, promising to return the child to his mother within a few weeks. The mother agreed, but fearing Castro would not keep his promise, she had Fidelito kidnapped and returned to Florida. Eventually, Mirta Diaz-Balart and son returned to La Habana, where they lived for five years, but when the Castro government took a more pronounced Marxist turn, Mirta left for Madrid without Fidelito. Some claimed he chose to stay with his father; others insist that Castro would not let his son leave the island. Fidelito would eventually study in the Soviet Union, becoming a geophysicist, marry a Russian (whom he eventually divorced), and serve as the head of Cuba's nuclear power program. Ironically, Miami Congressman Lincoln Diaz-Balart, nephew of Mirta and cousin of Fidelito, was one of the major advocates of keeping Elián in Miami. Could it be that the Elián custody battle was motivated by family events that had occurred some forty years earlier?

Regardless of Castro's true motivations, the fact remains that he wanted Elián returned. "We will move heaven and earth to get the child back!" he exclaimed during a TV interview (Bikel 2001). Yet more than forty years of fighting *la lucha* against Castro has conditioned Miami Cubans to oppose blindly whatever Castro wants. Because Castro publicly demanded something, the Exilic community felt compelled to take the contrary position: if Castro wants Elián, then he simply cannot have him. Spiting Castro by keeping Elián in Miami became more important than the child's welfare. Father Santana, confidant to Elián's Miami relatives, quoted Lazaro González, the boy's great-uncle, as stating, "to send Elián back to Cuba is to send him to hell. . . . I truly believe . . . that it was even better for the sharks to have eaten Elián in the waters than to go back to a country in which he's going to be manipulated by the system, in which he's going to be—they are going to teach him everything that are really in contradiction with human nature" (Bikel 2001).

Judaism has also been used to show the significance of Elián as the miracle child. Some even claimed that Elián was the linear heir to Moses.[17] Roberto Sánchez, sixty-five, an Exilic Cuban Jew, waved Israel's flag in front of Elián's Miami home, saying, "Elián is the Moses of the year 2000. This is a sacred child, so the flag of the Holy Land is appropriate here, because this street is holy land."[18] Like Moses, Elián was drawn from the waters, escaping the Pharaoh (Castro). The hopes were that, like Moses, Elián would lead his people to the promised land (Cuba). One Exilic Cuban magazine pictured Elián on its back cover with the caption "A Cuban Moses." Christian Exilic Cubans have even quoted the Talmud to justify the struggle to keep Elián in the States: "To save a human is to save the entire world."[19]

One of Elián's lawyers, Spencer Eig, an Orthodox Jew who made frequent television appearances, was fond of comparing Elián to "a Jew from communist Russia making it to Israel and then having to be sent back."[20] Rabbi Solomon Schiff, vice president of the Rabbinical Association of Greater Miami, compared the Elián saga to that of the *St. Louis,* a ship that in 1937, while carrying 937 Jewish refugees from Germany, was turned away from Cuba and the United States. To Rabbi Schiff, Elián represents the immense value of human life. Schiff points out that Christians, Jews, and Muslims (and I would add santeros/as) have identified with Elián for different reasons, but with the same idea: "Every human being is like an only book which deserves respect, dignity, and a quality of life."[21] The name Elián, a combination of Elizabeth and Juan — the names of his parents — has been misread by the religious faithful as Elías (Elijah). For Jews, Elián is the prophet who fought the false prophets of darkness. For Christians, Elián is the name those present at the Crucifixion thought Jesus called out when he said, "Eloi, Eloi, lama sabactani?" (My God, my God, why have you forsaken me?). For Muslims, Elián is the messenger who comes to warn the people of evil while bringing salvation.

History is simply repeating itself, according to Santiago Aranegui, professor of antiquity and history at Florida International University. Every new age occurs when a "chosen" person sets out on a grand, earth-changing mission. These epochs are usually announced by the appearance of a child, as with Moses and Jesus. For Adventist pastor Charles Vento, an Exilic Cuban, Elián, like the prophets of old, has the divine power to change the destiny of nations and to liberate oppressed people.[22] Mirta Rondon, sixty-one, who led a chant in front of Elián's Miami home, believed Elián to be a messiah: "I have a feeling that he will be the one. He will be the one who brings change to the history of Cuba."[23] In the streets of Miami, protestors routinely shouted, "Elián is king of the Cubans."[24] Exilic Cuban superstars like Gloria Estéfan, Willy Chirino, Arturo Sandoval, and Andy Garcia made pilgrimages to Elián's house. The Fox Family Channel produced the first Elián movie, which aired in September 2000.

Why all the fuss over Elián? Because Exilic Cubans read their story in the story of Elián. Frank Calzón, executive director of the Center for a Free Cuba (CFC) in Washington, D.C., put into words the feelings of the whole community: "Each one of us sees himself in that small child, in the suffering of his tragedy."[25] According to Silvia Iriondo, president of Mothers Against Repression, "In that child, we saw all the pain and all the suffering of forty-one years. Elián symbolizes the pain of the Cuban family, the Cuban families that throughout forty-one years of oppression have been divided by one man and one system" (Bikel 2001). Elián represents the ultimate sacrifice of a parent seeking liberty for their child. Many Cubans gathered at Elián's house somehow to prevent what they themselves experienced. The story of Margarita Aguiar, fifty-six, a Miami-Dade Community College counselor who took time off work to stand before Elián's house, is typical of those who came to pray. She recalls her brother being shot when Castro's soldiers took over her parochial school and invaded her church in February 1961. She states that her father placed her on a plane, exchanging being with her for her freedom, the same choice she wants for Elián. "He was a father who loved me enough to say, 'I'll never see her again, but she will live in freedom.' "[26]

Part of the Exilic Cuban collective memory is the *Pedro Pan* (Peter Pan) flights, a massive Catholic operation that removed more than fourteen thousand children from Cuba during the early 1960s. Even with the importance of the family unit, since the Revolution, Exilic Cubans have subordinated the parent-child relationship to "saving" the child from communism. Ernesto Betancourt, founding director of Radio Martí, the station responsible for broadcasting U.S. propaganda into Cuba, explains, "We [Exilic Cubans] see that the repression of a regime still pursues the child, the world only sees that he still has a father."[27]

During the last days of the custody standoff, when it appeared as if the battle to keep Elián in Miami was lost, the community continued to expect God to perform a miracle. When a flock of birds in V formation flew over Elián's Miami home on April 13 at 2:40 A.M., it was immediately taken as a sign from God. This sign notwithstanding, in the predawn hours of April 22, 2000, U.S. federal marshals raided Elián's home, and, in less than three minutes, removed him from the house, eventually reuniting him with his father, who was waiting in Washington, D.C. His forceful removal occurred on Holy Saturday, and the religious symbolism was not lost on the Exilic community. Pastor Humberto Cruz illustrated the connection by stating, "They say in the Scriptures that a shadow fell on Jerusalem when Jesus was crucified. A shadow has once again fallen, this time on our city [of Miami]."[28]Again, Catholic and Protestant ministers joined forces, believing that unless they came together, the Exilic community would be lost. They denounced the gov-

Cuba in bondage: Lisset Verra personifies a shackled Cuba in 1975 during the José Martí celebrations. Courtesy of the Historical Museum of Southern Florida.

ernment's sacrilege of violating Holy Week and called the community to prayer and peaceful demonstration.

On Easter morning, the day after the raid, congregations throughout South Florida prayed for Elián, his Miami family, and the community at large. At St. Juan Bosco, the church Elián's Miami relatives usually attend, eleven-year-old Milena Libertad (whose last name means "liberty"), herself a rafter who came to Miami the previous year, belted out a song she composed about Elián: "If you love me, hear me, Dad. I don't want to go back to Cuba." She brought the church to tears. Concepción Pelaez, seventy-six, summed up the importance of worship when she said, "I cry for the child. The Mass did me good because as we cry, we release our pain."[29] Later that evening, during the evening mass at Our

Lady of Charity shrine, Elián's young cousin, Lazarito Martell, prophesied, to the delight of the three hundred attendants, that Elián would stay in the States. The congregation, carrying prints of Jesus Christ on the cross with his blood dripping down over the island of Cuba, heard the Reverend Santana proclaim, "Elián is staying, and Fidel is leaving." When Elián's Miami family stood before the congregation, the parishioners waved miniature Cuban flags as they burst into the Cuban national anthem.[30] These services, and the events that led up to them, epitomize the merging of the Exilic Cuban political agenda with religious fervor. But when and how did this fusion occur?

A Cuban-Based Religious Experience

The animosity expressed during the Elián saga illustrates that politically speaking, there are basically two Cubas, one *allá* (there) and one *aquí* (here). On the island are revolutionaries who combat any attempt to subjugate Cuba's spirit to U.S. hegemony. In Miami are pro-U.S. capitalists who look to the United States to be the guiding hope in revitalizing a post-Castro Cuba. Owing to these fundamental political, economic, and ideological differences, the Cuban community has become a people divided against itself. The Cuban individual, Exilic or Resident, who chooses to address her or his community from any perspective other than the official one would be suspect of secretly abetting the opposing camp and might only succeed in uniting both groups in condemning her or his initiative.

The Resident Cuban calls you a traitor, a *gusano* (worm), for leaving. The Exilic Cuban calls you a traitor, *un comunista,* for saying anything about the Castro government that falls short of a condemnation. But in Miami worse things than being called a communist happen: for a Miami Exilic Cuban even to suggest any positive accomplishment of the Revolution invites violence. In 1979 Carlos Muñíz was assassinated in Puerto Rico for his leadership role with the Antonio Maceo Brigade, an organization helping to build the Revolution, composed mainly of Exilic Cuban college students who supported the social justice goals of the Revolution, the end of the United States blockade, the normalization of relationships, the independence of Puerto Rico, and the U.S. civil rights movement. Luciano Negrín, also a member of the Antonio Maceo Brigade and a prominent dialogue supporter, was killed in Union City, New Jersey, that same year. Ramón Donestevez, a Hialeah boat builder, was assassinated because of his suspected ties to the Castro government.

Exilic leader José de la Torriente was murdered in 1973 on suspicions of embezzling funds from his Cuban liberation organization. José Peruyero, Exilic war hero and president of the Brigade 2506 Veteran Association, was killed in 1976 for condemning Brigade 2506 veterans who participated in terrorist activities. Three months later, Emilio Milián, a radio commentator, had his legs blown off in a car bombing for criticizing Exilic paramilitary politics. From 1973 to 1976, more than one hundred bombs went off in Miami. Because these events occurred in the 1970s, the tendency of those recounting Exilic Cuban history is to insist that such terrorist actions were limited to that era.

Yet in 1989 alone, eighteen bombs exploded in the homes and businesses of Exilic Cubans who called for an approach to Cuba contrary to the official hard line. From May to October 1996, twelve bombs exploded in Miami for the same reasons. These actions led the FBI to name Miami the capital of United States terrorism. Recently, the archdiocese of Miami received numerous bomb threats for collecting and sending emergency relief to Resident Cubans suffering catastrophic damage when hurricane Lili directly hit the island in October 1996. (Ironically, the aid was returned by the Castro administration because the word *exilic* and the phrase "love conquers all" were written on the cans and boxes.) The Cuban Museum of Art and Culture in Miami received bomb threats for exhibiting the works of Tomas Sánchez, a Resident Cuban, which led Americas Watch, a human rights organization, to title their report on Miami's lack of freedom of expression "Dangerous Dialogue."

Cubans in La Habana are likewise silenced. Resident Cubans who criticize the present regime from within or who become active in human rights movements are accused of being agents of the United States and are subsequently jailed for violating laws that prohibit the right to assemble.[31] Four such dissidents, Marta Beatriz Roque, Vladimiro Roca, Felix Bonne, and René Gómez Manzano, were detained for criticizing Cuba's one-party system. On March 15, 1999, Roca, son of the late Cuban Communist Party Leader Blas Roca, was sentenced to five years in prison. He was released months before his sentence expired as a gesture of "goodwill" toward Jimmy Carter, who visited the island in 2002. Both lawyer Manzano and engineer Bonne were sentenced to four years, and economist Roque received a sentence of three and a half years. All defendants had an opportunity to avoid prison terms if they would voluntarily leave the country. They chose to stay.[32] Elizardo Sánchez, head of the Cuban Commission on Human Rights, estimates that 381 political prisoners are in Cuban jails. According to Amnesty International, Cuba has the longest-term political prisoners in the world, and, along with Colombia, was listed as the worst human rights offender in 1999. While a critical sociopolitical analysis of the present Cuban regime may be profitable, it remains beyond the scope of this book.[33]

Relations between these two antagonistic communities notwithstanding, they do share a common religious trajectory that helps to explain the fusing and confusing of religiosity with politics. Unfortunately, in spite of the many excellent Cuban scholarly works currently available, few specifically deal with how the religiosity of Cubans affects, if not determines, the political positions occupied by so many in Miami. Although significant works in the fields of anthropology, sociology, psychology, political science, economics, and history have been written, works on which this book heavily relies, conspicuously missing is a close examination of the Exilic Cuban political dilemma of *el exilio* as a religious response to the existential space of displacement. By religious response, I do not mean any specific religious or spiritual action Exilic Cubans *ought* to take to be faithful to some overall sense of dogma or religious ethics; rather, religion is understood here as a binding substance providing moral justifications for the political actions a given group undertakes. In short, the present Exilic Cuban political culture is itself a reflection of a constructed religious system indigenous to Miami.

The religiosity of Exilic Cubans in Miami determines their social, political, and economic reality through morals—ideals—that justify the Exilic Cubans' worldview. Religious faith becomes a special form of consciousness containing specific consequences for political will. Satisfaction of theological questions is not the ultimate goal. Rather, the longing to answer the unanswerable questions of their alienation (from the *patria* and from compatriots ninety miles away) becomes a religious quest for meaning. The attempt to make sense of an alienation that marks the Exilic Cuban identity creates a sacred space in which Exilic Cubans can grapple with their spiritual need to reconcile with their God and their psychological need to reconcile with their compatriots on the other side of the Florida Straits (De La Torre 2002a, 117–18). Besides the obvious political alienation existing among Cubans, as a people they are also divided along lines of sexism, racism, and classism. Hence, any Cuban religiosity capable of healing the ruptured relationships of Cubans, both Exilic and Resident, must take into account all aspects of their alienation.

To understand better the foundation of this Cuban religiosity, I suggest the term *ajiaco* Christianity.[34] *Ajiaco* is a Cuban stew consisting of different indigenous root vegetables. A native dish, it symbolizes who

Cubans are as a people and how their diverse ethnic backgrounds came to be formed. According to famed Cuban scholar Fernando Ortiz, the Amerindians gave us the *maíz* (corn), *papa* (potato), *malanga* (arum), *boniato* (sweet potato), *yuca* (yucca), and *ají* (pepper). The Spaniards added *calabaza* (pumpkin) and *nabo* (turnip), while the Chinese added spices. The Africans contributed *ñame* (yams). Cubans are, according to Ortiz, "a *mestizaje* [mixture] of kitchens, a *mestizaje* of races, a *mestizaje* of cultures, a dense broth of civilization that bubbles on the stove of the Caribbean."[35] In effect, Cubans are nourished by the combination of all their diverse roots.

Ajiaco symbolizes *cubanidad's* (Cubanness) cultural attempt to find harmony among diverse roots, aspiring to create José Martí's idealized state of a secularized vision of Christian love that is anti-imperialistic, antimilitant, antiracist, moral, and radical.[36] Unlike the North American melting pot, in which all newly arrived immigrants are placed into a vessel where they somehow "cook down" into a new culture that nevertheless remains Eurocentric, the Cuban *ajiaco* retains the unique flavors of its diverse ingredients, which enrich one another. Some ingredients may dissolve completely, while others may remain more distinct. Yet all provide flavor to the simmering stew, which by its very nature is always in a state of flux.

Although the Taíno—the original Amerindians of the Arawakan nation who first inhabited Cuba—left few visible traces of existence after their decimation by the 1600s, they continue to influence Cuban culture, popular memory, and imagination. Runaway slave communities incorporated the cultural influences of the Taínos' dwindling population, reintroducing them to Cuban culture. While all these distinct racial and ethnic groups representing the "ingredients" originated outside the island, they all repopulated the space called Cuba as displaced people. While not belonging, they made a conscious decision to be rooted to that particular land. The decision to belong brought together a mixture, an *ajiaco*, of different cultures. I propose that the metaphor of the Cuban *ajiaco* should form the basis for an authentic religious reality, a *locus theologicus*, from which Cubans approach the world (De La Torre 2002a, 121).[37]

Most Latina/o theologians, however, use the term *mulato* Christianity (when referring to Hispanics from the Caribbean) and/or *mestizo* Christianity (when referring to Hispanics from Mexico and Central and South America) to describe the Hispanic Christian perspective. While the term *mestizo* is mainly used to describe those of Spanish and Amerindian origins, *mulato* connotes a mixture of Spanish and African stock. Yet it is a racist term owing to its association with the word *mule*.[38] The negative connotations associated with the word *mule* carry over to the word *mulato,* regardless of the efforts made by Exilic Cuban religious scholars to construct a more positive definition. Because of its inability to reproduce itself, the mule is sterile; yet any religious understanding constructed from the Cuban perspective requires fecundity, one reason I consider the metaphor of the *ajiaco* to be so apt. I still recall from childhood that whenever my mother made an *ajiaco,* she would comment on its hearty qualities by stating, *"Hice un ajiaco que levanta los muertos"* (I made an *ajiaco* to raise the dead). *Ajiaco,* the collection of Cuba's diverse roots, becomes a life-giving substance, something with the power to give new life. Additionally, the predominately white Cuban population in Miami would find it repulsive to associate their religious sensibilities with the term *mulato,* insisting that they are pure whites whose religious expression is devoid of African influences. Is the insistence of Exilic Cuban religious scholars on using the term *mulato* truly a grassroots self-description rising from Christian believers, or is it an academic fabrication imposed on, yet not accepted by, the Miami Exilic community? While Latino/a religious scholars use *mulato* to indicate the positive mixture of races and cultures, creating what José Vasconcelos termed *la nueva raza cósmica* (the new cosmic race), the racist connotation of the word and its rejection by most white Exilic Cubans detracts from its ability to define properly the Exilic Cuban experience.[39] Furthermore, the term fails to encompass all Cubans. Cuban roots are more than just *mulato* (black and white) or *mestizo* (Amerindian and Spaniard). Cubans are also Asian, and because of both U.S. imperialism during the twentieth century and their present *exilio* in Miami, Cubans are also Eurocentric.[40] Cubans are heirs of a Taíno indigenous culture, of a medieval (Catholic, Jewish, and Muslim) Spain, of Africa (primarily Yoruban culture), and of Asia (specifically Cantonese).[41] Cubans are truly a multicultural people, belonging to five cultural inheritances yet fully accepted by none of them, making them simultaneously "outsiders" and "insiders." They can claim that the blood of the conquerors and of the conquered converges in their veins. From this existential space, Cubans can create a religious understanding influenced by these multiple traditions.

But why an *ajiaco* Christianity in particular? Until now, most Exilic Cuban religious scholars have dealt with the Exilic Cuban experience from an overall Hispanic and Christian context. Absent from the discourse has been the application of a self-critical analysis. Although it is important to position the Exilic Cuban within the larger "Latina/o" community, misunderstanding occurs when Cuban religious scholars fail to realize the radically different social space occupied by Exilic Cubans, specifically those residing in Miami. When Exilic Cubans are lumped together with Mexicans, Puerto Ricans, and other Latin Americans under the term Hispanic and/or Latina/o, the power and privilege achieved by the Miami community, largely composed of those with light skins and of upper- and middle-class status, is masked by the religious discourse claiming a Latino/a religious commonality. Also absent from the discourse is the Exilic Cubans' attempt to identify themselves with the Euroamerican dominant culture, and thus against other Hispanic groups. The desire of Latino/a religious scholars to evoke a pan-ethnic unity diminishes the reality of how sexism, racism, and classism are alive and well within the Exilic Cubans' constructed religious and political space. Solely casting Exilic Cubans as victims of Euroamerican oppression obscures the dubious role they play as victimizers. Exilic Cubans find themselves simultaneously the oppressed and the oppressors, a fact that is inconvenient and therefore sometimes ignored by those who would lump together Exilic Cubans with all other Latinos/as, rendering them all the Hispanic Other to U.S. hegemony.

Yet lumping these groups together does not completely work. According to the Census Bureau, Exilic Cubans' 1997 mean family income of $35,616 is closer to the U.S. population's mean income of $49,692 than that of any other Hispanic group. Contrast the Exilic Cuban mean income with the Mexican American mean income of $25,347 or the Puerto Rican mean income of $23,646. Sixty-three percent of Exilic Cubans own businesses (the highest rate among Latin Americans), contrasted with 19 percent of Mexican Americans and 11 percent of Puerto Ricans. Unemployment rates of 4 percent for Cubans are lower then the national average, while Mexicans are at 11 percent and Puerto Ricans are at 8 percent. Only 14 percent of Exilic Cubans find themselves below the poverty line, as opposed to 25 percent of Mexicans and 37 percent of Puerto Ricans. Finally, 22 percent of Exilic Cubans hold managerial or professional positions, much higher than the 9 percent of Mexicans or 12 percent of Puerto Ricans (De La Torre and Aponte 2001, 22).

These figures illustrate the difficulty Exilic Cubans have finding room within an overall Hispanic theological viewpoint that constructs a perspective solely from a position of marginality and poverty. While discrimination against Exilic Cubans is a reality and is reflected in the distribution of income (their mean income is about $14,000 less than that of the general U.S. population), Exilic Cubans, more than any other Hispanic group, earn higher average incomes and more frequently hold professional-level jobs. Yet this ascension of Exilic Cubans to positions of power is a relatively new phenomenon. In the early 1980s, anti-Cuban referendums in the form of antibilingual ordinances passed overwhelmingly in Miami. An attempt to solidify the political hold of the Euroamerican elite was in full swing.

The endeavor to disenfranchise Exilic Cubans created a backlash among the Exilic community, leading to a concerted effort to wrest control from the old Anglo guard. Tactics included the formation of Facts about Cuban Exiles (FACE) to combat anti-Cuban stereotypes, the intensification of activism by the Spanish American League against Discrimination (SALAD), and a political grassroots effort prior to the 1984 presidential election, which culminated in nine thousand Cubans becoming U.S. citizens and for the most part registering as Republicans. These efforts resulted in Miami becoming the only city in the United States where first-generation Latin American immigrants have become dominant in city politics. By the 1990s, the majority of city commissioners were Exilic Cubans, as was the mayor. The superintendent of Dade County public schools, the state chairs of the Florida Democratic Party, and the local chairs of the county's political parties are Exilic Cubans. Further, the president of several banks (about twenty) and of Florida International University, the Dade County AFL-CIO, the Miami Chamber of Commerce, the Miami Herald Publishing Company, and the Greater Miami Board of Realtors (a post I held) are or have been Exilic Cuban. It is common to find Exilic Cubans occupying top administrative posts in City Hall, at the *Miami Herald,* and in the city's corporate boardrooms (De La Torre 2002b, 21–22).

Listing such middle-class accomplishments on the part of Exilic Cubans is not an attempt to minimize the pain and suffering that came with being uprooted and the discrimination faced during the initial exilic experience, nor does it imply that all Exilic Cubans have achieved economic success. Yet, more than other recently arrived immigrants, as a group Exilic Cubans have generally ceased to be marginalized. By 1990, Exilic Cubans had become an integral part of Miami's political, economic, and social power structure. Indeed, Exilic Cubans have adopted a hypercapitalist ideology, propelling them into an ultraconservative Republicanism.[42] Many are more "American" than the Euroamericans and more "Cuban" than those who continue to reside in Cuba.

When economic and political achievements such as these are reviewed, seldom is a connection made between them and the religious sensibilities of Exilic Cubans. As mentioned earlier, few Cuban scholars approach *el exilio* from a sophisticated religious studies perspective. The religiosity of

Exilic Cubans is seldom taken into consideration when scholars attempt to understand the Miami ethos, even when it plays a prominent role, as witnessed during the Elián saga. Rather, religious sensibilities are usually relegated to the area of private faith, inconsequential to scholarly analysis. Yet a culture can never be truly understood without first examining the implicit connection between the religious beliefs constructed by that culture and its practices. Because cultures are born out of religious traditions, any thorough examination thus needs to be embedded in a religious discourse. What modern scholars call the secular space is in fact the product of former religious traditions (Foucault 1978a, 33).

Additionally, few Exilic Cuban religious scholars address Exilic Cuban religious expression in the context of the sociopolitical power achieved in the Miami community. While claiming to do "grassroots theology," they seldom consult the political "grassroots" in Miami. When the Exilic Cuban perspective is discussed among Cuban religious scholars, it is usually done from the pre-1980s rubric of the Cuban immigrant as alien. Why is present-day Miami ignored?

Most Exilic Cuban religious scholars are highly influenced by the liberationist tendency of Latino/a theology.[43] Rooted in the theological movement of Latin America known as liberation theology, these scholars are not averse to using Marxist economic analysis to elucidate the religious impetus of those who are most economically oppressed. Because liberation theology has been cast as a communist movement by those in power, and an overall abhorrence exists among Exilic Cubans toward communism, why then should we be surprised that Exilic Cuban religious scholars find little if any reception of it among *el exilio?* Consequently, Exilic Cuban religious scholars have contributed to the overall Hispanic liberationist discourse by speaking either within a constructed pan-ethnic space or within some other Latino/a tradition. One finds Exilic Cuban religious scholars writing about such subjects as the Mexican Virgen de Guadalupe or the socioeconomic misery of the Puerto Rican *barrio* in *el Bronx*.

Along with rejecting anything that might appear communist, Exilic Cuban religious scholars generally ignore present-day Miami because of the obvious difficulty of "doing theology as an oppressed people," when in fact the Exilic Cuban community is, for the most part, economically well-established; has a most effective U.S. lobbying group, the Cuban American National Foundation (CANF); and is the center of the political, economic, and social power in Dade County, Florida. It is difficult to cry "oppression" once a solid middle-class status has been achieved.

Yet if religion is understood as a "second act," that is, as a reflection of the actions and ideologies of a particular people, then what form and shape does the religiosity of Exilic Cubans in Miami take? In answering this question, this book does not attempt to create a new body of theology under the rubric of *ajiaco* Christianity, nor does it reflect any specific religious movement in Miami. Instead, it tries to elucidate how the political culture of the Miami Exilic community arose from a religious expression formed in the Miami diaspora.

The Importance of *Ajiaco* Christianity

The demonstrations of religious fervor on the streets of Miami over the fate of Elián were not an attempt by the community to manipulate religious sensibilities or beliefs to justify a political position; rather, the religious sentiments of the Exilic Cuban community facilitated their political stance. The Elián saga cannot be fully understood apart from an exploration of the different, and at times conflicting, religious roots that contribute to what I have been calling an *ajiaco* Christianity. *Ajiaco* Christianity, as an expression of religiosity, contradicts Durkheim's sociological, Freud's psychological, and Marx's economic functionalism, each of which insists that societal structures powerfully determine religious beliefs and rituals. *Ajiaco* Christianity resists the trend of reducing religion to a by-product of the so-called underlying social reality. Rather, I claim the reverse: religion shapes society; it is not simply a dependent variable of other forces. Society, psychology, and economics affect religion, but their influences are neither dominant nor determining. Rather than a mere expression of sociological dynamics, religion is a cultural fact in and of itself, needing explanation on its own terms. Religious phenomena, like those surrounding the Elián drama, can only be understood when examined on their own terms. Any attempt to elucidate such phenomena by means of physiology, psychology, sociology, economics, linguistics, art, or any other area will ultimately prove ineffective. Such approaches usually ignore the one unique and irreducible element of religion: the element of the sacred (Eliade 1963, xii). Only those aware of this sacred element can truly grasp *ajiaco* Christianity's impact on the Exilic Cuban social reality.

Yet Exilic Cubans have interpreted the sacred as a civil religion that supports, gives meaning to, and provides hope for *el exilio,* a term mainly used by Exilic Cubans to name their collective identity. The term connotes the involuntary nature of displacement and constructs them as so-journers in a foreign land. *El exilio* is an in-between place, a place to wait and hope for a return to the promised land. It is more than a geographic separation; it encompasses dis-connection and dis-placement. *El exilio* is a culturally constructed artifact imagined as a landless nation, complete with its own history and values. As travel writer David Rieff observes, "The country of which Miami is the capital is an imaginary one, that of *el exilio*" (1987, 149). *El exilio* exists in a reality apart from what Cubans long for, *la patria*.

In Miami, the longing for Cuba, or the "rhetoric of return," has become the unifying substance of the Exilic Cuban's existential being, yet this aspiration is slowly being replaced by a stronger desire to adapt to and capitalize on residence in this country. Taking their cue from Martí, they render *el exilio* a sacred space, making morality synonymous with nationalism. Living in exile is a sacrifice constituting a civic duty, representing a grander moral standing (*OC* III, 303–05; IV, 289; and XX, 397). Religion is understood as a moral mandate to rid the island of its atheist's regime. In like fashion, Resident Cubans also use Christianity to "baptize the revolution."[44]

Theology of the Diaspora

Ajiaco Christianity can be categorized as a theology of the diaspora. Such a theology is deeply rooted in the theoretical contexts of postmodernism, postcolonialism, and liberation theology. Diaspora theology as a post-modernist theology claims that absolute truths are mere constructions of any given society within a particular time period. Postmodernity, as one of the bases for a diaspora theology, argues for a multitude of matrices and voices, not only outside itself but also within, thoroughly committed to self-analysis and self-criticism. As a postcolonial theology, diaspora theology becomes grounded at the margins of society, engaged in decolonization both from within and from the center of power and privilege. Additionally, as a liberation theology, diaspora theology seeks to "review, re-claim, and re-phrase" its own matrix and voice in the midst of a dominant theological perspective. At its core, it becomes a theology of flesh-and-blood exile (Segovia 1996, 201).

As a postmodern theology, *ajiaco* Christianity encompasses the radical diversity of the Cuban ethos, in contrast to the modernist attempt to emphasize the objective universality of only the European element. Such objective claims to universality are basically understood as an exercise in power, and postmodernity in general is skeptical of these claims.[45] An objective, outside voice is replaced by a hermeneutical self-implication situating the discourse within the "reality" of *el exilio* and the construction of the Cuban ethnicity, a construction that attempts to mask the power and privilege achieved *el exilio* in Miami. The challenge facing Exilic Cubans is to perceive initiatives that are different from the value imperatives of the dominant Eurocentric culture undergirding how Cubans see themselves.

As a postcolonial theology, *ajiaco* Christianity becomes a response to the consequences of colonialism. Postcolonialism emerged from the Cuban pain of being domesticated by global imperial powers. Cubans suffered greatly while on the periphery of empire building, first with Spain and then with the United States.[46] As a liberation theology, *ajiaco* Christianity counterbalances the reductionist tendencies of postmodernity and postcolonialism. The creation of a theology of diaspora creates tension between liberation theology and postmodern discourse, two disciplines considered mutually exclusive by many scholars. Specifically, tensions exist between postmodernity's claims of radical plurality and the liberationist insistence of the hermeneutical option of those oppressed, between an arbitrary history and the celebration of the God of history. If postmodernity denies the existence of all metanarratives, then all new metanarritives, like liberation theology, which claims to account for and explain the reasons for oppression and the actions to overcome it, are futile.

Regardless of the good intentions of individuals or religious movements like liberation theology, new metanarratives eventually become an instrument of oppression. For example, the writings of Rousseau, the lover of freedom, were used during the terror of the French Revolution to justify a model of social oppression. Likewise, the writings of Marx led to Stalinism. Postmodernity concludes that people are much freer than they may feel (Foucault 1988, 10). Metanarratives like liberation theology are reduced by the postmodern discourse to movements that are unable effectively to confront or change the status quo. If history is reduced to an asynchronic movement, lacking a universal understanding that goes beyond history, then no metanarrative exists to describe the present and discern the future.

For those living under oppressive structures, postmodernity offers a stoic acceptance of one's social location. This approach fails to challenge present systems of oppression by seducing the disenfranchised into accepting their lot with the logic that it could be worse. Such an approach hampers any attempt to seek concepts like justice. For this reason, *ajiaco* Christianity as a liberation theology serves as a counterbalances to the postmodern discourse, attempting to deconstruct social frameworks and emphasize the fragmented plurality of experiences and perspectives, while opting for unitary concepts as a way to understand the Exilic Cuban social location. In this way, postmodernity is subversively positioned within the struggle to understand the Miami's Exilic Cuban religious and political fervor.

A Mixed Methodology

Here a note about my position as the author of this volume is in order. I approach the task of understanding the development of the Exilic Cuban political positions, via their religious sensibilities, as an indigenous ethnographer, an insider studying my own culture and offering a fresh perspective. Liberation theologians have taught us to reflect on autobiographical elements to avoid creating a lifeless religious understanding. Including one's story powerfully connects theory with reality. Throughout this book, I will set out to challenge the predominant assumption that all interpretations of the Exilic Cuban religious phenomena occur independent of the interpreter's social position or identity. Yet for some scholars, considering the interpreter's identity or social position somewhat adulterates the intended meaning of the religious phenomena. They insist that a person's identity interferes with the job of ascertaining a so-called objective rendering of events (De La Torre 2002b, 3).

Nonetheless, the approach I employ in this book challenges the assumption that the religious fervor expressed by Exilic Cubans, as in the case of the Elián saga, can be understood apart from what the interpreter brings to the analysis. Hence the analysis conducted in this book is at times autobiographical, and though at times academia considers the hermeneutics of the self to be unscholarly, I maintain that Exilic Cubans themselves consistently use such a strategy in the construction of their worldview, since it collapses the dichotomy of the religious and secular spheres. On the streets of Miami, few differences really exist between the religious and secular voice because of the understanding that all interpretations are either directly or indirectly influenced by one's identity and the social position of living and existing in *el exilio*. While it is not my intention to write my memoir, I find it essential to situate myself within *aji-*

aco Christianity. To situate myself in the geopolitical space of *el exilio* acknowledges my circumscribed location and particular perspective.

Although my family came to this country during the first wave of immigrants from Cuba (1959–1962), we were among the very small minority who did not belong to the departing elite, even though my father was a *batistiano,* an active supporter of the military dictatorship of Fulgencio Batista, and worked for the Buró de Investigaciones (Bureau of Investigations). My uncle was a famed political broadcaster who dedicated the remainder of his life fighting the Castro regime on the New York and Miami airwaves. My first memories are of a tenement building in the slums of New York City. Like other Exilic Cubans of the Northeast, we migrated to Miami in the early 1970s to take advantage of the warm sun and the economic enclave being developed there. It was a time of economic and political struggle for the sociopolitical control of Miami, so anti-Cuban sentiment was at its peak. By the age of nineteen, I had established a successful real estate firm, eventually employing more than a hundred associates. Prosperity led to community activism and a brief political career as campaign manager (and a candidate for the Florida House in 1988). I had achieved success within Miami's business world and was a respected community leader and right-wing political activist.

When our family moved from Miami to Kentucky, we encountered institutionalized racism (as opposed to individual prejudices) for the first time as adults, both in the workplace and the church. The day we moved, I woke up "white" in Miami, but that night in Louisville I went to sleep as a man of color. This experience illustrated that while in Miami, I benefited from the power and privilege obtained by Exilic Cubans, yet once I left Dade County, I suffered because I was seen as a Latino. As one who came of age in Miami when Exilic Cubans were creating Dade County's structures of power, as a religious scholar I now attempt to understand our unique location, striving to elucidate the religious fervor that affects political positions routinely taken in Miami, as demonstrated so clearly during the Eliàn saga.

CHAPTER 2

La Lucha

The Religion of Miami

Cuba is a fantasy island, an illusion, a construction of outsiders' imaginations. The dream of Cuba, in one form or another, has lasted for centuries. This imaginary space becomes superimposed on the island as the viewer's fantasies are projected onto Cuba as object. Yet these fantasies have nothing to do with Cuba's reality. Alan West, an Exilic Cuban linguist, illustrates how such illusions have victimized the island and its people:

From other shores, the island has been imagined and expressed in a series of more familiar discourses with a plethora of images: Pearl of the Antilles, tropical paradise, whorehouse of the Caribbean, Cuba as gold mine, cane field (slave trade), military outpost (strategic location/geopolitical pawn), tourist haven/exotic folkloric locale (flesh depot, fun in the sun, shed your inhibitions), investment opportunity (source of cheap labor), or revolutionary menace/terrorist haven (as U.S. nightmare). Cuba's images of "otherness" come from outside observers or covetous foreign powers. (1997, 2)

If we define history as the memory of a people, who are at times intoxicated by false memories, how do Cubans then recall their own history apart from the imagery imposed on them by the colonial gaze? How can they faithfully represent the historical development of *ajiaco* Christianity? How did historical religious events shape and form the reaction of the Exilic Cuban clergy during the Elián custody battle (De La Torre 2000, 267)?

Antecedents to the Elián Saga

The reaction of Catholic priests and Protestant ministers to the Elián saga can never be understood·apart from the historical fight of the Cuban Church against "godless communism." The Cuban Catholic Church, prior to the Revolution of 1959, was highly influenced by the denunciation of communism presented in the papal encyclical *Divini Redemptoris,* which understood Catholicism and Marxism as mutually exclusive. This 1937 pontifical document was written as a reaction to the excesses of the Spanish Civil War and the religious persecutions that occurred in Mexico and Russia. The Cuban clergy was predominately from Spain. Of the three thousand Catholic priests in Cuba on the eve of the Revolution, approximately twenty-five hundred were from Spain, trained during the Franco dictatorship and highly influenced by the bitter Spanish Civil War victory over communism, a victory with heavy religious overtones (Thomas 1971, 683–84). These priests transplanted the atmosphere of a religious crusade against communism from Spain to Cuba.

The Cuban Revolution occurred before the churches in Latin America became radicalized by the Vatican II (1962–65), which brought the Church in step with the modern world, and by the 1968 conference of Latin American bishops in Medellín, Colombia, which articulated the basic tenets of liberation theology. These gatherings emphasized the responsibility of Christians toward the poor and afflicted. Not benefiting from these theological developments, the pre-Revolution churches of Cuba concentrated on running schools, which were staffed by foreigners, located in the cities, and, owing to their high tuition, exclusive both of people of color and of low-income families. In an effort to increase their political power, these churches attempted to establish and maintain friendly links with the different conservative political regimes that ruled Cuba, regardless of their corruption and disregard of socioeconomic justice.

Paradoxically, during the Cuban Revolution, before Castro proclaimed his Marxist-Leninist orientation on December 1, 1961, both Catholic and Protestant chaplains actively served in the columns of the Castro brothers and Juan Almeida. Many Protestant leaders cooperated with the guerilla forces in their nationalistic attempt to eliminate Batista. Two early martyrs of the Revolution were Frank and Josué Pais, Baptists who were killed by Batista's soldiers for leading an uprising in Santiago. Esteban Hernandez, a Presbyterian, was also tortured and killed by Batista's police. The boat that brought the rebels to Cuba, *Granma,* was purchased with the help of a donation from a Presbyterian staff member with the National Council of Evangelical Churches. Additionally, the homes of Protestant leaders served as underground headquarters for the Revolution.

Catholic leaders also participated in the insurrection. Father Guillermo Sardiñas served as chaplain to the rebel army and was promoted to the rank of *comandante,* Father Madrigal was treasurer of the July 26 Movement, Father Chelala was treasurer of the movement in Holguín, Father Antonio Albizú's offered his house in Manzanillo as a rendezvous for rebel messengers, and Father José Chabebe relayed coded messages to the rebel forces via his religious radio program.[1] Although the Church hierarchy remained silent during the insurgence, a significantly large percentage of Catholics, like the martyred Catholic student leader José Antonio Echevarría, participated in the uprising, fighting the forces of Batista (Kirk 1988, 48–49). If Christ's mission was to bring about a just social order, then as followers of Christ, these Catholic Cubans felt called to this task. They saw the Revolution as the vehicle through which they could put their faith in action, specifically through solidarity with those who were marginalized and oppressed in Cuba.

After helping to eliminate Batista, the churches returned to their ministries. Many of them were pleased at first with the government's initial move to end gambling, prostitution, and political corruption. However, this early optimism gave way to disillusion as the new regime tilted to the left. The government's increasingly close relationship with the Soviet Union, the promoters of "godless communism," and its sponsorship of land and education reform (which curtailed Church autonomy), led to the eventual break between the Church and Castro's regime a few years after Batista's overthrow. Catholics as well as Protestants became engaged in counterrevolutionary activities, openly supporting and praising the United States, which was intent on quashing the Revolution and reestablishing its former authority on the island (De La Torre 2002a, 96–97).

The Church eventually took the position that Cuba needed to be "saved" from atheism. By Christmas 1960, Archbishop Pérez Serantes, social reformer, critic of the Batista regime, and early supporter of Castro, wrote a pastoral letter that presented Cubans with an ultimatum, titled "With Christ or against Christ." In it he clearly laid out the existing dichotomy in eschatological tones: "The battle is to wrestle between Christ and the Anti-Christ. Choose, then, each to who they prefer to have as *Jefe*" (Maza 1982, 91). By 1961, the government nationalized all church schools and declared most foreign clergy personae non gratae, in response to three Spanish priests and at least one Methodist minister who participated as chaplains in the April Playa Girón (Bay of Pigs) invasion. One of the priests, Father Ismael de Lugo, was to have read a communiqué to the Cuban population:

The liberating forces have disembarked on Cuba's beaches. We come in the name of God. . . . The assault brigade is made up of thousands of Cubans who are all Christians and Catholics. Our struggle is that of those who believe in God against the atheists. . . . Have faith, since the victory is ours, because God is with us and the Virgin of Charity cannot abandon her children. . . . Long live Christ the King! Long live our glorious Patron Saint! (Kirk 1988, 96)

As retribution for opposing Cuba's new Marxist orientation, both Catholics and Protestants faced expulsion, were forbidden to run schools as a source of income, and had their private media nationalized. Church members were routinely watched by political organs of the government, while bishops, priests, and ministers were placed under house arrest. Christians were refused entry into the Communist Party, allegiance to which guaranteed economic advancement, and denied high-level positions in the government and university. Many, mostly the middle class, chose flight, rather than fight, as an alternative, creating a brain drain on the island and further weakening the Church's power base. Monsignor Pérez Serantes, now a combative critic of Castro's Marxist leanings, best summed up the Church's predicament. Prior to his death, he said, "All that is happening to us is providential. . . . We believed more in our schools than in Jesus Christ" (Büntig 1971, 111).

Those Christians who chose Miami in response to Castro's crackdown on the Church brought with them the religiously cloaked sentiments about communism that originated with Franco's victory in Spain. The dialogue that developed between the left and the Church after Vatican II and the rise of liberation theology came too late for Cuba. The Exilic Cuban mind was set. To be an Exilic Cuban Christian meant to participate in the crusade against communism and Castro, period. To recognize any of Cuba's achievements, or to voice an opinion that might in any way be construed as a compliment of present-day Cuba, was to betray God and to proclaim an allegiance with Satan. During the custody battle over Elián, several demonstrators, armed with "Pray for Elián" placards and posters of then–attorney general Janet Reno (a Miamian) shown with diabolical horns sprouting from her head, took their protest to her Miami home.[2] One poster read "Elián is Christ. Reno is

Lucifer. Castro is Satan."[3] Immediately after the federal raid of Elián's Miami home, Mayor Joe Carolle denounced the seizure in religious terms: "What they did was a crime. These are atheists. They don't believe in God."[4]

In one of the protest marches following the raid, Cubans dressed in black and laid flowers, a silver cross, and the Cuban flag beneath a photo of Elián's mother, which was erected at the Playa Girón monument. Many cooled themselves with circular paper fans that read "I vote Republican." In this environment religion, politics, and power were fused and confused. What arose was a new religious expression diametrically opposed to the Cuban *ajiaco,* one I have labeled *la lucha.* As a religion, *la lucha* challenges the inclusivity of the Cuban *ajiaco* by establishing as the starting point the Exilic Cuban social space, a space that is vehemently committed to fighting the forces of darkness, here defined as anything with a leftist slant. *La lucha,* also known as *la causa sagrada* (the sacred cause), becomes a religious expression that legitimizes the role Exilic Cubans play in Miami.

La Lucha: Miami's Religion

Some Latina/o religious scholars have used the term *la lucha* to refer to a form of Latina feminism known as *mujerista* theology.[5] This is not how the term is being used here. Instead, I am reclaiming this Cuban idiom by returning to its original usage. The term *la lucha* has its roots in Cuba's nineteenth-century struggle against Spain for liberation. Later it became *la lucha* against the United States, as represented by the U.S.-backed Machado and Batista regimes. Today the typical Exilic Cuban on the streets of Little Havana understands *la lucha* as the continuing struggle against Castro and all who are perceived to be his allies.

In the previous chapter we examined how *ajiaco* Christianity is understood to signify the overall religious milieu of Cubanness. If *ajiaco* Christianity symbolizes an inclusive Cuban religiosity, then *la lucha* symbolizes an exclusive one. *La lucha* becomes a sacred space in which the Exilic Cuban's religious fervor becomes intertwined with the community's political convictions. As such, *la lucha* comes to represent the cosmic struggle between the "children of light" (Exilic Cubans) and the "children of darkness" (Resident Cubans), complete with a Christ (Martí), an Antichrist (Castro), a priesthood (CANF), a promised land (Cuba), and martyrs (those who gloriously suffer in the holy war against Castro). Add to this cosmology a messiah—Elián.

But to insist on themes of reconciliation out of a religious or biblical conviction is to participate in this cosmic struggle as a false prophet. The use of Christian motifs and biblical precepts about reconciliation has in the past brought about only unfortunate consequences. During the 1970s, the Reverend Manuel Espinosa, pastor of the Evangelical Church in Hialeah and former captain in Castro's military, used his pulpit to preach on themes of intra-Cuban reconciliation. In 1975 his sermons earned him the label *comunista* and a severe beating. By 1980, the good reverend publicly admitted he was a secret agent for the Castro government (García 1996, 139–40). His admission only confirmed in the hearts and minds of the émigré community that anyone who actively sought or supported reconciliation with Resident Cubans must somehow be connected with the regime and hence a promoter of evil.

The mecca of this new religious expression known as *la lucha* became the South Florida city of Miami. While small ethnic enclaves of Cubans can be found in New Jersey, New York, Puerto Rico, and California, 65 percent of all Exilic Cubans have migrated to Florida. Although Miami is located within the boundaries of the United States and operates within its legal, political, and judicial systems, in a very real and profound sense, Miami is the capital of the imaginary nation of Exilic Cubans. To visit Miami at the start of the new millennium is to visit the ideal Cuba of the 1950s and to participate in the Cold War that marked that era but has, everywhere else, at least, long since dissipated. As the Exilic Cuban postmodern capital of the Americas, the city serves as a museum to the Cuba of yesteryear. If a person wants to buy Cuban bread, Gilda crackers, Materva soft drinks, café Pilon, malt, or Cuban sandwiches, they must go to Miami, for these items no longer exist in Cuba. Well-known pre-Castro restaurants like La Carreta, El Caney, Río Cristal, and El Patio continue to operate in Miami. Even the Spanish spoken in Miami maintains its 1950s La Habana accent—which no longer exists in La Habana. Likewise, members of Miami's Cuban community express the same religious views as they did when they opposed Castro during the early 1960s, when the only choice that existed was between Christ and the Antichrist.

Exilic Cubans internalize, naturalize, and legitimize their religious view, *la lucha*, in order to mask their position of power as they shape Miami's political and economic structures according to the tenets of this religion. They construct an ethnic identity, complete with a long and complicated genealogy, so that they can blame Resident Cubans for their own problems. They (re)member their (dis)membered past as a white people coming from a white nation, fleeing tyranny with only the clothes on their backs and leaving behind *la Cuba de ayer* (the Cuba of yesterday), which to them represents an idyllic way of life. The construction of this fictitious *Cuba de ayer* becomes an economy of truths and lies. (Re)membering *la Cuba de ayer* is a strategy against oblivion, a survival tactic. Its construction creates a common past, symbolically linking them to the land they left behind, while defining their new Exilic identity. If ethnic memory is oriented toward the future, not the past, then *la Cuba de ayer* traps them in a social construction that prevents them from moving forward.

To re-create *la Cuba de ayer* on U.S. soil is to create a landless Cuban territory, with its distinct cultural milieu and idiosyncrasies, that serves to protect Cubans from the pain of economic and psychological difficulties caused by their initial uprooting. Cuba became more than just the old country; it grew to be the mythological world of Cubans' origins. Cuba becomes some ethereal place where every conceivable item *es mejor* (is better), where the sky is bluer, the sugar sweeter, the bugs less pesky, and life richer. Everything *aquí* (here), when contrasted with *allá* (there), is found lacking. Unlike other immigrant groups, who left painful memories of the old country behind while joyfully anticipating a country where "the streets were paved with gold," many Cubans did not want to come to what many considered a country with an inferior culture.

Cuban poet and writer Reinaldo Arenas captures the pain of being uprooted by *el exilio* and the need to remember what was left behind. He wrote: "Someone who's been uprooted, exiled, has no country. Our country exists only in our memory, but we need something beyond memory if we're to achieve happiness. We have no homeland, so we have to invent it over and over again" (Suárez 1999, vix). According to cultural anthropologist James Clifford, "Perhaps there's no return for anyone to a native land—only field notes for its reinvention" (1988, 173). Exilic Cubans avoid the pain of displacement by constructing a mythical Cuba where every *guajiro* (country bumpkin) has class and wealth, where no racism exists, and where Eden was preserved until the serpent (Fidel) beguiled Eve (the weakest elements of society, such as the blacks and the poor) and brought an end to paradise.

La lucha, as a religious expression, is rooted in the socioeconomic status of Exilic Cubans, which is radically different from that of other Latino/a groups. Of the more than one million Cubans living in the United States, about 73 percent arrived as refugees (Pedraza 2001, 411). When Batista departed from Cuba on New Year's Day, 1959, he triggered panic as party-goers rushed to their homes to collect their sleeping children, money, and valuables. Batista's children and money were already out of the country. He was able to accumulate a personal fortune of about $300 million, representing one-quarter of all government expenditures (Bethell 1993, 89–90). Those who were able to leave arrived in the United States still in their tuxedos and dress uniforms, their formal gowns and high heels. Unlike other contemporary refugees to the States, these first Exilic Cubans belonged to a privileged social class. Although they were not particularly numerous, they represented the top echelons of their country's governmental and business community. Their status facilitated their reestablishment in a foreign land, at the same time creating a brain drain that emptied the Resident community of trained personnel indispensable to the socioeconomic development of the country. Undoubtedly, the mass exodus of Cubans from the island created regrettable consequences for both communities. It is even possible that if the wealthy, educated elite had remained in Cuba instead of seeking safety and security in the United States, Castro may not have lasted this long. Responding to the glittering allure of the States outweighed the need to plot resistance on the homeland.

The economic restructuring of Cuba by the United States prior to the Revolution created these presocialized refugees.[6] A pro-U.S. Cuban elite with connections to upper-class groups in the United States and Latin America was created to protect U.S. interests. Clearly, these refugees represented the political, economic, and social structures of the pro-U.S. presence in the Republic of Cuba. As a way of protecting themselves economically against Cuba's political instability, they hoarded their capital and educated their children in the United States. Few reinvested on the island, instead transferring abroad considerable amounts of Cuban capital. According to the U.S. Department of Commerce, Cubans, by the mid-1950s, were estimated to have more than $312 million in short-term (liquid capital) and long-term (stocks) investments in the United States. Real estate investments totaled more than $150 million, mostly in South Florida (Pérez 1988, 299). Most of those belonging to this elite managed to transfer their assets out of Cuba before Castro's victory, while others held the bulk of their investments abroad (Pérez-Stable and Uriarte 1993, 135). This protection of capital eased the transition to Exilic existence for some refugees.

The first wave of immigration to the States occurred from the day of Batista's departure on January 1, 1959, until the missile crisis of October 22, 1962.[7] This wave brought 153,534 refugees, who were considered "political exiles." These immigrants mainly left the island on their private yachts or on commercial flights and ferries.[8] Demographically, these new

Cuban refugees were quite homogeneous. The vast majority was an elite of former notables who were mostly white (94 percent), middle-aged (about thirty-eight years old), educated (with about fourteen years of schooling), urban (principally residing in La Habana), and literate in English (Fagan, Brody, and O'Leary 1968, 19–28). They represented the vast majority of the upper-class elite, middle-class businessmen, professionals, managers, and technocrats whose socioeconomic interests were jeopardized by revolutionary policies calling for wealth redistribution (Azicri 1988, 67). They were not so much bound to Batista as they were to the political and economic structures that accorded them privilege (Amaro and Portes 1972, 10). They were united in their bitterness over their lost status and in their commitment to overthrow Castro and regain their assets.

In spite of their cultural status and their whiteness, these early refugees still faced ethnic discrimination in housing and employment. It was common to find signs on apartment buildings throughout Miami that simply stated "No Cubans, no pets, and no children." Yet while I do not want to minimize the trauma and hardship of being a refugee, those who settled in Miami were entering a social environment made familiar through years of prior travel and business dealings, an advantage other immigrant groups never had. These Cubans, especially the *habaneros/as* (those from La Habana), saw South Florida as a pleasant vacation hub from which to await Castro's immediate downfall. With time, those who belonged to Cuba's elite attempted to re-create their golden past. For example, those who belonged to the five most exclusive yacht and country clubs in La Habana established a new club in *el exilio,* nostalgically named the Big Five, thereby creating a socioeconomic space for former notables (Pedraza 2001, 419).

The second wave (1962–1973) consisted of two stages. The first stage occurred from the end of the missile crisis until the Camarioca boat lift (the first of its kind) in November 1965, when Exilic Cubans sailed to that port to pick up their relatives. Although commercial flights between the United States and Cuba were suspended owing to the missile crisis, many arrived either through the Camarioca boat lift or through a third country. This stage brought 29,692 refugees. The second stage constituted the airlift from Varadero Beach to Miami, which continued until 1973. A total of 268,040 refugees arrived in this country through these "freedom flights."

The total number of refugees who came to this country during the second wave was 297,732. More than half of all Cubans who migrated to the United States arrived during this second wave (Azicri 1988, 67). Additionally, the majority of these refugees were women, children, and seniors. Males of military age (fifteen to twenty-six years old), political prisoners, and certain skilled technicians were refused permission to leave Cuba. The second-wave immigrants were predominately white, educated, middle-class, and willing to work below minimum wage. While in Cuba, they largely constituted the group directly relying on economic links with the United States. As those links came to an end with Cuba's tilt toward Marxism, most sought to escape. On average they were semiskilled working-class people who capitalized on the emerging economic enclave being established by the first-wave Cubans. Their departure from Cuba consolidated the power of Castro's Revolution by exporting any serious internal opposition.[9]

Because of their light skin color, first- and second-wave Exilic Cubans identified with white Americans and succeeded in avoiding certain racial barriers that persist in the United States. Unlike any other group of immigrants who has come to U.S. shores, Cubans, as we saw in the last chapter, have risen to the top echelons of a city's sociopolitical structures within one generation. While poverty continues to exist among Exilic Cubans, their national average family income is closer to that of Euroamericans than to that of any other Hispanic group.

According to a 1997 survey conducted by *Hispanic Business Magazine,* of the eighty U.S. Latino/a multimillionaires, thirty-two are Exilic Cubans, even though Exilics represent only 5 percent of the Hispanic population. Consider this in light of the fact that only twenty-six are Mexican, even though 64 percent of Latinas/os are of Mexican origins. Or that only seven are Puerto Ricans, who represent 11 percent of the Hispanic population. Roberto Goizueta, the late CEO of Coca-Cola, was worth $836 million; the Mas Canosa family, which heads the anti-Castro lobby group, is worth $586 million; while superstar Gloria Estéfan reaches the $100 million mark.[10] Of the top fifty largest Hispanic-owned firms in the United States, about a third are located in the Miami area. "No place in the United States has a Latin community like Miami's" boasts Telemundo (a Spanish-language television station) boss Joaquín Blaya. "Here we are members of the power structures."[11] When we consider that these families arrived on U.S. shores a generation ago, their financial success is quite impressive.

Their quest for economic success, which seemed motivated by a desire to prove that they are not the *gusanos* Castro says they are, coupled with their anticommunist ideology, formed an integral aspect of *la lucha*. Their financial success in the States became evidence that God favored the Exilic Cubans, while the hardships in Cuba confirmed God's displeasure. This rise to economic power, however, was not due to divine intervention but rather to four cultural texts. Individually these texts are insufficient in explaining the political and economic rise of Exilic Cubans, but together they shed light on the potency of *el exilio*.

The first text is the Exilic Cubans' ethnic composition as early refugees. The social class of Exilic Cubans affected the construction of their ethnicity once they were in the United States and spared them from the minority status of other Latinas/os. Suzanne Oboler's social scientific work shows how middle- and upper-class, college-educated Hispanics measure their incorporation into U.S. dominant culture against the experiences of Southern and Eastern European immigrants, who were categorized and seen as "white," thus allowing them to assume status as "first-class" citizens. Exilic Cubans' socialization within Cuban hierarchical society created the expectation of immediate inclusion into the upper echelons of U.S. society. Once here, Exilic Cubans shifted their self-identity according to the predominant ethnic and racial classifications of the United States. As a result, Exilic Cubans have attempted to distance themselves from the ethnic term Hispanic or Latina/o by emphasizing instead their nationality. In contrast, those resembling the working class, whether Mexicans, Puerto Ricans, or Exilic Cubans known as *Marielitos* (those who came in the third wave of 1980, which will be discussed in the next chapter) measure their progress against their life changes since immigration (1995, 138–41, 163–63). *Marielitos,* and all subsequent Exilic Cuban immigrants, were brought up under a Castro regime and thus lacked their predecessors' business acumen, contacts, and familiarity with capitalist paradigms. Even though they faired better than other migrating Hispanic groups, and suddenly improved their standard of living simply by arriving in Miami, they have yet to replicate successfully the rapid economic development enjoyed by immigrants of the first two waves.

It is also important to note that while all strata of Cuban society were represented in the first two waves of Cuban migration, the vast majority consisted of those from the upper echelons and the middle-class who most benefited from the pre-Castro regime. The concept of the "habitus" can help illuminate how these Exilic Cubans ascended in the socioeconomic institutions of Miami. Habitus can be abstractly defined as the system of internalized dispositions that mediates between social structures and practical activities, shaped by the former and regulating the latter (Brubaker 1985, 758). Being born into a position of privilege in Cuba, these Exilics had a socially constructed lifestyle that facilitated their rise to the top echelons of Miami's power structures. In a sense, this lifestyle unconsciously taught them how to behave to achieve economic and social success once they immigrated. The social constructs of this lifestyle, manifested as customs, language, traditions, values, and so on, existed prior to their birth (Bourdieu 1977, 72–3, 78–87). As the "memory of the body," these constructs have been imposed on Exilics since before their birth, molding their childhood and guiding them through adulthood by decoding and helping them adjust to new situations. To protect their self-interest, Exilic Cubans merely had to assert what they had been all along in order to become what they will be, something accomplished with the lack of self-consciousness that marks their so-called nature as part of *el exilio*.

The second text is rooted in the propaganda value of Cubans fleeing communism, especially at the height the Cold War, which made it advantageous for the United States to ensure the economic success of these arriving refugees. Exilic Cubans' hatred of communism furthered their usefulness in West-East global tensions. Stated then–U.S. representative Walter H. Judd (R-Minn.), "Every refugee who comes out [of Cuba] is a vote for our society and a vote against their society" (Masud-Piloto 1988, 33). The refugees' arrival in Miami was used to discredit the Castro regime, as a place of "golden exile" was constructed to contrast with Castro's Cuba. Still, their migration to the United States was not so much motivated by a search for the so-called American Dream as it was a direct response to the political situation in the homeland. As such, they adamantly rejected the identity of "immigrant" and instead insisted on being classified as "refugee." This refugee label helps explain why many Exilic Cubans refused to identify with the civil rights movement, resulting in their belief that they were not morally entitled to government assistance in the form of welfare or affirmative action.

Ironically, for the first time in its history, the United States became an asylum to a large group of refugees by assuming the financial burden of resettling them. Total aid of approximately $2 billion was disbursed through the Cuban Refugee Program, providing assistance to more than seven hundred thousand Exilic Cubans. This does not include the millions spent by church and voluntary agencies, which were never fully reimbursed. Over a twelve-year period, aid consisted of direct cash assistance, guaranteed healthcare, food subsidies, retraining and retooling programs, college loans, English-language instruction, and financial assistance in establishing small businesses. Even though most succor was contingent on resettlement to another part of the United States, Miami's economy, which at the time was undergoing a recession, was greatly affected by the arrival of so many refugees, triggering the transformation of South Florida from a quaint tourist trap to the center of Latin American trade. Loans granted by the United States Small Business Administration to Miami businesses from 1968 (when the agency began keeping racial and ethnic statistics) until 1979 show that Hispanics received 46.9 percent (or $47,677,660) of available funds, Euroamericans received 46.6 percent (or $47,361,773), and African Americans received 6.3 percent (or $6,458,240) (Pedraza-Bailey 1985, 4–34; Pérez-Stable and Uriarte 1993, 155; Porter and Dunn 1980, 194–97).

The third text is the construction of an ethnic economic enclave by *el exilio* that was dependent on a large number of immigrants with substantial business experience acquired in Cuba, access to labor drawn from family members, and access to capital through "character loans." The flight of capital from Latin America to the economic and political security of the United States provided an economic space in which Exilic Cubans could manage said funds, leading to the creation and growth of banks. Once these Exilics were secured in banking positions, they provided "character loans" to their compatriots to encourage business. It mattered little whether the borrower had any standing within Euroamerican banks, whether they had any collateral, or whether they spoke English. Loans (usually from $10,000 to $35,000) were provided based on the borrower's reputation in Cuba. This practice contributed to the development of an economic enclave in Miami (Portes and Stepick 1993, 132–35). It was discontinued in 1973, because the new refugees, who were not part of the more elite first wave, were unknown to the lenders.

This Exilic Cuban economic enclave was organized to serve the needs of the Exilic Cuban's own market. Doctors, dentists, electricians, plumbers, construction workers, and other professionals who lacked proper licenses or proper documentation from regulatory boards continued to work in their professions, either from their homes or from the backs of their pickup trucks, and they were diligent in avoiding the authorities. Little overhead, cut-rate prices for fellow Exilic Cubans, and reliance on informal word-of-mouth networks allowed these early entrepreneurs to establish themselves financially before eventually competing with older Euroamerican Miami firms. Many took advantage of the recession occurring in Miami at that time and of the resulting boarded-up storefronts in economically depressed areas. Inexpensive leases minimized the risks associated with going into business, leading to the transformation of this area into what today is known as Little Havana.

This enclave also allowed Exilic Cubans to avoid the economic disadvantages that usually accompany racial segregation. The creation of an economic enclave fostered upward mobility not available to other Hispanic groups or to African Americans. Not only did the original entrepreneurs benefit, but later arrivals found established community networks providing opportunities for employment and further entrepreneurship. For example, six years after the 1980 Mariel boat lift, half the refugees were employed by Exilic-owned businesses, while 20 percent became self-employed (Portes and Clark 1987, 14–18).

Labor, needed to ensure the success of any business venture, was easily obtained from both family members and from other more recent refugees. With time, Exilic Cubans, with business acumen acquired in La Habana, filled an economic space in Miami by offering U.S. products to Latin America. Even though Exilic Cubans constitute 4.8 percent of the Latino/a population in the United States, as already mentioned, a third of all large Hispanic corporations are based in Miami. Exilic Cuban Guillermo Grenier, head of Florida International University's sociology department states, "As the Western Hemisphere becomes more Hispanic, Miami has become the frontier city between 'America' and Latin America" (Booth 1993, 82–85). Exilic Cubans took advantage of this emerging "frontier" space.

Additionally, this ethnic economic enclave provided a secure and familiar space in which Exilic Cubans could avoid losing their identity and hence being absorbed by the dominant culture. While other ethnic enclaves established in this country by European immigrants facilitated gradual assimilation into the dominant culture, the Exilic Cuban enclave created a space that preserved the culture by firmly establishing its economic success. This enclave eased the shock and stress of adjusting to a foreign culture. A psychological need was thus met, as Exilic Cubans developed social networks to protect them from assimilation, forging a group identity in the process. This group's religious expression developed simultaneously with their economic enclave as a holy hatred for the one responsible for causing the pain of *el exilio*. Castro becomes the sole cause of and reason for this pain, and therefore, acceptance into this enclave was conditional on allegiance to their religion, *la lucha*.

The final text involves the Central Intelligence Agency (CIA) and its contribution to the influx of capital into the Miami region, facilitating Exilic Cubans' socioeconomic success. The formation in 1961 of the Consejo Revolucionario Cubano, a provisional government in exile, created a financial relationship between Exilic Cubans and their benefactor, the

CIA (Gonzalez-Pando 1998, 24). According to reports published in the mid-1970s, reports prompted by hearings held by the U.S. Senate Select Committee to Study Government Operations with Respect to Intelligence Operations, Zenith Technological Services, known by the codename JM/WAVE, served as a front operation on the campus of the University of Miami. By 1962, JM/WAVE was the largest CIA installation in the world outside of Langley, employing thousands of Miami Cubans, making it one of the largest employers in Dade County.

It is no secret that the CIA, under the direction of then–attorney general Bobby Kennedy, conducted a secret war against Castro from Miami, code-named Operation Mongoose. Recent declassified U.S. documents show a continuous attempt to undermine and overturn Castro's government. The CIA tried to hatch a scheme for a second invasion of Cuba months after the failed Playa Girón invasion. The development of these plans continued even after the United States made a "no-invasion" pledge with the Soviet Union in order to end the October 1962 Cuban missile crisis. Some of these schemes included "Operation Good Times," which proposed airdrops of doctored photos of Castro consorting with beautiful women, sporting the caption "My ration is different." Operation Free Ride proposed airdrops of one-way airline tickets to other Latin American countries. Operation Dirty Tricks was designed to blame Cuba in the event that John Glenn's Mercury orbit failed. Evidence was manufactured to prove electronic interference from the island. Operation True Blue planned to disrupt Cuban radio and television transmissions with degrading comments about Castro. Operation Bingo would justify an August 1964 invasion by simulating a Cuban attack on Guantánamo Bay Naval Base. Other operations included planning the assassination of Castro, even hiring Chicago Mafia crime boss Sam Giacana, who formerly profited from casinos in La Habana, for $150,000 to do the job. Ironically, the assassins hired where on the FBI's most-wanted list and on Bobby Kennedy's target list of organized crime figures.[12] The Museum of the Ministry of the Interior in La Habana provides displays and documentation of more bizarre plots. One example is a plot to supply Castro with cigars containing botulism or explosives. In another plot, thallium salts (a depilatory) were to be sprinkled on Castro's boots in hopes that his trademark beard would fall off.

Operation Mongoose involved more than five hundred caseworkers, handling more than three thousand Exilic Cubans, at a cost of more than $100 million a year (Baker 1999, 42). Funds to carry out CIA missions made possible the operation of more than fifty-four front businesses, including airplanes that served as an air force known as Southern Air Transport and a navy whose ships were disguised as merchant vessels (Didion 1987, 88–91; and Forment 1989, 47–81).[13] Some businesses, while never proven to be CIA funded, maintained a very close relationship with the agency. For example, Radio Swan involved E. Howard Hunt, later convicted for the Watergate break-in, in its operations. In fact, prior to the CIA-planned Playa Girón invasion, Radio Swan broadcasted coded messages informing counter-revolutionaries in Cuba of the upcoming assault (Frederick 1986, 6–7). The proactive presence of the CIA in numerous businesses provided Exilic Cubans with substantial funds for covert operations to destabilize the Castro government, as well as employment opportunities in numerous service industries associated with the agency, including boat shops, gun shops, travel agencies, and real estate agencies.

Exilic Cubans Bernard Barker, Virgilio González, and Eugenio Martínez, who in 1972 allegedly burglarized the Democratic National Committee in the Watergate complex, were Miami realtors previously associated with JM/WAVE. Their involvement in the burglary was an attempt to document a Castro-McGovern conspiracy. Under the rubric of the Exilic Cuban religion of *la lucha,* the convicted Watergate burglars became *mártires de la lucha* (martyrs of the struggle), the highest honor one can expect to receive in Miami. CIA-trained Cubans have also allegedly been used by foreign governments to carry out terrorist acts in the name of the global struggle against communism. For example, it is believed that in 1976, the Chilean state police reportedly hired Exilic Cubans to assassinate Orlando Letelier, former Chilean ambassador under Salvador Allende, critic of the Pinochet military dictatorship, allegedly linked to the Castro regime. His car exploded close to Dupont Circle in Washington, D.C. (García 1996, 142–43).

Ironically, while the CIA continued to support several anti-Castro schemes, as in the case of armed raids on the island between 1963 and 1965, the Justice Department began to clamp down on Exilic Cuban military activities. While the CIA provided support to these groups, FBI agents infiltrated them in an attempt to collect sufficient evidence to prosecute its leaders. When the U.S. Justice Department brought criminal charges against these anti-Castro groups for violating the U.S. Neutrality Act (which forbids U.S. citizens from taking hostile actions against a foreign country), they were prosecuting the same groups that had received their training and funds from the CIA.

The socioeconomic success achieved by Exilic Cubans within a capitalist system in Miami, and their expulsion from a communist homeland,

made them more likely to embrace the Church's Franco-influenced attitude about the evils of communism. Their hatred of Marxism and the
U.S. financial support provided to those of refugee status facilitated their
adoption of the dominant Euroamerican capitalist value system. Soon
they became exaggeratedly "American." With a consistent voter turnout
of over 75 percent in national and local elections, Exilic Cubans have
learned to translate their worldview into public policy. This worldview
and spiritual understanding revolve around the central theme of the Sa-
tanic nature of communism in general and of Castro in particular, a
theme constructed in *el exilio*.

Miami's Panopticon

Most societies create for themselves a series of opposing systems designed
to define what is good and what is evil. This binary system contrasts what
is legal with what is illegal, what is acceptable with what is unacceptable,
what is criminal with what is not criminal, and so on. Societies can con-
strue political assassinations, restriction of free expression, or brute in-
timidation as necessary evils in the advancement of a sacred cause. Yet not
all people within that society, though they may agree with the ultimate
end, may agree with the tactics used to achieve the goal. The question becomes, How do these violent tactics become acceptable in the eyes of a
society at large? The answer is, It can be done only by reducing what is
good and what is evil to a simple opposition between what is "normal"
and what is pathological (Foucault 1973, 73).

When a society is engaged in a holy war—such as *la lucha* against
Satan, personified as Fidel Castro—warlike activities, killings, bombings,
and censorship must be employed to ensure the final victory of good. It
becomes normal, regardless of how distasteful it may be, to accept the
spilling of blood. In fact, it becomes a moral imperative. According to
Rodolfo Frómeta, the commander of Commandos F-4 who served three
years in federal prison for trying to buy U.S. armaments to be used in
Castro's assassination, killing Castro would not be murder but rather "an
attempt to do justice about a person who has killed thousands and thousands of persons."[14] These victims include his son, father, and brother.
For Frómeta, and for the rest of his community, a new definition of justice is at work in which the actions taken to bring about this justice about
become rationalized and justified. In addition, determining what is normal by mounting the social structures of power becomes a way of pre-

serving Exilic Cuban culture. The power achieved by Exilic Cubans in Miami facilitated the construction of the indigenous religion of *la lucha,* which determines what is good and what is evil. Power has the ability to traverse and produce things. It creates pleasure, constructs knowledge, and produces discourse. Power can be positive, producing reality and creating the subject's opinion of what is "truth" (Foucault 1984, 60–61). It will be tolerated if those subjected to power are unaware that power structures exists, hence the importance of power being able substantially to mask itself (Foucault 1978, 86). Exilic Cubans effectively accomplished this masking by constructing *la lucha.* Through power, as voiced in the daily discourse concerning Castro's Cuba, the religion of Miami was created and normalized in the minds of Exilic Cubans as "true." The "truth" created is complete with religious justification for the power and privilege Exilic Cubans achieved in Miami and the power they exercise in the holy war against Castro.

Because the "enemies of Cuba" (read, those who are not us) are a threat to "truth," they must be silenced at all costs. A holy war has been waged for more than forty years against the Castro regime, presented to the general public as part of the "evil empire," á la then-president Ronald Reagan. This holy war includes the bombing of the Mexican (1979) and Venezuelan (1983) consulates in Miami, the 1979 bombing of the TWA terminal at Kennedy Airport, the 1978 Avery Fisher Hall bombing at Lincoln Center, the multiple bombings of the Cuban Mission to the United Nations, the machine gun assassination of Cuban attaché Félix Garcia Rodríguez, and the attempted assassination of Cuban United Nations ambassador Raúl Roa Kouri. Other terrorist acts include, but are not limited to, the unsuccessful 1964 bazooka shelling of the United Nations during Che Guevara's speech, the 1978 bombing of the offices of the newspaper *el Diario-La Prensa,* the 1979 bombing of the Soviet Mission to the United Nations, and the 1980 bombing of Aeroflot ticket offices.

During the 1970s, Exilic Cuban militants formed secret organizations like Frente de Liberación Nacional (National Liberation Front), Acción Cubana (Cuban Action), Omega Siete (Omega Seven), Gobierno Cubano Secreto (Secret Cuban Government), and Jóven Cuba (Young Cuba) to participate in violent confrontations against both Resident and Exilic targets (Gonzalez-Pando 1998, 54). In 1979, after Muñiz Varela was assassinated in San Juan, Puerto Rico, by "Comando Cero" for his participation in the inter-Cuban dialogue, Comando Cero released a statement to the United Press International: "Any Cuban or Puerto Rican,

Guerrilla training camps: About eight hundred Exilic Cubans trained in 1981 at a camp near Miami for possible guerrilla operations in Nicaragua, Cuba, and/or Panama. Weapons are AR-15, civilian versions of M-16 rifles. Courtesy of the Historical Museum of Southern Florida.

just as any American who travels to Cuba, regardless of his motives, is considered our enemy. Any Cuban who goes to Cuba, in tourist groups or by himself, we will be forced to be judged as we did with Muñiz Varela." In a different communiqué, he warned: "[Muñiz Varela was] the first to die, but not the last" (Masud-Piloto 1988, 77).

The 1997 bombings of tourist locations in La Habana, which killed an Italian tourist, wounded seven, and caused extensive property damage, was masterminded by a seventy-year-old Exilic Cuban named Luis Posada Carriles, who has claimed responsibility.[15] Posada allegedly was trained by the CIA in the 1960s, was the centerpiece of the Reagan administration's efforts to supply arms to the Nicaraguan Contras, and has been linked to assassination plots in Colombia, the Dominican Republic, Guatemala, La Habana, and Honduras. During his *New York Times* interview, Posada alleged a financial relationship with the deceased CANF cofounder, Mas Canosa, whose organization allegedly provided more than $200,000.[16] Posada chuckled when he stated that the money would arrive with a message from Mas Canosa, "This is for the church." More recently, the FBI uncovered a plot allegedly masterminded by

Posada to assassinate Castro during his August 1998 trip to Santo Domingo.[17] Ultimately, Posada absolved CANF of any responsibility in bankrolling his activities and publicly renounced terrorism.[18] Regardless of their actual involvement, those who participated in, or who were rumored to have participated in, such activities became *mártires de la lucha* when convicted. They did not become martyrs because they were falsely accused by the United States but because they fought against "evil," making them sacred heroes of the Exilic Cuban community. As José Basulto, cofounder of the rafter-rescue group Brothers to the Rescue, said, "Violators of the Neutrality Act are, in my eyes, patriots."[19]

That *mártires de la lucha* are regarded as patriots is evident in how the Exilic community venerates Orlando Bosch. The U.S. Department of Justice has linked Bosch to terrorist attacks in Miami and Latin America. Such alleged terrorism included a 1963 aerial strike at a Cuban refinery that killed three children, the shelling of a Polish freighter in the Port of Miami (for which he was convicted in 1968), and a 1976 bombing of an Air Cubana jetliner that claimed the lives of seventy-three passengers, most of whom were teenage members of Cuba's national fencing team (for which Bosch was acquitted in Venezuela in 1986). An unsupported allegation was also made during the 1978 House Select Committee on Assassinations placing Lee Harvey Oswald at Bosch's Miami home two months before Kennedy's assassination and both in Dallas around November 20 (Didion, 1987, 134–35). Yet the Miami City Commission, recognizing Bosch as a *mártir de la lucha,* declared March 25, 1983, to be "Dr. Orlando Bosch Day."

More recently, a grand jury indicted seven prominent Exilic Cubans accused of conspiring to assassinate Castro during the 1997 Latin American summit at the Venezuelan Island of Margarita, a clear violation of the U.S. Neutrality Act. The U.S. Coast Guard, responding to an October 27 distress call from the forty-six-foot yacht *La Esperanza* (the Hope), discovered five alleged assassins (between sixty and seventy years old) carrying two .50-caliber semiautomatic rifles, night-vision goggles, and satellite positioning devices. One of the men, Angel Manuel Alfonso, blurted out the plot. Among those indicted with the five on the yacht was Jose Antonio Llama (owner of the yacht), who sits on the executive board of CANF, and Francisco "Pepe" Hernandez (owner of one of the weapons), who replaced Mas Canosa as chairman of CANF. These indictments occurred during the Clinton administration, leading Juan Masimi Soler, lawyer of one of the defendants, to profess the veneration of such *mártires de la lucha* when he said, "If this were Ronald Reagan, or

Mártires de la lucha: A year after the event, Orlando Gutierrez kneels before pictures of the fallen Brothers to the Rescue downed in 1996 by Cuban MiG fighters. The Miami Exilic Cuban community recognizes these men as martyrs in the struggle for a free Cuba. Photograph © A. Enrique Valentin/*The Miami Herald*.

George Bush, they'd be giving these people a freedom medal." Ultimately, by 1999 all the men were acquitted or had the charges against them dismissed.[20]

Although Exilic Cubans consider themselves "free," in reality Miami can be understood through the paradigm of the "panopticon" as offered by philosopher Michel Foucault. Panopticism describes a model prison in which the center is occupied by a guard tower enabling guards to gaze at the prisoners in their individual backlit cells, while the prisoners are unable to gaze back at the guard. The guard's ability to gaze confers power on the observer while setting a trap for those being observed, even when the surveillance is not constant. The mere possibility of being watched forces the prisoners as Objects to internalize the power relation. In Foucault's words:

He who is subjected to a field of visibility, and who knows it, assumes responsibility for the constraint of power; he makes them play spontaneously upon himself; he inscribes in himself the power relation in which he simultaneously plays both roles; he becomes the principle of his own subjection. By this very fact, the external power may throw off its physical weight; it tends to the non-corporal; and, the more it approaches this limit, the more constant, profound and permanent are its effects: it is perpetual victory that avoids any physical confrontation and which is always decided in advance. (1995, 202–3)

It would be naive to view power as belonging only to the elite. Power is everywhere, forming and passing through a multitude of institutions. It is most effective when it is exercised through a coercion that appears natural and neutral, a coercion based on the simple ability to observe. The panopticon, as a mechanism of exercising power, serves as a model for how oppressive power works on the streets of Miami. The bomb that is overtly targeted at one offending "heretic" is symbolically directed at all potential "sinners." For this reason the public display of punishment must be spectacular, seen by all as a triumph of "justice." The excess of violence becomes a religious ritual that purifies the whole society through the sacrificial death of the heretic who bears the sins of those who defile what has been defined as good. Public punishment, at its extreme, brings into play the dissymmetry between the heretic who has dared to go against the doctrines of *la lucha* and the constructed all-powerful will of the Exilic community, which displays its power by communicating what will happen to those who refuse to conform to the "truth" as established and defined by that community.

These public demonstrations are not intended to establish justice but to manifest power, and, through that power, to prevent the repetition of the heretic's peccadillo. In light of several militant groups having declared, as the common phrase has it, "war against the enemies of Cuba's freedom," past punishment serves as the instrument for preventing others from straying from the official religious doctrines of *la lucha*. Punishment, above all else, is always directed at all potential heretics. Hence it is never a mechanism solely of prohibition but also of production—the production of political and social subservience. All must know about the possibility of violence because all must be made to feel afraid; and all must bear witness to its infliction so as to, to a certain extent, partake in its unleashing. Only an inefficient social structure will continue to constrain through the use of brute force when the religious fervor of *la lucha,* normalized as truth in the minds of the community, provides a better way of obtaining conformity.

With time, the fear of punishment in the form of bombs and machine guns is no longer needed to maintain discipline within the Exilic Cuban community. These weapons have been so effectively used in the past that the guard's ubiquitous gaze has been internalized. A shift in the "technology of power" takes effect when yesterday's tortured public bodies scattered on Miami's sidewalks in the wake of a bombing become today's docile private bodies confined to their individual "cells." As Exilic Cubans committed to memory the terror of swift punishment, a system of diminishing penalties took hold. Instead of brute force, public ridicule or ostracism from the socioeconomic spaces of Miami became sufficient to ensure obedience. Although the use of brute force may still occasionally be required as a reminder of the punishment awaiting heretics, the bomb-throwing patriots operating within the theater of punishment have increasingly become the bureaucratic patriots working within the sociopolitical hierarchy.

La lucha thus includes a comprehensive system of domination. Exilic Cuban radio stations and numerous *periodiquitos* (tabloids) of Miami become the unblinking eye of *la lucha,* serving as the guard tower.[21] The gaze of the radio stations and *periodiquitos* produce conformity to the religion of *el exilio*. These stations are not the terminal points of power. Rather, they serve as the official pulpit whose sermons spread news, disseminate rumors, denounce heretics, and constantly call for the punishment of in(Fidel)s. The airwaves and printed pages of Miami normalize the "sinner's" punishment, not as vengeance in the hands of terrorists but as a result of divine retribution. And when the instruments of God's wrath are prosecuted by the U.S. government, these instruments become martyrs of the faith. The guard in the tower, the power that demands obedience, is disguised as the basic democratic right to a free press.

Because power cannot be possessed, it can only be exercised by those privileged enough to position themselves within the dominant culture. But if misused, power can be lost and used against those who previously benefited from it. Bernardo Benes, considered one of the leading Exilic Cubans in the late 1970s, lost his position of power and privilege when he met with Castro to explore the possibilities of reconciliation. Benes's trip to Cuba resulted from Castro's appeal (stimulated by secret normalization talks with the Ford and Carter administrations) to engage in a dialogue about possible reconciliation with Exilic Cubans. An olive branch was offered when Castro publicly stated he might have "misjudged" the "Cuban community abroad."[22] *El diálogo* divided the Exilic community when what became known as *el comité de los 75* (the committee of the seventy-five), headed by Bernardo Benes, traveled to la Habana to discuss reconciliation. The participation of Exilic Cubans in *el diálogo* led to the bombing of Miami's Continental Bank (where Benes worked) and of Padrón Cigars (owned by another participant of *el diálogo,* Orlando Padrón); the boycott and vandalizing of businesses of participating owners; beatings; and the assassination of two *dialogueros* (participants in the dialogue): Eulalio José Negrín and Carlos Muñiz Varela.

Those who participated in *el diálogo* were labeled traitors, communists, *vendepatrias* (sellouts), *tontos inutiles* (useless idiots), and *mariposas* (butterflies, a euphemism for homosexuals) by Miami's Exilic Cuban radio stations and *periodiquitos.* One Exilic Cuban *periodiquito* (*La Crónica,* translated as the "chronicle" or the "story") published the names, addresses, and telephone numbers of those supporting *el diálogo* so that "real" Cubans could personally express their anger.[23] On several occasions, as late as 1986, some Exilic Cuban radio stations were fined by the Federal Communications Commission for inciting riots. Benes described the panopticon function of these radio stations and tabloids when he stated, "A million Cubans are blackmailed, totally controlled, by three radio stations. I feel sorry for the Cuban community in Miami. Because they have imposed on themselves, by way of the Right, the same condition that Castro has imposed on Cuba. Total intolerance. And ours is worse. Because it is entirely voluntary" (Didion 1987, 113). To live in *el exilio* of Miami is to consent to one's own subjugation while hoping that *la lucha* will radically provide salvation from one's estranged existence.

The events surrounding the scheduled performance of Dolores Prida's one-act play, *Coser y cantar* (Sew and sing), during the First Annual Festival of Hispanic Theater in 1986 also illustrates how Miami's panopticon functions. *Coser y cantar* explores the struggle of an Exilic Cuban woman caught between two cultures. A bilingual monologue develops between the Spanish-speaking "Ella" who represents her cultural heritage, and the English-speaking "She" who represents her Angloization. As both sides of her personality bitterly bicker for mastery, Ella/She concludes that both selves are crucial for survival. The play was canceled because of numerous radio denunciations and bomb threats. Why? Dolores Prida was suspected of communist leanings. Her experience in Miami led her to claim that the only city besides Miami where she has been afraid to express herself, "where people look over their shoulder to see if they can say what they were going to say," is La Habana. And on October 19, 1998, someone lit fire to Club Amnesia in Miami Beach in response to a sched-

Protesting Bernardo Benes: A group of Exilic Cuban women protests across the street from the Continental National Bank (where Bernardo Benes was a vice president), in spite of the pouring rain. Posters read "Dialogue is treason to our martyrs," "Dialogue is treason to a free Cuba," and "Benes is an agent of Fidel." Courtesy of the Historical Museum of Southern Florida.

uled performance of Resident Cuban Manuel Gonzalez Hernandez, simply known as Manolin, *el Médico de la Salsa* (the Salsa Doctor).

In Miami former comrades can easily become deadly enemies. Forty years after the CIA-backed Playa Girón invasion, a conference was held in Cuba to discuss the events of 1961. Nine members of the Brigade 2506, who fought to dethrone Castro, now accepted his invitation to the conference. They were exploring a new strategy for dealing with Castro's government, one of open dialogue. Yet, in spite of their membership in the Brigade, seen as a badge of honor among the faithful, they were now seen as enemies of *la lucha,* backsliding sinners who had lost their way, traitors *sin vergüenza* (with no shame). Hence they were officially kicked out of the Brigade 2506, becoming personae non gratae. Mario Cabello, who was among those ousted, had to be escorted out of the building for his own safety. "It's ironic that forty years ago when I was captured by

Cuban soldiers, I was called a traitor and today, forty years later, I'm being called a traitor by my friends," said Cabello. Juán Pérez-Franco, president of the Brigade, justifies the righteous indignation exhibited against those who break from *la lucha*'s doctrines because they "betrayed the martyrs of the invasion." According to Pérez-Franco, "Our position is one of total and complete intransigence. We are at war. War is not just shooting. We are fighting them ideologically, intellectually, in a war of principles. We have no army, no money for an army and no country to help us. The only weapon we have is our intransigence."[24] This intransigence is maintained through the panopticon of Miami, where inhabitants believe one thing privately yet confesses quite another thing publicly. Joan Didion captured the pain caused by Miami's panopticon when she wrote, "The [wounds] *el exilio* inflicts upon its own do not entirely heal, nor are they meant to" (1987, 114–15, 120).

These wounds are not inflicted by a centralized Exilic Cuban elite. Rather, the power to inflict wounds on the docile body resides in a multitude of networks (such as radio stations and *periodiquitos*) woven into the political economy of the elite. Therefore, replacing the elite would not suffice in eliminating these networks, which are ingrained in Miami life. Benes's experience proves the autonomy of a disciplinary structure designed to punish dissenters of *la lucha*, even those among the elite. The tragedy of Miami's panopticon is that those who exercise power are not necessarily aware of their complicity in the power structures of the Exilic community or of their own self-subjugation to those structures owing to their belief in the holy cause of *la lucha* (De La Torre 2001, 196–200).

CHAPTER 3

Psalm 137

Constructing Cuban Identity while in Babylon

The U.S. occupation of Cuba after the island's 1898 war for independence brought in its wake economic domination by Euroamericans. The war created huge debt, providing cheap land and labor to U.S. capitalists, who were able to step in and replace the bankrupt Cuban ruling class. By paying back taxes, for example, they could easily acquire properties that had been foreclosed on. Through the Reciprocity Treaty signed in 1903, the now-defunct hegemonic Cuban ruling class was replaced by a Euroamerican elite. Overnight, the traditional oligarchies virtually disappeared (Donghi 1993, 202).

Between 1909 and 1929, U.S. capital investment in Cuba increased by 700 percent. Approximately 80 percent of Cuba's imports and 60 percent of her exports came from or went to the United States. During the 1920s, 95 percent of Cuba's main crop, sugar, was United States bound; 40 percent of all raw sugar production was owned by U.S. capitalists, two-thirds of the entire output of sugar was processed in U.S.-owned mills (mostly in Baltimore and other U.S. cities), and the product left the island through the Havana Dock Company, also in U.S. hands. Additionally, 23 percent of the nonsugar industry, 50 percent of public service railways, and 90 percent of telephone and electric services were owned by U.S. firms. Investments in Cuba ranged from $700 million to $1 billion, controlling Cuba's most profitable sectors. Nickel deposits were mined and processed by Nicaro, a U.S.–built plant. During military occupation, Military Governor Wood granted 218 tax-exempt mining concessions, mostly to U.S. firms. Of the four oil refineries in Cuba, two were owned by U.S. companies. All banks were in United States and British hands, with one-quarter of all deposits being made in U.S. and British branches. Approximately 90 percent of the export trade of Havana cigars went through the United States, which controlled half the manufacturing process (Huberman and Sweezy 1989, 5–7; Thomas 1971, 466; Newman 1965).

The U.S. domination of the Cuban market bordered on the absurd. Cuba exported raw sugar to the States while importing candy. It exported tomatoes, and imported all its tomato paste. Cuba exported fresh fruit and imported canned fruit. It exported rawhide and imported shoes. It produced vast quantities of tobacco yet imported cigarettes (Benjamin et al. 1984, 13). How right was José Martí, who was fond of saying "The country that buys, controls; the country that sells, obeys" (*OC* VI, 160).

Without a doubt, territorial invasions and the exploitation of the island's natural resources by U.S. corporations led to conditions that fostered the Castro Revolution in 1959. Fervor for national independence fanned anti-imperialist fires and began to play a central role in Cuban politics. Disgust at the "emasculation" of Cuba meant that any revolution on the island would be anticapitalist and anti-United States. Hence Castro's Revolution was more a product of Third World nationalism than of Marxist ideology. In fact, the early reforms implemented by Castro were not all that radical. Initial agrarian reforms were based on moderate principles used in Bolivia and Mexico, and rent-control policies similar to those implemented by Castro were already in place in many Latin American countries (Donghi 1993, 290–91).

In essence, Cubans find themselves as refugees in the very country responsible for putting them there. They have lost the land of their birth and have had to accept that their bodies will be laid to rest in alien soil. In short, Exilic Cubans are a people without a land, marginally welcomed in this country but also disliked because of their refusal to assimilate. Like other Hispanic groups, they face hostile congressional laws and proposals; however, as discussed in earlier chapters, they have also learned to capitalize on the space they occupy in Miami.

Most liberationist theologians focus on the biblical book of Exodus as a source of hope for their existential situation. A God who hears the cries of an oppressed people and personally leads them toward liberation serves as a powerful motif. Exodus, however, is not the story that best describes the Exilic Cubans' social location. Rather, it is the Babylonian captivity that best resonates with Exilic Cubans. Like the psalmist, Exilics sit by the rivers of their host country, singing about their inability to sing

God's songs in a foreign land. Psalm 137, which describes the Jews' captivity in Babylon, reads as follows:

By the rivers of Babylon, we sat and wept when we remembered Zion. On the midst of the willows we hung our lyres. There, our captors asked us for the words of a song, and our plunderers joyfully said, "Sing us a song of Zion." How shall we sing the song of Yahweh on foreign land? If I forget you Jerusalem, let me forget my right hand, let my tongue cleave to my palate if I do not remember you — if I do not bring up Jerusalem above the head of my joy. Remember Yahweh for the sons of Edom on the day of Jerusalem said, "Lay it bare, lay it bare, even to its foundation!" O daughter of Babylon, O destroyed one, blessed is the one who shall repay your reward with what you rewarded us. Blessed is the one who seizes and dashes your little ones against the stones.[1]

The Hebrew word *galut* is defined as exile, banishment, or the diaspora. As the physical condition of forced removal, it is more than just the result of international forces. To the one being cast into the diaspora, *galut* becomes a religious condition, a condition that forces the displaced person to ask the basic theodicy question: How can a loving and powerful God allow such unbearable pain to befall God's people? This deeply political psalm is also deeply religious. For the captive Jews in the foreign land of Babylon, their faith became a means of coping with their existential situation, giving meaning to the shame and humiliation of displacement and providing hope. In interpreting the sacred text as literature, narratives such as this one best explain the Exilic Cuban's social location because they depend less on the intention of the original narrator than they do on the imagination of those who reading the text.

The fervor of Exilic Cubans protesting the return of Elián to La Habana caused great division within the community and within individual families. Yet regardless of what individual Exilic Cubans advocated, all agreed that the overall geopolitical situation that gave rise to the Elián custody battle was caused by the shared pain of hanging their lyres in the willow trees, or better, of "leaving their conga drums by the palm trees." Hence to understand better the raw emotions expressed during the Elián confrontation, we must look at what it means to be an Exilic Cuban struggling for a sense of identity while residing in the "Babylon" of the United States.

Belonging neither to the United States nor to Cuba, Exilic Cubans turn inward in their struggle to define their identity (de los Angeles Torres 1995, 213). This struggle is in reality a (re)invention of a community's vision of itself that is both religious and future oriented. As the community struggles to find a unifying self-definition, grounded in a connection to the past, it ascertains the meaning abstracted from that past as an important criterion for coherence (Fischer 1986, 196). This unifying self-definition both can be culturally specific, as in the case of *la lucha,* and can dialectically function as critiques of the prevailing ideologies.

In trying to define the ethnicity of Exilic Cubans we come to a better understanding of the Exilic community's fervid ethical and religious response to Elián. How does the social location of Exilic Cubans contribute to their views about Elián, views that were grounded in religious convictions and that were expressed throughout the saga? I will explore this question by juxtaposing the biblical story of the Babylonian captivity articulated in Psalm 137 with the experience of Exilic Cubans. The task will be to conduct a social analysis, shedding light on the submerged convictions that led to a religious crusade, manifested in the multiple prayer vigils and parades held during the Elián saga. This chapter will accomplish this task by examining the Exilic Cuban ethnicity through a biblical-theological lens. First I will define the "we" sitting by the river weeping by exploring the similarities between the Jewish and Cuban exilic experiences. Second, I will attempt to spell out intra-Cuban power relations. If Exilic Cubans are reduced to a U.S.-subjugated Other, how can they begin to understand the relationship between a privileged segment of the Exilic Cuban community and a disenfranchised segment? Finally, I will explore the sociopolitical ramifications of a postexilic community in a post-Castro Cuba. If the goal of the Exilic Cuban community is eventual return to the land and therefore unification with the people they left behind, how can this reconciliation be harmonized with the biblical call to "dash [the enemies'] babies against rocks"? Should this be the official advocated view? Please note that it is not my intention in this chapter to provide a theological perspective or an ethical response; rather, it is to use biblical text (specifically Psalm 137) as well as the religious symbols used by Exilic Cubans to uncover the community's attempt to hide political power behind the religious facade of *la lucha.*

By the Miami River

By the Miami river, we sat and wept at the memory of La Habana, leaving our conga drums by the palm trees.

About his exile Reinaldo Arenas wrote:

I have realized that an exile has no place anywhere, because there is no place, because the place where we started to dream, where we discovered the natural world around us, read our first book, loved for the first time, is always the world of our dreams. In exile one is nothing but a ghost, the shadow of someone who never achieves full reality. I ceased to exist when I went into exile. . . . The exile is a person who, having lost one, keeps searching for the face he loves in every new face and, forever deceiving himself, thinks he has found it. (1993, 292)

Arenas makes powerfully clear why Exilic Cubans weep at the memory of the land that witnessed their birth. How do people create a new identity in a new place while not losing their connection to the old? From *el exilio,* Cubans are forced to reconstruct their identity in order to survive their new social location, which they do by gazing into the mirror that defines them.

In *la sagüesera* (southwest Miami), on Calle Ocho (Eighth Street), is a restaurant called Versailles, dubbed *"el palacio de los espejos"* (the mirrored palace). What makes this restaurant unique are the glistening chandeliers obtained from a Las Vegas casino and the mirrored walls. Sitting in the crowded salon, you constantly see yourself reflected. The restaurant, which recently celebrated its thirtieth anniversary, has served as a political space where politicians seeking the all-important Cuban vote stop to drink *un cafecito* (Cuban coffee) while glad-handing. Even then-president Bill Clinton made the necessary pilgrimage to the restaurant to thank the few Cubans who supported his last election. Supposedly Versailles is the place to be seen by those aspiring to higher community positions. But seen by whom? As Exilic Cubans look into the mirrors that surround them, they are in fact searching for their ontological origins—not so much what they are, but what they see themselves as.

When I was growing up in Miami, on Sunday nights my parents and I occasionally went to Versailles to enjoy a hot plate of Cuban food, even though we ate Cuban food at home throughout the week. We would put on our fine clothes and jewelry in preparation for dining on *palomilla* (steak) with *arroz con frijoles negros* (rice and black beans) and *plátanos maduros* (fried plantains), always gazing at ourselves in the mirrors that surrounded us. I often wondered if we dressed in our conspicuous attire so that we could be seen or so that we could see ourselves. As I looked in the mirror, I assumed that what I saw was a faithful (more or less) reflection of my existing self. Yet the opposite is true.

Instead of being a *reflection* of my self, the image in the mirror served the function of *forming* my self, my "I." To gaze into the social mirror of exilic existence is likewise to discover an image that constructs the self. The elusive reflection of the Cuban in the mirror constructs an Exilic Cuban self captivated by its belief in the projected "imaginary," in which both future and past are based on an illusion. In short, the ideal formed in the mirror situates the agency of the "ego" in fiction, while projecting the formation of the "self" into history. This mirror emphasizes the alienation necessary for self-recognition by introducing an illusionary element into the construction of the ego, leading to the creation of a self-image that occurs outside the self. As a function of the mirror's ability to reflect the self, the perspective is reversed so that the appearance of the reflected self differs from that of the ego. Additionally, the mirror's size creates a perspective in which the ego sees the self as if from a distance (Lacan 1977, 1–7). Hence my history, as an Exilic Cuban being seen by an Exilic Cuban (me), is a mirage of someone anticipating the maturation of the power I strive to possess.

Here I am deciphering my self-identity as an Exilic Cuban as a recollection of images and fantasies designed to fulfill my desires. Because my Cuban eyes see in the mirror the maturation of the political and social power that I desire to possess in exile, reading my history as an illusionary "golden exile" becomes of paramount importance. I go to the restaurant well dressed, wearing my jewelry, not so that others can see me but so that I can see myself as someone with power—or the potential to obtain it. By striving for power in Miami, Exilic Cubans create a history in which they tell themselves that before they got there, *"Miami era un campo con luces"* (Miami was just a village with fancy lights).

Those Exilic Cubans who possessed the power to transform a sleepy tourist town into the epicenter of U.S. trade with Latin America see themselves as superior to other ethnic groups that have not transcended the *barrio,* or ghetto. But which is the illusion, the self or the reflection? Seeing an Exilic Cuban from the mirror's "imaginary" perspective places the subject "I" in a privileged space of observation, while imposing an oppressive gaze on other Cubans, such as those who came through Mariel in 1980 or those who stayed in Cuba. These Cubans (along with other non-Cuban Latinas/os) become the Exilic Cuban's Other, categorized by their class and skin pigmentation.

How Cubans "see" their Other defines their existential self. The ability to "see" implies a position of authority, a privileged point of view, as illustrated by the panopticon model discussed in the previous chapter. "Seeing" is not merely a metaphysical phenomenon involving the transmittance of light waves. Rather, it encompasses a mode of thought that radically transforms the Other into an object for possession. The subjective "I" exists only when it tells itself who it is not; it is defined when it is contrasted with the seen objects—in this case Resident Cubans and Marielitos. Socially constructing the "I" out of the differences with the "them" involves established power relations that give meaning to these differences. Specifically, when an Exilic Cuban man striving to be part of the elite looks in the mirror, he does not see a Resident Cuban, an African American, a woman, a homosexual, or a non-Cuban Hispanic, all of whom he perceives as inferior. By projecting his "I" onto the Other, he is able to define himself as a white macho man who is successful and religious. This mirror image normalizes the Exilic Cuban's self-definition, while legitimizing the Other's relationship to it (De La Torre 2001, 187).

Also important in the creation of this self-definition is the belief that the frustration, humiliation, and alienation caused by *el exilio* are by no means the fault of those forced into the diaspora. Foundational to the self-definition of the Exilic Cuban is the concept of betrayal—betrayal by Batista, who abandoned the island, betrayal by those Cubans who supported Castro, betrayal by Castro to the ideals of the revolution, and betrayal by the United States at the Bay of Pigs. Even though the Exilic community may now be surmounting local power structures, and in effect, may be responsible for oppressing others, it is inconceivable for Exilic Cubans to see themselves in the role of oppressor. In their minds, they are the perpetual victims. To complete the mirror image's hold on Exilic Cubans, a narrative with an absolute appeal to the "truth" of religion revelation is required. The importance of *la lucha,* as this religious expression, is that it provides the psychological reassurance of legitimacy. When Exilic Cubans compare their own position with that of the less economically privileged Resident Cubans, they fail to be content with their success; they feel they have earned the right to their happiness. No matter how mythical the "golden exile" may be, the "success story" is crucial in the construction of the Exilic Cuban ethnic identity. This story dictates that they have earned their wealth and privilege and that Resident Cubans have brought about their own misfortune by supporting Castro or by refusing to accept capitalist ideology. Their failure proves their illegitimacy as "true" Cubans, and therefore they must be envious of Exilic Cubans, who have proven their legitimacy.

For Exilic Cubans to see themselves as "true" Cubans in the social mirror of exile is to internalize, naturalize, and legitimize their reflection, allowing them to mask their power in reshaping Miami's political and economic structures according to the tenets of *la lucha.* They actively construct a new identity, complete with a complicated justification of privilege, so that they can blame their Other for their constructed space, which the Other deserves because of their inferiority or their refusal to emulate Exilic Cubans. The ethnicity they construct is an attempt to imitate the dominant culture, the same culture whose neocolonialist ventures on their island forced them to be refugees. Emasculated by U.S. neoimperialism, those who financially benefited from this relationship now look toward the former imperialist to define their machismo (Freire 1994, 44–45). Unable to discern how the previous U.S.-Cuba relationship contributed to the oppression of most Cubans, Exilics developed a "submerged consciousness" that allows them to ignore or forget this history. The first two waves of Exilic Cubans refugees desired at all costs to resemble their oppressor, yearning for equality with the eminent men of the United States.

La lucha, as holy war, is a product of mirror imagery, where religious fervor and political convictions become merged to create a self-imposed ethnic identity. Yet the self-deceptive gaze, influenced by the pain of living in *el exilio,* creates a history that supports and justifies the construction of the Exilic Cuban ethnic identity. This history includes three necessary beliefs: (1) that Exilic Cubans pulled themselves up by their own bootstraps; (2) that Exilic Cubans fled tyranny; and (3) that Exilic Cubans are not racists. Before continuing with our analysis, let us first turn to debunking these myths.

The Exilic Cuban–constructed ethnicity stresses the fact that the refugees of the two waves of immigration before the Mariel boat lift were model citizens who always embraced the Euroamerican work ethic. During the early 1960s, the U.S. media broadcast numerous stories of penniless Cubans rising from adversity to success. These stories stereotyped the Exilic Cuban as being part of the "Cuban success story," obscuring the difficulties faced by the majority of *el exilio.* While the rags-to-riches mythology benefited both the United States and the elite of the Exilic Cuban community, the myth of the success story prevented Exilic Cubans from creating alliances with other disenfranchised minority groups. In fact, it pitted them against the Miami black community as they competed for jobs, governmental services, and other forms of public support, such as small business loans.

In a letter to then-president Lyndon Johnson, Donald Wheeler Jones, president of the Miami Beach branch of the National Association for the Advancement of Colored People, outlined the concerns of the Miami black community:

A cursory observation of the employment patterns of many Miami and Miami Beach hotels, restaurants, and other businesses will substantiate the fact that the Cuban has displaced the Negro and other personnel formerly employed there in many capacities such as waiters, bell-hops, doormen, elevator operators, and other similar occupations. There are many other categories of employment, almost too numerous to mention, that Negroes no longer enjoy as a direct result of the Cuban influx which apparently is about to be extended. In short, the Cuban influx of immigrants to this country have had their most severe effect upon that group of citizens least able to afford it, the uneducated, non-highly skilled, non-professional Negro, who prior to the Cuban influx could eke out a fairly decent standard of living through menial, service-type jobs that require a minimum of formal education or training. (Masud-Piloto 1988, 63)

The Cuban success story was created at the moment the civil rights movement was making its mark on Miami. Just as the city's black community began organizing to make demands for justice, Cubans began to arrive. Their arrival created a diversion, allowing the white establishment to ignore the issues raised by the black community. Racist employers preferred the lighter-skinned Cubans to the blacks who traditionally occupied these jobs. Praising the Cuban "work ethic" implied that other groups (read, Miami blacks) had not yet adapted to the "American" work ethic. Euroamericans holding positions of power in Miami were able to point to the Cubans and in effect say to the black community, "Stop whining, look at these amazing Cubans who came with only the clothes on their back, not speaking the language. They've pulled themselves up by their bootstraps. What's your excuse?"

As we've established, one's identity as an Exilic Cuban is a social construction created out of the pain of living in *el exilio*. And a foundational tenet of this construction claims that Exilic Cubans remember the homeland as a white nation, a construction that is detrimental both to biracial Cubans and to African Americans in Miami. In 1980, as more than one hundred thousand Mariel Cubans crossed the Florida Straits on their journey to Miami, Miami experienced its worst race riot. In March of that year a black insurance salesman named Arthur McDuffie was pulled over by several police officers who proceeded to crack open his skull with their flashlights because he had attempted to outrun them on his motorcycle, after allegedly making a vulgar gesture. Two months later an all-white jury took three hours to find all the white officers involved not guilty. Within two hours of the verdict, rioting, killings, burning, and looting erupted throughout Liberty City, Miami's primary black neighborhood, lasting several days. The reaction of the Cuban community was to perceive the civil unrest as a North American phenomenon. After all, in their minds, racism was not a Cuban vice. During the riots, Exilic Cubans sat on the sidelines, telling both Anglos and Africans Americans how much better Cuba handled its "black problem." Although the cause of the riot was more complex than the introduction of a new wave of Cubans to the Miami area, the Euroamerican community linked the race riots with the arriving Cubans, insisting that the cause of the riots was black frustration at losing jobs to incoming Cubans, ignoring the obvious connection to McDuffie's murder.[2]

African Americans found themselves in a city where the power structures were transforming as a lighter-skinned immigrant group pushed them aside, contributing to their invisibility. McDuffie was the spark igniting the rage caused by the double subordination of Miami's black community: subordination to Euroamericans and now subordination to the emerging Cuban community.

It was important to both Euroamericans and Exilic Cubans that this emerging community succeed. On a local level, its success served as a counterpoint to problems with the black community. On a national level, it served as a viable alternative to communism by perpetuating the myth that *any*body can make it in the United States. The titles of several newspaper articles point to the Cuban success story: "Cuba's New Refugees Get Jobs Fast," "Those Amazing Cubans," and "Cuban Success Story in the United States."[3] The Exilic Cubans' success helped them to replace the Miami Euroamerican establishment. Including the "rags-to-riches" myth in the formation of their identity served as a form of resistance to the Euroamerican dominant culture. Paradoxically, since they themselves were struggling as new immigrants, it was necessary for the elite within the Exilic Cuban community to master the structures of oppression not only to get the attention of the dominant culture but also to replace it.

The successful communication of power and authority, as with the success story, produces a self-fulfilling prophecy. While being socialized into an Exilic Cuban ethnicity, Exilics learn how to act with the authority and self-assurance that both results from and reinforces the success story. If others believe in their story, the impression will contribute to their emerging power (Scott 1990, 48–49). While the success story may veer from the reality of the 1970s, the construction of this story served the domestic and foreign interests of the United States, while transforming the Exilic Cubans from refugees into model immigrants, then into Miami's ruling elite whose political and economic power is felt in Washington, D.C., as well as around the world. This social and political construction of the Exilic Cuban success story created a public narrative that reflected and reinforced the changing character of power and politics, forging the "truth" of the story and linking it to power (Croucher 1997, 102–8).[4]

Since Exilic Cubans weren't ostensibly searching for opportunities, the second foundational tenet of their ethnic construction claims that they are victims who "fled" tyranny. The image of Exilic Cubans constructing rickety rafts and braving shark-infested waters to escape communism for the land of freedom has become a key motif of the exilic story, defining both the determination and the machismo of the immigrants. The first two waves of refugees have claimed this model as the norm. Yet from 1960 to 1980, only sixteen thousand, or 2 percent, of all Exilic Cubans left Cuba on small boats or rafts (Allman 1987, 302). Most left by airplane. The heroic actions of the few who actually braved the treacherous Straits are minimized and adulterated when the raft experience becomes the normative experience for everyone. The reality notwithstanding, the dramatic tales of "fleeing communism" were necessary because of their advantages to the U.S. government. In the 1960s, the United States lost Cuba to the communists (assuming Cuba had belonged to the United States in the first place) and was defeated at Playa Girón, major setbacks in the ideological struggle against the Soviet Union. But the image of Cubans climbing off rafts and kissing U.S. soil provided powerful propaganda showing the superiority and desirability of capitalism over communism.

The Exilic Cuban pro-U.S. performance on the global stage of the Cold War afforded them benefits, specifically $2 billion in resettlement aid and immediate resident status, that simply did not exist for other immigrating groups. Additionally, these developments hid the fact that later refugees were not so much fleeing tyranny as they were seeking economic prosperity. They closely resembled "classical immigrants" who were "pulled" by the glittering allure of economic opportunities found in the United States, as opposed to being "pushed" by the Castro regime (Amaro and Portes 1972, 10–14). This economic pull to the United States complicates the reductionist argument that the sole motivation for Cuban immigration is political, a necessary belief in forging a privileged exilic identity. It ignores the natural flow of people from underdeveloped to developed countries, a trend that has existed in Cuba since Hernán Cortés left to seek riches of Mexico. While the basic motivation for an individual to leave any country may be dissatisfaction with the situation there, it is impossible to discern any clear dividing lines between political, economic, and psychological reasons.

The 1971 Cuban airlift: A newly arrived Cuban lies on the ground and kisses U.S. soil. Courtesy of the Historical Museum of Southern Florida.

The 1980 Mariel exodus, comprising the third wave of refugees, best illustrates this point. As the end of the 1970s the Cuban economy experienced a sharp decline in commodity prices, rising interest rates, a rapid increase in costs of industrial goods, and a budget deficit that reached $785 million by 1982. The situation was exacerbated by natural disasters, crop diseases, and machinery breakdowns, reducing the industrial output. In 1979 these conditions contributed to a 25 percent loss of the sugar harvest, and the near-total loss of the tobacco and coffee crops due to "blue mold." Additionally, pork production was literally wiped out because of African swine fever, and fishing revenue decreased by 25 percent because of an oil tanker spill.[5] Further, 1979 witnessed more than one hundred and fifteen thousand Exilic Cubans returning to the island for visits, spending more than $100 million, flooding the island with durable goods, and demoralizing Resident Cubans, who marveled at the economic success of those living in *el exilio* (Hamm 1995, 45–49).

As Cuba's economic situation worsened, in the late 1970s the country curtailed spending in the social economy, eliminating previously subsidized services such as bus transportation, utilities, and infant day care (Knight 1990, 254). In spite of the vehement denunciations of the Castro regime by U.S.–bound Mariel refugees, it appears that they migrated to the United States, as did many Haitians, to escape economic difficulties in the homeland. Yet an estimated thirty thousand Haitians were turned away during the same time as the Mariel exodus for being too "black" and for lacking the political or economic clout that was emerging among the established Exilic Cuban community.[6]

3 The third component of the construction of the Exilic Cuban identity is the myth of racial equality among Cubans, a theme that will be analyzed in greater detail in the next chapter. As mentioned above, most Exilic Cubans remember Cuba as a white nation, a construction that was challenged by the Mariel boat lift. Unlike the elite first wave of refugees, or the middle-class second wave, this wave of Cubans more closely resembled a cross-section of the population. Forty percent of these refugees were biracial, of mixed African and European lineage. The arrival of so many nonwhites transformed the Exilic community from 99 percent white before the Mariel boat lift to 80 percent white, 5 percent black, and 15 percent biracial after. Even with the arrival of many black and biracial Cubans, these groups remain the most under-represented among the émigrés. The double difficulty of being black immigrants (discriminated against among Cubans for being black and among blacks for being Cuban) prevented them from belonging to the kind of community that has sheltered the rest of the Exilic community. Many of these nonwhite Cubans settled in the Northeast (specifically in New York City and Union City, New Jersey) to escape residues of the South's Jim Crow tensions. Yet even in those cities they experienced racism from both Euroamericans and white Cubans. For example, as late as 1990, the income of nonwhite Cubans in the United States lagged behind white Cubans by as much as 40 percent, clearly indicating the economic toll of racism.[7]

Because of both racism and classism, an immediate distancing between the established Exilic Cuban community and these new arrivals from Mariel occurred. They came to be known pejoratively as *Marielitos;* this label was given them in an effort to differentiate this group of refugees from all previous groups. Most *Marielitos* held few memories of a pre-Castro Cuba; most were children of the Revolution, coming of age in the late 1960s or early 1970s. Some Exilic Cubans refused to support or assist the *Marielitos,* who found themselves stereotyped by both Exilic and Resident Cubans as criminals, patients in mental institutions, *mariposas* (slang for homosexuals) and *escoria* (scum). During the Mariel boat lift, the press in both La Habana and Miami found agreement in vilifying *Marielitos.*

According to then-mayor Maurice Ferre, Castro had "flushed these people on us" (García 1996, 70). The negative images of *Marielitos* that surfaced in the established community (both Euroamerican and Cuban) were mostly the result of articles published in *The Miami Herald.*[8] While it is true that more than one-fifth of all *Marielitos* had prison records, the vast majority of them were incarcerated as political prisoners or for acting as traders in the underground market. Less than 2 percent were hardcore, recidivist criminals, and only a few thousand suffered from any mental illness. The vast majority were blue-collar workers from the lower economic classes of society, and most were young single men without families (Peterson 1982, 81–86).

Additionally, a high proportion of *Marielitos* were black, and their darker skin left them open to scapegoating. They were seen by the established white Exilic community as a threat to their social construction of "model immigrants." According to a publication sponsored and funded by CANF, "Criminal activities became particularly significant after the 1980 Mariel exodus due to the actions of hardcore criminals that were forced to leave the country by Castro's government. Those criminal activities cast a dark shadow over this particular sector of Cuban immigration, but its effects subsided by the mid-1980's" (Jorge, Suchlicki, and de Varona 1991, 22, 56).

A 1982 poll of overall public attitudes toward U.S. ethnic groups, conducted two years after the Mariel boat lift by the Roper Organization, showed that only 9 percent felt Cubans have been good for the country, while 59 percent felt they had made the country worse. The remaining 32 percent had mixed feelings or no opinion. This transition from being considered "model citizens" during the first two waves of immigration to being the least favored ethnic group in the nation caused the established community to blame the new arrivals from Mariel (Portes and Stepick 1993, 30–33). Cubans seemed to have become the most stigmatized immigrant group in the history of the United States, as illustrated by the release of the movie *Scarface,* starring Al Pacino as a vicious *Marielito* drug lord.

Not surprisingly, three years after arriving, 26 percent of polled Mariel refugees believed they were discriminated against by Euroamericans, while 75 percent believed they were discriminated against by established Exilic Cubans (Portes and Clark 1987, 14–18). *Marielitos* quickly became the Exilic Cuban's Other, partially disparaged for not having left Cuba earlier. José M. Szapocznik, an Exilic Cuban psychologist, might best have unmasked some of the animosity many Exilic Cubans felt toward the *Marielitos* when he wrote, "Mariel Cubans carried the shame we all felt in having Castro outsmart us" (Levine and Moisés 2000, 52).

The fourth and latest wave of immigrating Cubans also needs to be considered. Since the Mariel boat lift, Cubans have continued to migrate to Miami. These Cubans, drawn to Miami as the Cuban economy crumbled as a result of the collapse of the Soviet Union and the Eastern European communist bloc, boarded various crafts to cross the Straits. These "boat people," known as *balseros* (rafters), began to arrive in the late 1980s, their numbers increasing as the Cuban economy spun out of control. The United States immigration policy for Cubans, unlike that for any other ethnic group ever to arrive on U.S. shores, facilitated speedy naturalization. Any Cuban who arrived in this country was labeled a political refugee and within two years obtained residential status. Yet interviews conducted with *balseros* revealed that their departure was motivated more by economic than by political concerns (Eckstein 1994, 121). With the end of the Cold War, however, Exilic Cubans lost their symbolic importance. Then–attorney general Janet Reno (a Miamian) declared in September 1994 that Cuban refugees were no longer welcome and would not be admitted into the United States. This declaration was in response to the latest wave of more then forty thousand *balseros* to this country. Tragically, many perished at sea.[9]

However they define their collective identity, it is certain that Exilic Cubans interpret this identity through a religious lens, through belief in a God who blesses them for having suffered so greatly because of the diabolical political ideology known as communism. *Gracias a Dios y todos los santos* (Thanks be to God and all the saints), reason most Exilic Cubans, they have been able to achieve economic and political success, in spite of the efforts of Satan's representative, Fidel Castro. This achieved success proves God's favor and serves as a testimony to the world that these exiles are not the *gusanos* Castro claims them to be but rather God's chosen people called to bear witness against the evils of communism in general and Castro in particular. This belief in a divine commission to crusade against God's enemies helps Exilic Cubans maintain the hope that, just as God returned the Jews of the biblical story to their homeland, so too will Exilic Cubans one day be returned home.

How Can We Sing?

"Sing," they said, "some mambo." How can we sing our rumba in a pagan land? Mi Habana, if I forget you may my right hand wither.

Those who arrived in the United States from Cuba as infants or small children struggle with the realization that they do not belong to the

Cuban rafters: An official U.S. Coast Guard photograph of rafters crossing the Florida Straits in 1976. Courtesy of the Historical Museum of Southern Florida.

mythical *Cuba de ayer* of their parents. In spite of their determination not to forget La Habana lest their "right hand wither," their situation provokes them to ask the paradoxical question, "How can we forget that which we can not remember?" On a personal note, when I look at my two children, born in the early 1990s, I realize that in spite of my efforts to raise them as Cubans (a term I struggle daily to define for myself), their skin is light enough and their lifestyle sufficiently middle-class for them to assimilate easily into the dominant culture. Their blond hair and blue eyes allow them to "pass" as Euroamericans. By 2030, when my children are my age, will they define themselves as Cubans? Will the names they give their children, names like Ashley Gómez or Jordan Perez, betray the extent of their assimilation, an assimilation similar to that of the exiled Jews who lived in Babylon some 2,500 years ago?[10]

The pain that prevents me, and many Exilic Cubans like me, from "singing our rumba" in a foreign land is the knowledge that while my parents, my children, and I belong to the same biological family, we live in separate cultural families. My parents will die as brokenhearted Cubans who will never again bathe at Cuba's warm tropical beaches. I will die as an unfulfilled Exilic Cuban, for even though I have visited my homeland on several occasions, I am deeply pained when constantly told by island inhabitants, "You may have been born here, but you are no Cuban." I am accepted neither in the United States because I am too Cuban nor in Cuba because I am too Americanized. My children will die as new "Americans," remotely remembering their roots. They are no more Cuban than my parents are "American." They exist in two different worlds, connected only by my generation.

Exilic Cuban sociologist Rubén Rumbaut has labeled those in this in-between space the "one-and-a-half" generation. While the first generation, consisting of our parents from the "old" world, faced the task of acculturation, managing the transition from one sociocultural environment to another, the second generation, consisting of our children from the "new" world, face the task of managing the transition from childhood to adulthood. We who are caught in between these two spaces are forced to cope with both crisis-producing and identity-defining transitions (1991, 61).

Every Exilic Cuban has heard Celia Cruz sing the popular tear-jerker "Cuando salí de Cuba" (When I left Cuba). No other song better summarizes the pain of the Exilic Cuban's existential position. "Never can I die, my heart is not *here*. Over *there* it is waiting for me, it is waiting for me to return *there*. When I left Cuba, I left my life, I left my love. When I left Cuba, I left my heart buried [emphasis mine]." This popular Cuban ballad, written by an Argentine (Luis Aguile) and sung as a hymn of faith, illustrates a certain poignant denial of Exilic Cubans, who will certainly live, and most probably die, on foreign soil.

Both the exiled Hebrews of the Bible and the Cubans of today were forced to deal with the incomprehensible pain of exile. Judaism as a religious expression was constructed in Babylon out of the pain of questioning the sovereignty of a God who would tear the chosen people from their homes and plant them in an alien land. A major concern for those in exile was their status as deportees. Did removal from the "promised land," by which their identity as Hebrews was constructed, indicate a divine rejection, voiding any future participation in God's plan? The prophet Ezekiel (11:14–25) addressed the exiled Hebrews' anxiety by attempting to construct a new covenant upon "a single heart" and "a new spirit." Moreover, with the fall of Jerusalem and the devastation of the Temple, which marked the end of the Jews' political sovereignty and the beginning of the Babylonian exile, concerns were again raised about an everlasting rejection by God, or worse, the inability of God to prevent these destructive forces. For Ezekiel (8–11) the fall of the city was not a result of God's powerlessness but of God's deliberate desertion, a belief qualified by the hope of restoration. Additionally, Ezekiel stressed the continuation of God's fidelity to Jerusalem and to the exiled. While comforting, Ezekiel's words failed to initiate repentance among those in exile (18). Instead, the experience of exile led the Jews to forge a new identity (De La Torre 2000, 271–72).

La lucha serves a similar purpose in constructing identity. As we have seen, Exilic Cubans subconsciously reconstructed themselves according to the imagery of the mirror. They internalize and naturalize their mirror image so that they can shape outside structures, always masking their drive to master them. If we define power as repressive, then a purely juridical understanding of power can develop. Power, identified with law, says "no." Such a view of power is wholly negative and narrow. Power is not defined as a group of institutions or social mechanisms ensuring obedience from those who are disenfranchised. It is neither a mode of subjugation nor a form of domination exerted by one group over another (Foucault 1978, 92; 1984, 60–61). Instead, power creates: it creates the "truth" of ethnicity for the one gazing into the mirror. Looking in the mirror, Exilic Cubans reread their history as the story of a people who escaped. Unlike other examples of refugees, both the Babylonian-bound Hebrews and the United States–bound Cubans belonged to the privileged upper class.[11] The surreal scene at the Miami airport, as well-dressed refugees disembarked, resulted from the same forces that brought about the Babylonian exile of the Bible. In both cases, the hegemony of the north (Babylon for the Jews and the United States for the Cubans) was responsible for the circumstances making flight necessary. Cuba's political system, since the formation of the Republic in 1902, was designed to protect the commercial interests and assets of the United States. Dictator Batista's utility to the United States was best expressed by William Wieland, Cuban desk officer at the U.S. State Department, who said, "I know Batista is considered by many as a son of a bitch . . . but American interests come first . . . at least he is *our* son of a bitch, he is not playing ball with the Communists" (Thomas 1971, 971). As vassals, both the Cuba of the first half of the twentieth century and Judah of the Bible were desirable prizes: Judah as a buffer zone between the north and south and Cuba as a key to the entire hemisphere. While Judah's exile was triggered by the physical invasion of Babylon, Cuba's Revolution was a backlash against the hegemony of the United States. The majority of the elite from both Cuba and Judah found themselves in *el exilio,* cut off from the land that defined who they were.

Is it any wonder that when Exilic Cubans read Psalm 137 they are stirred to the core of their beings? Exilic Cubans fully comprehend the tragic pain of sitting by the rivers of an alien land unable to sing to a God whom the psalmist secretly holds responsible. Landlessness, which comes with the ninety-mile crossing of the Florida Straits, radically disenfranchises them. The hope of returning to their land becomes fundamental to the construction of their Exilic Cuban ethnicity, yet each passing year, the cemeteries of Miami sprout more headstones bearing Cuban surnames.[12] Rather than proclaiming, "next year in Jerusalem," as do Jews at the conclusion of the Passover meal, Exilic Cubans tell each other, "this year Castro will fall," as if this one person were the only thing preventing them from "going home." In reality, the hope of returning home has been replaced by a private desire to adapt and capitalize on their presence in their new country.

The prophet Jeremiah wrote a letter to the exiled Jews telling them to stop hoping for a speedy return. He tells them "to build houses, live, plant gardens and eat their fruits; . . . [they are to] seek the peace of the city [to which they are exiled] . . . and pray to Yahweh for its peace, for in its peace there will be for you peace (29:5–9)." Like these exiled Jews, Exilic Cubans are forced to relinquish the old world and embrace the realities of the new space they occupy. Their adherence to Jeremiah's dictates was facilitated by their former contacts with elites in other Latin American countries; the possession of the necessary language skills and cultural links to deal with these contacts; their confidence in succeeding due to their habitus; and their connections with U.S. corporations, developed when they acted as their representatives in Cuba.

Success exists in exile. In the closing chapter of 2 Kings, the disgraced king of Judah, Jehoiachin, is allotted a seat at the Babylonian king's table "above those of the other kings (25:27–30)." From the former Judean elite arose leaders like Nehemiah, who occupied the post of "cupbearer" for the Persian king Artaxerxes.[13] While life in exile contained numerous hardships, the exiled Jews from the elite circles of Judah possessed the necessary habitus and resources to overcome their predicament. In Babylon, exiled Jews constructed a community whose legacy is felt to this day. This independent and powerful community participated in the life of postexilic Israel by providing financial support to the Palestinian community until the Roman destruction of the Second Temple. The importance of the Babylonian Jews in the construction of Judaism is evidenced by the monumental development of the Babylonian Talmud (which has taken precedence over the Jerusalem Talmud) in subsequent centuries.

Like the exiled Hebrews, Cubans suffered no unusual physical hardships. On the contrary, for some life in exile opened up opportunities that never existed in the homeland. Exilic Cuban sociologist Lisandro Pérez, who heads the Cuban Research Institute at Florida International University, states, "In Miami there is no pressure to be American. People can make a living perfectly well in an enclave that speaks Spanish" (Booth 1993, 84). As a unilingual Exilic woman told me, "Even though I hate Fidel, I thank him every day. In Cuba I had nothing, living in a dirt floor hut. But now, look at me. My two sons went to college and make a lot of money, and I own a house with Italian tiles." Like the Babylonian Jews, Cubans entered trades and grew rich, with some ascending the political structures to hold power over those who did not go into exile, just as Nehemiah did. In spite of the "rhetoric of return," the United States became the place where Exilic Cubans put their hope.

Even while Jerusalem was falling, Jeremiah bought a plot of land there (32:9–11). His message juxtaposes God's judgment—exile—with God's deliverance—repatriation. The true hope for Jerusalem did not lie in Babylon; rather, it was rooted in the homeland. Similarly, Exilic Cubans, especially YUCAs and Generation Ñ, see their exilic experience as positive because of their individual economic advancements.[14] While they look to the United States to define the future of Cuba, they also look to Cuba to define their present situation in the United States. The greatest danger of landlessness is the ending of a people's history. The historical activity of remembering *la Cuba de ayer* protects Exilic Cubans from this apocalyptic danger and creates the hope of one day returning to the "promised land" (De La Torre 2001, 192–93). During the 2002 centennial celebration of the establishment of Cuba as a republic, held in the heart of Miami, Rafael Peñalver, one of the celebration organizers, said, "We're in exile but can't forget that a dream for a free Cuba began more than a century ago. When Fidel Castro is just an asterisk in the story of Cuban history, there will always be a Cuban people."[15]

Remember What the Communists Did

Yahweh, remember what the communists did—a blessing on him who takes and dashes their babies against the stones.

The author of Psalm 137 prayed for the enemy's babies to be dashed against the stones. In his pain, the psalmist dreams of exacting revenge on those perceived to be responsible for expatriation. Revenge becomes part of the religious ethos of a wounded community. *La lucha* can never be understood apart from the deep desire for punishment, defined as justice, for those whom the community holds responsible for the pain of displacement. *En el noventa, Fidel revienta* (In 1990, Fidel will burst) was a slogan proudly worn on the T-shirts of Exilic Cubans in 1990. After the U.S. invasion of Panama and the fall of the Sandinista government in Nicaragua, crowds chanted, *"Ayer Daniel, hoy Manuel, mañana Fidel"* (Yesterday Daniel, today Manuel, tomorrow Fidel). But *mañana* never came. Castro, it appears, has outlived his obituaries. Even though historians write about the Cold War in the past tense, Miami remains the only place on earth that still excites Cold War hatred and fervor. As Joe Garcia, executive director of CANF, reminds us, "The Cold War didn't end for us" (Bikel 2001).

Mimicking the psalmist, the Exilic Cuban United States congressman Lincoln Diaz-Balart (ironically a nephew of Castro) called for a post-Castro Cuba to launch a campaign of retribution against anyone who participated in "collaborationism with tyranny." Ten years in prison would not be adequate punishment for those who are guilty. The congressman even called for foreign investors presently doing business with Cuba to be abducted and brought back to Cuba to be punished (Kiger 1996, 57). Diaz-Balart assumes that the vision held by Exilic Cubans is also the hope of the majority of Resident Cubans.

Sociologist Egon F. Kunz's theory is that the "majority-identified refugees are firm in their conviction that their opposition to the events [in their homeland] is shared by the majority of their compatriots" (1981, 42). Every Cuban Exilic community, whether in New Orleans in the 1850s, Tampa in the 1890s, New York in the 1930s, Miami in the 1950s, or Miami in the present, has assumed that their view of Cuba has been shared by those remaining on the island. This assumption provided them with moral justification in their struggle to change the island's economic and political reality (Poyo 1975, 76–98). The assumption that Resident Cubans desire to be rescued by Exilic Cubans is rooted in José Martí's words and actions. Martí's plight as an Exilic was central to his construction of Cuba Libre (liberated Cuba). The concept of two Cubas—the real Cuba that is *aquí* (here) as opposed to the morally degraded Cuba *allá* (there) and the responsibility of Exilic Cubans to continue the holy war of *la lucha* to "save" *la Cuba de allá*—is illustrated in a speech he delivered in Tampa, Florida, on November 26, 1891:

You [Exilic Cubans] must create, *allá* where the corrupt proprietor rots whatever he looks upon, a new Cuban soul . . . *Aquí* where we keep watch for the absent ones . . . where we create what must replace the things destroyed for us *allá—aquí,* no word so closely resembles the light of dawn, no consolation enters our hearts with greater joy, than this ardent and ineffable word: Cuban! . . . To our fatherland crumbling to pieces *allá,* and blinded by corruption, we must take the devout and farseeing country being [constructed] *aquí.* (1977, 252–64)

To the Exilic Cuban, Martí's words are as true today as they were more than a century ago.

When they look in the mirror, both Exilic and Resident Cubans see what they consider to be true Cubans. Patriots and traitors are presented in mirror-image reversal, depending on which side of the Florida Straits you look from. *La lucha*'s maintenance of *la Cuba de ayer* ensures the condemnation of the perceived enemies of Exilic Cubans while mythically creating the Cuba of tomorrow, a post-Castro Cuba based on horizontal oppression, where Resident Cubans will be subjected to Exilic Cubans. The overwhelming support of the embargo by Exilic Cubans denies Resident Cubans basic medical supplies and causes death among the sick, the elderly, and infants. According to recent polls, even though 25 percent of Exilic Cubans feel that the embargo has not worked, 78 percent strongly support its continuation, and 70 percent advocate increasing international economic pressures against foreign corporations dealing with Cuba (Grenier and Gladwin 1997, 10, 12).[16] From a sanitizing distance, Exilic Cubans are dashing the "enemy's" babies against rocks when they deny insulin to those born diabetic. Viewing the embargo in light of the Elián story, some have raised questions concerning the Exilic Cubans' desire for wishing one child a good life while denying it to countless others.

According to a 1997 study conducted by the American Association for World Health titled *Denial of Food and Medicine: The Impact of the United States Embargo on the Health and Nutrition in Cuba,* the newest United States embargo restrictions have contributed to an increase in low-birth-weight babies and nutritional deficits, such as neuropathy and anemia caused by vitamin deficiency. Further, a decrease in available medicines from 1,297 in 1996 to 889 in 1997 and a decline of water quality due to a lack of treatment chemicals and spare parts for the nation's water system have contributed to a deteriorating public-health infrastructure. The pope's call for the end of the embargo during his January 1998 visit to Cuba has spurred a heated debate in Washington. The staff of Senator Jesse Helms (R-N.C.) drafted a bill to modify the embargo to allow donations of federal food, medicine, and medical equipment. Both CANF and the Clinton administration expressed support for such a bill, yet Exilic Cubans like Congressman Diaz-Balart have continued their opposition, even though the final bill was self-defeating in its requirement of cash-only purchases.[17]

In 1998 Cuba petitioned the U.N. World Food Program to alleviate widespread shortages produced by two years of El Niño–related drought (the worst in forty years). The $20.5 million (less than 10 percent of the estimated $267 million crop loss) requested for food aid would be targeted at six hundred thousand people in Cuba's eastern provinces, mainly children, pregnant and nursing women, the disabled, and the elderly. The U.S. State Department normally approves such requests, even when made by countries like North Korea, Ethiopia, and Sudan, countries without diplomatic relationships with the United States. Nonetheless, Exilic Cuban congressional representatives Lincoln Diaz-Balart and Ileana Ros-Lehtinen urged the State Department to reject the request.[18] In their minds, sending one aspirin to Cuba would enrich Castro and ensure his continued political survival. President George W. Bush, in a speech to two hundred Exilic Cubans attending a celebration of the ninety-ninth anniversary of Cuban independence held in the East Room of the White House, reiterated his firm stand on continuing the embargo as "a moral statement."[19] Yet Eloy Gutiérrez Menoyo, who took up arms against the Castro government, and for his actions spent twenty-two years in Castro's prisons, expressed the futility of "dashing the enemy's babies against the stones" when he stated, "How do you explain to a Cuban mother who cannot find medication for her child . . . that the purpose of the embargo is the democratization of Cuba?" (Baker 1999, 76)

The panopticon paradigm discussed in the previous chapter can be expanded to explain how Exilic Cubans morally justify exercising their power over the Resident Cuban community through the support of the U.S. embargo. As a morally correct action, it becomes a foundational tenet of *la lucha*. The embargo against Cuba, redrafted and maintained through the efforts of CANF, becomes an example of large-scale disciplinary structure. The embargo is a controlled space that represents a standardized action persisting over a period of time. It normalizes the "new world order" by punishing those who refuse to obey. Initially, policy planners for the Eisenhower and Kennedy administrations supported an embargo in the hopes that the hardship caused would foment internal dissent, leading to the downfall of Castro. Ironically, the embargo strengthened Cuban nationalism as well as resentment of the United States, which has historically been seen as the aggressor. Additionally, Castro was provided with a scapegoat for the economic woes of his country.

The embargo presupposes the hierarchical authority to gaze, a gaze facilitated by the U.S., allowing Exilic Cubans to qualify, classify, and punish Resident Cubans for not overthrowing Castro. The attempt to exercise power over Cuba presupposes a mechanism that coerces by means of observation. Once the United States, as the perfect eye, "sees" Cuba conforming, then the embargo will be loosened or lifted. "Conforming" was defined by George W. Bush during his 2002 visit to Miami as allowing opposing political parties to organize freely; allowing independent trade unions; freeing all political prisoners; allowing human rights organizations to visit Cuba to ensure that conditions are ripe for free democratic elections; allowing outside observers to monitor the 2003 elections; and eliminating discriminatory practices against Cuban workers.[20] Ironically, the United States does not take similar stances on other one-party communist regimes, specifically China, North Korea, or Vietnam. Engagement with these countries is based on the philosophy that they can be brought closer to democratic ideals through free trade. Commerce becomes the vehicle for establishing greater political freedoms. But not when it comes to Cuba.

Cuba's refusal to conform to the U.S. gaze translates as suffering for Resident Cubans. Yet the "babies dashed against the stones," the victims of this institutionalized violence, are blamed by the Exilic Cubans as the cause of the violence. A CANF publication concerning Resident Cuban suffering shifts the blame from the victimizer to the victims: "The argument that [the United States embargo is responsible for the deprivation and suffering of the Resident Cubans] confuses the cure with the curse. Castro's stubborn refusal to acknowledge the failure of his totalitarian regime and to relinquish his absolute control by allowing the introduction of basic political and economic freedoms remains the root cause of the Cuban people's suffering" (de Varona 1996, 11).

Meanwhile, the gaze creates on the island a "siege mentality," which serves to justify Resident Cuban acts of oppression. When asked about a lack of freedom and political repression in Cuba, the first deputy minister, Fernando Remirez de Estenoz, chief of the Cuban Interest Section in Washington, D.C., explained that the Revolution has little choice but to defend itself. When the most powerful nation in the world has consistently attempted to undermine Cuba's government, either openly on the world stage or covertly via the CIA, does the Revolution have any choice but to respond by restricting the threat of counterrevolutionary activities, which in turn curtail civil liberties?[21] Additionally, because *el exilio,* through *la lucha,* spends so much energy trying to eliminate Castro and bring the Revolution to an end, the Castro government sees it actions as a form of self-defense. A connection has been made between the bombs that exploded in La Habana, bringing death to tourists, and *el exilio.*

Whether these connections are real or perceived makes little difference in a society operating with a siege mentality.

In 2000, then-chairman of the Senate Foreign Relations Committee Jesse Helms and former vice presidential candidate Joseph Lieberman proposed $100,000 in aid over four years to Resident Cuban dissidents. Even though most nations consider it a crime for opposition groups within their borders to receive monies from foreign powers that would allow them to organize subversive activities, President George W. Bush has expressed his support for the bill, dubbed the Cuban Solidarity Act. It matters little that these monies may end up in the hands of the Castro government, or that the dissidents whom the monies are intended to help may become targeted by the government, or that some of the most prominent dissidents on the island are reluctant to accept the support, preferring a peaceful transition over against a U.S.-sponsored ouster of Castro.[22]

La lucha insists that the United States be placed in the role of observer so that it can punish Cuba for its moral violations. When U.S. Attorney General John Ashcroft visited Miami in May 2001, CANF lobbied to have Fidel Castro indicted for the 1996 downing of four Brothers to the Rescue fliers by Cuban MiG fighters.[23] These forms of punishment, like the embargo, lead Exilic Cubans to horizontal oppression, to Cubans oppressing Cubans. Yet ironically, while *la lucha* relies on the "rhetoric of return" to justify its actions, most Exilic Cubans have no desire to move back to Cuba.

Returning would mean a tremendous economic sacrifice. Like the exiled Hebrews who lived in Babylon during their captivity, Exilic Cubans have become well-to-do, taking away motivation for rushing back to the homeland. The hardships required in nation-building do not outweigh the luxuries of living in Miami. While a willingness to support financially the rhetoric of return may exist, polls suggest that few are personally willing to participate. A 1997 poll revealed that 23 percent would be likely or somewhat likely to return to Cuba if the country's economy significantly improved, while 29 percent would be likely or somewhat likely to return if Cuba adopted a democratic form of government. However, 49 percent would be likely or somewhat likely to return if both the economy and government changed for the better. This poll showed later-wave émigrés as more likely to express a desire to return than those of the first two waves (Grenier and Gladwin 1997, 33–34a).

While Exilic and Resident Cubans struggle with each other, the United States is positioning itself eventually to reimpose its hegemony.

Likewise, the "rhetoric of return" sung about by the psalmist became a reality when a new hegemonic power was allowed into the region. Seventy years after the biblical Jews were carted off to Babylon, Babylon fell to the Persians. The construction of a postexilic Judah was possible because it contributed to Persia's international goal of creating a buffer between Persia and its enemies, the Egyptians. As such, Judah's existence depended on Persia's goodwill (Ezra 7:11–18). The nation was rebuilt at the price of being a vassal for 250 years to its more powerful northern neighbor.

The parallels to modern Cuba are striking. In the same way that the Persian court created a postexilic community to secure its national interests, the United States has promised to "rebuild" Cuba, ensuring that any post-Castro government would sacrifice its sovereignty. A twenty-four-page report titled *Support for a Democratic Transition in Cuba,* submitted to Congress on January 28, 1997, by then-president Clinton outlines the administration's intention of providing $4 to $8 billion to establish an approved governmental and political system. The conditions for replacing the ongoing thirty-five-plus-year trade embargo with this assistance package includes the departure of the Castro brothers ("horizontally or vertically," per Senator Helms), the release of all political prisoners, the dismantling of the interior ministry, and the holding of a United States–style public election. The report also calls for a possible renegotiation of the soon-to-be expired lease of Guantánamo Bay, where a U.S. military presence still exists. Such a future could create a hierarchical community dominated by those dedicated to the economic concerns of the U.S. business elite.

If *la lucha* can be understood as a religion, then CANF is its priesthood. CANF, operating as the ultraright government in exile, was established as an attempt to move away from the negative stereotype of Exilic Cubans as terrorists held by some Euroamericans. Miami police investigators believed that as many as fifty exile groups participated in activities that included bombings and assassinations. According to Mas Canosa, "Miami was under a lot of bombings, explosions, and people that were killed in the streets. We made an effort to show them that there were other civilized ways to struggle for the democraticization of Cuba." CANF was an attempt to create a mainstream political organization that would combat Castro, elect politicians sympathetic to *la lucha*, and dispel the negative image held by Euromericans of Exilic Cubans. Richard Allen, who was at that time national security adviser to President Ronald Reagan, helped create the Exilic Cuban political action committee to funnel monies to U.S. candidates, thus affecting mainstream politics. CANF was started in 1981 when fifty Exilic Cuban businessmen paid $10,000 each to purchase a seat on the Board of Directors (Kiger 1996, 25). However, by subordinating CANF to the U.S. political system, the United States once again reinstated itself as the hegemonic power, supervising Cuban affairs by transforming U.S. foreign policy toward Cuba into a domestic interest group issue.[24]

CANF has written a constitution for a post-Castro Cuba, complete with legal codes and a sector-by-sector economic analysis. In the early 1990s, CANF created the Blue Ribbon Commission for the Economic Reconstruction of Cuba. Members of the Blue Ribbon Commission include Republican presidential candidate Malcolm Forbes Jr., former United Nation's ambassador Jeane Kirkpatrick, United States senators Bob Graham and Connie Mack, economist Arthur Laffer (whose "Laffer Curve" served as the foundation of Reaganomics), and Hyatt Hotels Corporation CEO Jay Pritzker. Ronald Reagan himself once made a special appearance (Kiger 1996, 31–32). The commission envisions a libertarian Cuba where all the nation's infrastructures would be run and operated by the private sector. Upon Castro's downfall, CANF plans to send to the island "a ship of hope," full of investors, stockbrokers, and bankers.[25] In the minds of the commission members, impoverished Resident Cubans lack the necessary capital to refurbish and run power plants, airports, railroads, or utility companies. The task of supplying this needed capital would fall to foreign corporations like Citibank, Burger King, General Cigar, Royal Caribbean Cruise Lines, and BellSouth Corporation, all of which were asked to contribute $25,000 apiece to underwrite financially the work of the commission; however, it is unknown who eventually contributed, since CANF refuses to disclose the list (Kiger 1996, 32).

By August 1990, the University of Miami's Research Institute for Cuban Studies began to collect data to produce the *Registry of Expropriated Properties in Cuba*. The purpose of these land registers is to compensate previous Exilic owners for the loss of their property and assets.[26] Yet CANF prefers that commercial properties be auctioned off to the highest bidder rather than seeing them go to the pre-Castro owners, giving a clear advantage to those who can outbid the previous owners.[27] Even if Exilic Cubans were to take advantage of the Helms-Burton Act, allowing those who lost properties during the Castro regime to sue corporations presently benefiting from their use, they still must wait for two years after all U.S. corporate claims have been made.[28]

During the late 1980s and early 1990s, different types of businesses held seminars for Exilic Cubans on the economic projections of a post-Castro

Cuba. After all, who better than Exilic Cubans to take advantage of the island's economic potential? As George Harper, an Exilic Cuban lawyer who organized one of these conferences, has pointed out, Cuba has

eleven million consumers who for thirty years have had little in the way of new or modernized housing, appliances, consumer goods, or automobiles; [the island had] beautiful beaches and mountains, located close to the U.S.A.; the world's largest reserves of nickel and other minerals, with an estimated value of two hundred billion dollars; fertile topsoil and a favorable climate for coffee, citrus, and other agricultural products; [and] investors and workers with the means, talents, and desire to export or invest in Cuba; some on a large scale, some on a small scale . . . [So many of the Exilic Cubans as prospective investors] have the same cultural background, ethnicity, language, and history as those now living in Cuba. (Rieff 1987, 183–84)

Proposed horizontal oppression among Cubans is thus masked by discourse about national identity and by patriotism—patriotism at a profit. Yet few ask what will happen to those presently occupying these properties.

From the periphery of the Jewish exilic community's epicenter of power, a prophet arose who became a subversive yet redemptive voice. While we do not know his name, his writings are found in the later chapters of Isaiah. Appealing to the community's memories, he plots a new trajectory for discerning reality, a reality that conflicts with the self-deception of the exiles. Second Isaiah's vision is inclusive (49:6; 56:1–8; 66:18–21), calling the exilic community to become "a light to the nations, that [God's] salvation [read, reconciliation] may reach to the end of the earth" (49:6). The focus is on a God who supports the afflicted. Such a God opposes the partisan politics rampant in the postexilic Jewish community.

Rejecting this kind of prophetic voice, Exilic Cubans are aggressively taking the opposite role, the same role taken by the Zadokite priestly party during the return of the Jews from Babylonian captivity. Just as CANF is supported by the U. S. government and has set out to create plans for the "restoration" of Cuba, the Zadokites were officially sponsored by the Persian court and given the task of restoring Judah as a vassal to Persia.

Ezra, with legal and financial support from Persia, was sent to create this buffer zone, where the inhabitants would strictly obey the "laws of your God *and the law of the [Persian] king*" (7:25–26; emphasis mine). Absent was any negotiation for land. Instead, land was to be controlled by the returning Jews. Like Ezra, Exilic Cubans are preparing to demand that Resident Cubans "put away their foreign wives."[29] Some of those "wives," however, may be worth keeping (such as high literacy rates, a 100 percent social security system, a high doctor-per-patient ratio, a low infant mortality rate, and long life expectancy).

Before the Revolution, Cuba placed among the top three Latin American countries in the delivery of social services. These social-service facilities, however, were concentrated in La Habana and other urban areas, while the rural areas lacked basic services. Rural peasants lived in thatched-roof shacks with no indoor utilities, no security of land ownership, no medical facilities, and no schools. The average peasant could expect to earn $91 a year, as opposed to the nationwide average of $374. Castro's reforms have diminished the income gap between the agricultural and urban sector. Even Castro's detractors admit that Cuba's social-service accomplishments (many of which were corroborated by UNESCO), specifically free education and public-health systems, rank among the best in the Third World and are on par with those of many industrial nations (Barkin 1973, 191–96).

Any dream of a reconciled future will not be realized if the accomplishments of the Resident community are ignored, discredited, or dismantled. When those returning from exile prevented those who stayed behind from determining the country's future, new oppressive structures were created. This was the case when exilic Jews returned to the homeland from Babylon and ignored the prophetic egalitarian call found in Second Isaiah. Soon the postexilic community found itself weakened by internal economic abuses. Exilic Jews benefited from the economic misfortunes of the Resident Jews, while disguising their profiteering as religious piety (Isaiah 58: 1–12; 59: 1–8). The poor Residents found themselves enslaved as they lost their lands to the returning exiles (Neh. 5:1–5) and cheated of their wages by returning Jews who set up new businesses (Mal. 3:5).

The danger of merging religious fervor with political convictions is that the newly created religion can become repressive. The biblical paradigm of domination established by the returning Jews can repeat itself. The planned post-Castro community can lead to the subjugation of Resident Cubans by Exilic Cubans, who in turn will be subjected to U.S. hegemony. The danger is that Exilic Cubans, like their Babylonian exilic Jewish counterparts, will follow the example of Ezra, forcing Resident Cubans to "put away their foreign wives," establishing a vassal political system that would enrich the Exilic community elite to the detriment of the Resident community (De La Torre 2000, 275–78).

CHAPTER 4

Machismo

Creating Structures of Oppression

Historically, it has always been easy to blame Euroamericans for Cuba's economic, social, and political situation. Yet not all Cuba's woes can be attributed to the United States and its neoimperialism, or to the embargo, or even to global capitalism. José Martí advises, "[i]n Nuestra America [Our America] it is vital to know the truth about the United States. We should not exaggerate its faults purposely, out of a desire to deny it all virtue, nor should these faults be concealed or proclaimed as virtues" (1977, 49).

In the previous chapter, I debunked fantasies of Cuban ethnicity, unmasking how structures of oppression were established within *el exilio* in the form of religious expression called *la lucha*. This chapter continues an examination of *la lucha* by investigating the foundations of intra-Cuban oppression. The division caused by the 1959 Revolution and its aftermath had deep roots in long-standing forms of oppression based on gender, race, and class, each reinforcing the other. These forms of oppression are not recent phenomena caused by the political ideologies created either by Resident or Exilic Cubans. Rather, they are traceable to Cuba's foundation. Thus it is important to examine the historical development of Cuba's different marginalized groups, remaining conscious of the fact that the official history of Cuba runs the risk of becoming a product of the imagination of its chroniclers, especially of those who benefit from the retelling of history.

In most cases, interpreting history has little to do with what actually happened and more to do with what is believed to have happened. It could even be argued that historians speak of things that have never existed except in their own imaginations. All perspectives are subjective. Interpreting Cuban history as a history of marginality alone, using the "insider-outsider" dichotomy, oversimplifies the problem. Just as when "outsiders" constructed Cuban history, thereby oppressing Cubans under the colonial gaze, so too does the construction of history by Cuban "insiders" oppress all that is Other to the Cuban elite. When those in power, either the inside elite or the "outside" colonizer, write history, they do not record the events of Cuba; rather, they recount their own stories in regard to all they have plundered and violated. Thus Cuban history has existed in its relationship to Spain, Britain, the United States, and the Soviet Union. Its history is the history of the dominant global powers. Its retelling contains the biases of the historian and the value-laden models used for interpreting past events, with the historian's ideological production becoming imposed on the narrative.

Specifically, before the colonizer's subjective "I," all Cubans occupy the space "I am not." And when posed before the white Cuban male elite's subjective "I," all Cuban nonmales, nonwhites, and nonelites occupy the object "I am not." For theological reflection to be relevant to Cuban reality, the identity of this "I am not," constructed by the dominant "I," must be exposed. Exhibiting the social fabrication of the "I" disrupts the prevailing normalization of gender, race, and class distinctions and unveils the hidden dynamics of Cuban oppression.

In maintaining the position of subject, both the colonizer and the Cuban elite are guilty of a "syntax of forgetting." Nation-building usually requires an epic tale of triumphant wars, heroic figures, and awe-inspiring achievements, elevating the dominant culture while disenfranchising the Other (Bhabha 1994, 160–61). History is retold to serve the interests of those who benefit from present societal structures. Cuba's national identity discourse and official history not only disguises the complex political forces responsible for bringing forth that history, but more important, it also suppresses sexual differences, racial divisions, and class conflicts.

To understand the intra-Cuban web of oppression, one must begin by examining the historical development of Cuba, a history involving several continuous stages of domination. If the domination of a certain people by others creates an ethical system, then historical writings justify this system and the social positions of those who are in the dominant position to write history. This relationship of domination is not a "relationship" per se but becomes fixed throughout history through meticulous procedures conferring and imposing rights on one group and obligations on another. The dominant culture reproduces itself in history and normalizes its power by engraving its memories on both things and bodies. In effect, "[t]he body manifests the stigmata of past experience" (Foucault 1984, 83–85). This exercise of power creates knowledge, which promotes power. The "truth" of *la lucha* is created by the prevailing of truth as constructed and defined by the Exilic Cuban ethos.

The victors of Cuban history inscribe their genealogies on the national epic, genealogies emphasizing military victories and political achievements. The accomplishments of these macho victors are a testament to their exaggerated manly pride, which celebrates their virile prowess. These deeds are rooted in a macho memory reconstructed for a macho future. This constructed history becomes the official history, mirroring the actions and values that arose from the forward thrust of white, elitist machos. Yet the truth of the macho subject cannot be found in the subject's history. In effect, "truth" resides in the "locus" of the subjugated Other (Lacan 1977, 286). Precisely for this reason, dominant power must constantly obliterate the Other's "locus." As Frantz Fanon so eloquently put it:

> Perhaps we have not sufficiently demonstrated that colonialism is not simply content to impose its rule upon the present and the future of a dominated country. Colonialism is not satisfied merely with holding a people in its grip and emptying the native's brain of all form and content. By a kind of perverted logic, it turns to the past of the oppressed people, and distorts, disfigures, and destroys it. This work of devaluing pre-colonial history takes on a dialectical significance today. (1963, 210)

To seek the voice of those who do not inhabit history destabilizes those with the power and privilege to substitute their history for the forgotten history of the oppressed or marginalized. Recounting the oppressed's history forces the dominant subject to view the Object as external rather than as simply a mirror projection of the ego's subjectivity. Ignoring the voices of history's neglected justifies yesterday's sexual, racial, and economic domination, while normalizing today's continuation of that oppression and preventing tomorrow's hope for liberation.

In 1998 Cubans celebrated the centennial of Cuba's "liberation" from Spanish rule. 1998 also marked the centennial of Cuba's subsequent and immediate subjugation to U.S. neocolonialism. José Martí dreamed of the construction in Cuba of *patria*.[1] Unfortunately, after the War for Independence, Cuba evolved into simply another oppressive society. This chapter explores the multidimensional aspects of Cuban oppression by way of debunking the sociohistorical construction of machismo. We engage in this task in order to comprehend the roots of the Exilic Cuban religion known as *la lucha*.

La lucha is the religion of *el macho*. Gender, race, and class oppressions do not exist in isolated compartments, nor are they separate categories of repression. They are created in a space where they interact and conflict with each other, a space I will call machismo. Because all forms of oppression are identical in their attempt to domesticate the Other, understanding machismo requires a full consideration of sexism, heterosexism, racism, ethnocentrism, and classism. The sexist, who sees women playing a less productive role than men, transfers upon the nonelite male Other effeminate characteristics, placing him in a feminine space for "easy mounting." Their subjugation (not just of the body) establishes the selfhood of the macho (De La Torre 1999a, 214–18). For Cubans, a serious examination of macho structures must be the first stage in the process of dismantling all forms of oppression, providing an alternative for the tenets of *la lucha*.

Sexism

To be a man, a macho, implies both domination and protection of those beneath you, specifically women. It becomes the macho's responsibility, his burden, to educate those who fall below his perceived superior standards. Because of their gender, most men are complicit with sexist social structures, a complicity motivated by personal advantage.[2] All things being equal, men prevail over women in the marketplace, in the church community, and within *cubanidad* just because they are male.

Historically, feminism was nonexistent in colonial Cuba, since women were limited to the domestic sphere (de Caturla Brú 1945, 155). As he was in other Latin American nations, the husband/father in Cuba was the head of the family, solely responsible for its wealth and for all relations with the public, under the patriarchal legal concept known as *patria potestad*.[3] When people married, a dependency relationship was created as women forfeited their personhood. Husbands assumed control over all property and legal authority over their wives and children, while wives, bound by law, were required to obey and submit to their husbands. Under such an arrangement, women, through marriage, were "saved" from having to work as domestic servants or prostitutes. As *el bello sexo* (the fair sex), women were taught, via Church and social norms, a pre-scribed behavior of gracious submission to the authority of their fathers and husbands. A well-bred woman was considered desirable if she was weak, beautiful, and meek. In theory, Cuban women were to devote themselves to the finer aspects of life (the arts, charity, and so on), while in reality, these activities were confined to the privileged space of upper-class Cubans. The vast majority of Cuban women, living in poverty, toiled in exhausting labor just to fend off starvation (De La Torre 2002a, 71).

The historical establishment of *patria potestad* without a doubt created a Cuban ethos that is male chauvinist and male supremacist. The former denotes an attitude of superiority, while the latter describes the actual existing power relationship. In such a system, women are defined according to their place within the home, as housekeepers meeting the needs of men, and according to their place within a sexual caste system, in which they are perceived in the extreme as either virgins or whores (Young 1981, 4). Defining themselves as superior, men deem women, as well as non-macho males, as inferior beings. Machos who are able to possess several different women (or even men) provide a testimony to their virility. The patriarchal cultural ethos of such a system creates and reinforces the supremacy of males as machos.

Traditionally, honor is bestowed on a family through the machismo of its men, while *vergüenza* (shame) befalls the family in which the men lack macho qualities, a deficit that is made most evident by how *their* women behave. In short, a man's worth is defined by his relationship to women. How he relates to other machos becomes dependent on how he treats nonmachos. Honor is principally maintained by fulfilling one's obligations and protecting the family, especially virgin daughters, from those who wish to impugn another's honor. The most devastating attack to a man's honor is to seduce his virgin daughter, not his wife, because, after all, another man has already had her. This *falta de respecto* (lack of respect) brings *vergüenza* upon the macho (Fox 1973, 276).

Women are to appear defenseless without men to protect them, which is why unmarried daughters must always be chaperoned, a practice rigidly continued by many in the Exilic community during the 1960s, 1970s, and 1980s. The expectation of a young woman's virginity signifies patriarchy, for it is based on the male desire to secure the heritage of his offspring (deemed his possession) by guaranteeing paternity. Additionally, virginity signifies purity, innocence, and submission, qualities of the ideal women (Leiner 1994, 82). Yet it was always acceptable to seduce young virgin women who were poor or nonwhite, because their inferior status meant that her family could not be dishonored. Nonwhites were, by definition, *sin vergüenza* (without shame), so they had no *respecto* to lose (Fox 1973, 277). The fact that they were not part of the white elite meant that their family lacked machos through which honor could be achieved.

A woman who worked outside the home served as public testimony to the inability of the man to provide. A woman who showed leadership qualities bore witness to the inability of the man to dominate her. And a wife who was unfaithful, or a daughter who was not a virgin, demonstrated that the man was unable to control his women. Thus, in the mind of the macho, it is the women, through their actions, who bring *vergüenza*. The only recourse for a man who has lost honor because of actual or perceived sexual activities of *his* women was vengeance. This explains the common nineteenth-century idiom among the upper class: "*La mujer honrada, la pierna quebrada y en casa*" (The woman of honor stays in the home with a broken leg).

Latina feminist theologies, as practiced in the Unites States, become a response both to the sexism existing within the Hispanic community and to the racial, ethnic, and class prejudice of the Euroamerican feminist community, which ignores the fundamental ways in which white women benefit from the oppression of women of color. These Latinas are attempting to find liberation as members of the Hispanic community by obliterating those institutions that cause suffering so that all, both women and men, can find fulfillment. Yet absent from the discourse is any discussion of the recent phenomenon that privileges Exilic Cuban women. Although Exilic Cuban women still face discrimination, especially outside Dade County, the existence of an ethnic economic enclave helped them to obtain higher-status jobs than those enjoyed by other Latinas.

Latinas recently arriving in the United States often obtain employment that is dangerous, low paying, and degrading. This was also the case with Cuban women arriving in the 1960s, who were able to gain employment faster than their male counterparts, since employers preferred women for unskilled jobs because they could be given lower wages. The role of wage-earner occupied by these Exilic Cubans was more a response to economic survival than to the feminist movement of equality (García 1996, 109). By 1970 Exilic Cuban women constituted the largest proportionate group of working women in the Untied States. In Cuba, only women of the lower economic classes worked, while those of the higher classes dedicated their lives to leisure. Once in the United States, these former middle- and upper-class women had to obtain employment to survive economically. This new role wreaked havoc on the machismo of the husband, who felt his inability to be the sole provider as a lost of prestige, respect, and honor. Meanwhile, the wife gained a new sense of power and independence owing to her ability to provide for the family. Nevertheless, while holding down a job, she was still expected to care for the house and children (without servants), and to boost her husband's morale (Rogg 1974, 76).

Eventually, the establishment of the economic ethnic enclave in Miami shielded more recent arrivals from the predicament faced by the Cuban women of the first two waves and still faced today by other non-Cuban Latinas. Economic upward mobility among some Exilic Cuban women allowed them to create status and social prestige. For many, success was measured by their ability to hire *una negrita* (a black girl) — regardless of age or *una india* (a mestiza) to clean the house.

Traditionally, gender has been defined as a set of innate social traits that are naturally linked to one's biological sex. Males are expected to behave aggressively, women submissively. These traits become universally accepted as the norm; however, in reality, such sets of behavior, deeply rooted in the political and religious heritage of a people, are socially constructed by a given society, imposed to legitimize the power of one group over another. This is ostensibly so that those who perceive themselves as "inherently" aggressive can dominate those whom they perceive as "inherently" weaker. Subscription to the male-female binary structure implements societal structures of oppression based on relatively minor and sometimes blurred biological distinctions. Gender-appropriate roles are not limited to the biological sex of a person. Only machos, who profess through attitudes and deeds to have *cojones* (balls), are males. All others are females. History is forged through one's *cojones*. Women, nonwhite males, and the poor fail to influence history because they lack *cojones*, a gift given to machos by the ultimate Macho, God.

To accuse a man of *lavándole los blumes de la mujer* (washing his wife's bloomers) is to question his machismo, because housework, by its very nature, is perceived as emasculating, while manual work outside the home is seen as defeminizing. *"El colmo"* (the ultimate sin) is to be called a *"maricón"* (a derogatory term meaning queer or fag), the antithesis of being macho. The cultural importance of having or lacking *cojones* was best captured by then-U.N. ambassador Madeleine Albright who, responding to the February 24, 1996, downing of two unarmed civilian planes flown by the Miami-based organization Brothers to the Rescue, denounced the bravado exhibited by the pilots of the Cuban air force by asserting, "This is not *cojones:* This is cowardice."

Those who are white Cuban elite males look at their reflections in the mirror and recognize themselves as machos through the distancing process of negative self-definition: "I am what I am not." The formation of the subject's ego constructs an illusory self-representation through the negation of *cojones,* now projected upon the Exilic Cuban Others, anyone identified as nonmachos. Ascribing femininity to the Exilic Cuban Other forces the construction of female identity to originate with the *macho,* as she becomes defined as the nonmacho. In fact, the feminine Object, in and of itself, is seen as nothing apart from a masculine Subject, which provides a unifying purpose. Once femininity is ascribed, domination follows. The macho's endowment of *cojones* provides the capacity to dominate Others, especially the macho's adversaries. The resulting gaze of the white Cuban elite male inscribes effeminacy on Others who are not macho enough to "make" history, "provide" for their family, or "resist" their subjugation to the dominant macho. Women, nonwhites, and the poor become the "not male."

The phallic signifier of machismo is the *cojones.* For Cubans, *cojones* become their cultural "signifier of signifiers." The Other, if male, may have a penis but lacks the *cojones* to use it. I conquer, I subdue, I domesticate *por mis cojones* (by my balls). A distinction is made between *cojones,* the male testicles, and *cojones,* the metaphoric signifier. Those with power and authority exhibit *cojones,* which are in fact derived from social structures, traditions, religious norms, laws, and customs created by those very *machos,* who are usually white and rich.

When those rendered Other by gender, race, or class demonstrate hypermacho qualities, they too can be praised for being *machos.* This was the case with both Antonio Maceo, who was black, and his mother. Maceo, Cuba's black general during the Ten Years' War and the Second War for Independence, not only symbolized the hopes of Cuba's blacks, but he also embodied the macho qualities of honor, bravery, patriotism, and the best that Cubans can hope to be. When the Ten Years' War was lost, all Cuban political leaders and military commanders capitulated through el Pacto del Zanjón (the Treaty of Zanjón). Maceo, who won every battle during the war and sustained seventeen gunshot and four bayonet wounds, agreed to meet his nemesis, commanding Spanish General Arsenio Martínez Campos, to discuss the terms of peace. They met on the morning of March 15, 1878. After enduring a lengthy discourse on Cuba uniting with Spain in order to "march toward progress and civilization,"

Maceo informed the good general that he came to speak of Cuba's in-dependence and the abolition of slavery (Thomas 1971, 267). Such "testosterone gall" has created the Cuban compliment *"como Maceo"* (like Maceo), commonly said while upwardly cupping one's hand as if to weigh the enormity of one's *cojones*.

Blacks who demonstrate the "white" qualities of machismo may re-ceive admiration and praise, even while being denied earned positions of power and privilege within Cuban society. Likewise, women who demonstrate macho attributes will receive praise for their manliness, while being denied positions of responsibility. As progressive as Martí was in his thinking, he still demonstrated chauvinism by equating polit-ical maneuvering with womanliness. Although he challenged North American racism, he glamorized North American sexist mores, disliking the women of the United States because they appeared "physically and mentally stronger than the young [men] who [court] her" (1975, 36). He honored Maceo's mother, Mariana Grajales Maceo, for impressive pro-creation of male patriots, while glossing over, if not totally ignoring, the efforts of Cuban women of all colors who raised funds, aided refugees, outfitted insurgent forces, attracted Euroamerican support, fought as *mambisas* (female freedom fighters), and served as spies and couriers. For patriots like Martí, women in Cuba Libre were to serve as repositories of inspiration, beauty, purity, and morality, lest the unleashed powers of fe-male passion provoke the destructive passion of men (Hewitt 1995, 23–32).

In reality, no one has *cojones*. Machos and nonmachos alike experience the absence of and desire for *cojones*. While one sex may possess physical *cojones,* neither sex possesses what they signify; all suffer from a fractured sexuality. The *macho* lives always threatened by the loss of power they symbolize, while the nonmacho is forcefully deprived of this power. The potent symbolic power invested in the *cojones* both signals and veils white elite Cuban male socioeconomic power. Perceiving those oppressed as feminine allowed white Cuban men with *cojones* to assert their privilege by constructing the Others as inhabitants of the castrated realm of the ex-otic and primitive. Lacking *cojones,* the Other does not exist except as des-ignated by the desire of the one with *cojones.* Like a benevolent father, a *patrón,* the one with *cojones* takes on the duty and responsibility to care for, provide for, and protect those beneath him. The castrated male (read, one made Other by gender, race, or class) occupies a feminine space where his body is symbolically sodomized as a prelude to the sodomiz-ing of his mind.

The nonmacho Others became enslaved by the inferiority engraved on their flesh by the Cuban ethos. Likewise, the macho is also enslaved by his own so-called superiority, which originates with his *cojones*. While nonmachos are forced to flee constantly from their individuality, the macho must constantly attempt to live up to a false construction. Both are alienated, both suffer from an obsessive neurotic orientation, and both require liberation from their condition.

How did this neurotic state develop? A patriarchal Spain created it as part of its colonization process. Cuba, unlike other Latin American nations that enslaved the indigenous people, reduced the Taínos to near extinction. To replace this vanishing population, Cuba imported Mayans and Africans as slaves. Later, the Chinese began to take their place. As slaveholder, Cuba's concern was the acquisition of cheap labor. Hence slave merchants did not bother to bring women to Cuba, contributing to a predominately male society. By the same token, the white overlords were also mostly men, searching for gold and glory. Cuba was a stop-off point on the way to somewhere else. Those passing through were on their way to discover riches on the mainland. Few women accompanied these conquistadors. Since the beginning of the Eurocentric period of Cuban history, the island's population has always lacked a significant number of women of any color. This absence of women contributed to the creation of an excessively male-oriented society, where weaker males (nonwhites) occupied "female" spaces. They washed; they cooked; they "entertained."

Cuba was the last Latin American nation to gain its "independence" from Spain. Rather than engaging in nation-building, Cuba spent the nineteenth century preoccupied with military struggles, contributing to a hypermacho outlook. The physical bravado characterizing a century of bloody struggle for independence fused manhood with nationhood. In fact, one argument used by those in power in Cuba to justify self-rule was based on its greater level of machismo as compared to Spain, which, after all, was "ruled by a woman."[4] Machismo became woven into the fabric of Cuban culture. Early during the 1959 Revolution, when the United States attempted to impose its will on the island, Castro accused Washington, D.C., on January 16, 1960, of seeking to "castrate" the Revolution because it desired independence, that is, because it desired to claim its machismo (Thomas 1971, 1077).

Both Castro and the late Exilic Cuban Mas Canosa (president-in-waiting of a post-Castro Cuba) served as public personas incarnating machismo, charismatic leaders par excellence. One is a bearded revolutionary with a cigar in his mouth and a rifle in his hand, living off the land.

The other was a cigar-smoking, suited capitalist conquering Miami's new concrete jungle.[5] The leadership style of both individuals is akin to a modern form of *caudillismo,* a four-century-old Latin American institution that grants complete power to *el jefe* (the chief), who incarnates the messianic hopes of the people. Both men govern by virtue of their unifying authority derived from the loyalty of the popular masses. Such a leadership style, which glorifies the larger-than-life feats of *el jefe,* are not conducive to democratic principles. A *caudillismo* of the left and a *caudillismo* of the right may significantly differ in ideologies, yet the consequences for nonmachos is the same: oppression. Both sides are intolerant of political opposition, deeming their authoritative rule as necessary to ward off the excesses of the opposing camp. Hence dictatorial practices and violent repression become necessary evils in the defense of liberation, as political pluralism becomes an unaffordable luxury. The present leadership vacuum within the Exilic Cuban community in Miami is mostly due to the failure of a new macho to ascend the power structures and take the reins after Mas Canosa's death. A similar fate appears to await Resident Cubans.

Meanwhile, Cubans on both sides of the Florida Straits proclaim the same message: the creation of *patria* is real man's work. Nonmachos are perceived as "ideologically weak" in both places. In the view of those who supported the Revolution, homosexuality is a product of former bourgeois decadence (Arguelles and Rich 1984, 691). According to Castro, "[Revolutionary Cuba] needed strong men to fight wars, sportsmen, men who had no psychological weakness" (Lumsden 1996, 53–54). Castro also said, "We would never come to believe that a homosexual could embody the conditions and requirements of conduct that would enable us to consider him a true Revolutionary, a true Communist militant" (Young 1981, 8). Additionally, in a 1965 interview for *El Mundo,* Samuel Feijoo, one of Cuba's most prominent revolutionary intellectuals stated, "No homosexual [represents] the revolution, which is a matter for men, of fists and not of feathers, of courage and not of trembling" (1981, 61).

Likewise, Exilic Cubans consider *patria*-building the task of real men of valor. Most of the *periodiquitos* that proliferate in the exilic community routinely discredit anyone suspected of being sympathetic with the Castro regime or question the normative anti-Castro stance by labeling them *mariposas* (butterflies, a pejorative term for gays). Ideological weakness is translated as a lack of machismo.

Ironically, an unusual compliment was paid Castro in these same *periodiquitos* when they claimed, "The only good thing about Castro was that he got rid of homosexuals" (Arguelles and Rich 1985, 122, 127).[6] Lourdes Casal, an Exilic Cuban who obtained her doctorate in psychology, studied the images reflected in more then 104 novels written by Cubans. She ascertained that "[t]o launch an accusation of homosexuality against a political enemy was one of the most terrible insults. To call a man a queer was a way of calling him a woman, a direct attack on his masculinity, on his value as a macho. It was a way of calling him weak and unworthy of holding power" (1975, 260).

Exilic Cuban anthropologist Ruth Behar best describes this merging of machismo with nationhood when she writes:

In seeking to free Cuba from its position as a colony of the United States, the Cuban Revolution hoped to redeem an emasculated nation. Manhood and nationhood, in the figure of the Cuban revolutionary hero, were fused and confused. . . . Manhood is an integral part of the counterrevolution too. As Flavio Risech points out, "neither *revolucionario* nor anticommunist *gusano* can be a *maricón*." . . . If national identity is primarily a problem of *male* identity, how are Cuban women on both sides to write themselves into Cuban history? (1995, 12)

With colonization by the United States immediately following "independence" from Spain, Cuba continued in its emasculated state. The long U.S. military occupation, the Platt Amendment, and the transformation of La Habana into a western hemisphere whorehouse for Euroamerican consumption meant that Cubans lost their manhood, their machismo. Those who came to the United States as infants or small boys sought to reinstate the machismo lost by their fathers. The one-and-a-half generation of Exilic-Cuban boys in their teen years experienced peer and at times parental pressure to "prove their manhood." For most Cubans, machismo means to be sexually ready for anybody, anywhere, anytime. According to Mirta Mulhare de la Torre, "The dominant mode of behavior for *el macho*, the male, [was] the sexual imperative. . . . A man's supercharged sexual physiology [placed] him on the brink of sexual desire at all times and at all places" (Lumsden 1996, 31). Conquering *la americanita* (the Euroamerican girl) became an adolescent ritual of machismo. Exilic Cuban boys were encouraged to date the *americanita* to prove their manhood, as long as they remembered to marry *la cubanita* (the Cuban girl—naturally a virgin).

This one-and-a-half generation of Exilic Cubans who arrived in this country as children were forced to navigate simultaneously sexual maturation and cultural adaptation. These processes became interwoven as gender and cultural identity became integrated. Thus cultural preference merged with sexual preference. In trying to become a mature man in exile, the Cuban male finds both regression and assimilation to be constant temptations as he creates an ethnic identity as a Cuban American (Firmat 1994, 41–45). I would add to these temptations that of the sexual conquest of the *americanita*. For as Fanon points out, "When my restless hands caress those white breasts, they grasp white civilization and dignity and make them mine" (1964, 63). For Fanon, the fantasy of the oppressed man is to occupy the space of power and privilege belonging to the oppressor. Conquering the *americanita* provided an opportunity for the Exilic macho to converse with the dominant culture from on top (pun fully intended).

An exploration of the relationship between so-called machos and *maricónes* is not solely a discourse about homosexuality but a study of the cultural deployment of power through the social assignment of nonmacho traits, linking power with sexual classification. Cuban homophobia differs from homophobia in the United States. Exilic Cubans do not fear the homosexual; rather, they mostly hold him in contempt for being a man who chooses not to prove his machismo (which might explain the low opinion many Cuban men have of priests). Unlike for Euroamericans, who think of both men engaged in a sexual act as homosexuals, for Cubans only the one who places himself in the "position of a woman" is the *maricón*. In other words, sex with another man does not define homosexuality; only the one penetrated is labeled *una loca* (a crazy woman, another way of saying *maricón* or *mariposa*). In fact, the man who is in the dominant position during the sex act, known as *bugarrón,* is able to retain, if not increase, his machismo (Arguelles and Rich 1984, 687).

Reinaldo Arenas, the famed Cuban poet who was persecuted by the Castro government for his homosexuality, recounts his experience of obtaining a permit to leave the island during the Mariel boat lift of 1980. Because "undesirables" were targeted for expatriation, a large number of homosexuals were able to leave Cuba. At the police station Arenas was asked if he was gay. After answering in the affirmative, he was then asked if he was active *(bugarrón)* or passive *(loca)* during sex. He responded passive, at which point the lieutenant yelled to another officer, "Send this one directly." Of importance is what occurred to those who confessed to playing the active role during the sex act. Arenas claimed that a friend of his who did this was denied permission to leave. For Cubans, those who function as *bugarrónes* are not considered real homosexuals (1993, 280–81).

Arenas further insisted that it is not the norm for one homosexual to desire another homosexual. Rather, "she" desires a macho who as *bugarrón* would enjoy the act of possessing as much as the homosexual would enjoy being possessed (1993, 108). For this reason, unlike in the United States, violence against gays is not the accepted norm, for *la loca* provides sexual gratification to *el macho* without bringing into question the partner's machismo, even though *la loca* is perceived as having a corrupting influence on the macho. Although Cuban *locas* continue to be held in contempt, they are usually tolerated with humor.[7]

A man is suspected of being homosexual if he fails to demonstrate macho qualities. Such qualities include, but are not limited to, an interest in rough games; a muscular physique; an absence of a gentle, quiet, or nurturing sensibility toward others; a desire to control others; and a drive to posture and aggressively compete with others. To appear strong, virile, and aggressive is the essence of machismo. Those who fall short of this macho paragon are seen as unfit for leadership positions (Leiner 1994, 22). This is why Cubans use the term *mariposa* in attacking their political enemies.

Carlos Franqui, former director of *Radio Rebelde* and one of Castro's twelve disciples, who came down from the mountain in 1959 to serve as editor of the newspaper *Revolución,* describes how machismo affects politics. He wrote:

[The politics of gang warfare in the mid-1940s is] disguised as revolutionary politics. Actually, it was a collective exercise in *machismo,* which is its own ideology. *Machismo* creates its own way of life, one in which everything negative is feminine. As our Mexican friends Octavio Paz and Carlos Fuentes point out, the feminine is screwed beforehand. . . . [*Machismo's*] negative hero is the dictator (one of Batista's mottos was "Batista is the Man"), and its positive hero is the rebel. They are at odds in politics, but they both love power. And both despise homosexuality, as if every *macho* had his hidden gay side. . . . The two brands of *machismo,* conservative and rebel, are quite different. The conservatives (generals, soldiers, police) always defend the establishment, while the rebels attack it. Nevertheless, both groups share the same views about morality and culture. They hate popular culture, and all the Indian and black elements in it. Anything that isn't white is no good. (1984, 150)

While visiting the home of a retired Exilic Cuban radio commentator (who contributed to the anti-Castro rhetoric common on Miami's airwaves), I noticed a statue proudly displayed on his desk. The statue was of a cigar-smoking Fidel Castro on all fours with his pants around his ankles, with a standing Ronald Reagan sodomizing him. In the mind of the sculptor and the Cuban men who view the statue, Ronald Reagan is not in any way a homosexual. Rather, the statue celebrates the machismo of Reagan, who forces Castro into a nonmacho position.

Missing from this analysis is the space occupied by lesbians, known by Cubans as *tortilleras* (a derogatory term translated as "dykes"). While *maricones,* as men forsaking their manhood, constitute a "scandal," *tortilleras* are usually ignored owing to the overall machismo of the society that grounds its sexuality on the macho's desires, repressing feminine sexuality. Tolerance of lesbians is partly due to their unimportance to the macho's construction of sexuality. They simply have no place in the dominant construction (Arguelles and Rich 1984, 687). For lesbians, as well as for homosexual men, the adage *"se dice nada, se hace todo"* (say nothing, do everything) remains the accepted closeted norm of both the Resident and Exilic Cuban community.

Both the creation of Cuban machismo and the establishment of *patria* occurred within the zones of imperial and anti-imperial power. Here land and nationalism are gendered. The land requiring subjection is assigned a female body. Nationhood rests on this male projection of identity. The construction of the religious-political discourse of *la lucha,* along patriarchal lines, can be understood as a gender discourse. For Resident Cubans, Fidel Castro serves as the father figure, *el señor.* For Exilic Cubans, the late Mas Canosa was the head of the household, *el patrón.* Below both exists feminine land, needing the masculinity of those who will construct *patria* upon her. During the 1980 Mariel boat lift, Resident Cubans viewed the departing refugees as scum, parasites, lumpen (from Marx, modified to mean "men without manhood"), and homosexuals, a construction that Exilic Cubans in Miami use to differentiate themselves from these new "darker" Cubans.

The first creation of Cuba required the reduction of women to the status of objects. The conquistadors' understanding of racism was unlike that of the Euroamericans, who passed laws prohibiting racial mixing. For Spaniards, having sexual relations was as natural as breathing or eating. Spanish men took indigenous women as bed partners, concubines, or wives. The children of these unions, claimed by the Spaniards as their own, took their father's names. It is estimated that by 1514, 40 percent of Spanish colonizers had indigenous wives. By 1570, in accordance with the Council of Trent's elevation of marriage to a sacrament, the Crown forbade married men from traveling to the Americas for more then six months without their family. This resulted in more single men heading West, stimulating the rise of a miscegenated population (Mörner 1967, 35–52; and Sauer 1966, 199).

The European conquest of Cuba began with the literal sexual conquest of the native woman. This becomes evident in an incident involving Miguel de Cuneo, who participated in Columbus's second journey. Cuneo attempted to seduce an indigenous woman given to him by Columbus—as if Columbus owned this living "object" and could dispose of it as he saw fit. When she resisted, he whipped her and proceeded to rape her (Todorov 1984, 48–49). The metaphor of land as feminine is further illustrated by how Columbus saw the world. To him, "[The world] is like a very round ball, and on one part of it is placed something like a woman's nipple" (1984, 16). This European was the first to gaze on the naked female bodies of the indigenous people and the virgin land under them. The entry in his travel diary for Thursday, October 11, reads:

Immediately [the morning of Friday the 12, after land was sited at 2:00 A.M.] they saw naked people, and the admiral went ashore in the armed boat. . . . The admiral called two captains . . . and said they should bear witness and testimony how he, before them all, took possession of the island. . . . They [the land's inhabitants] all go naked as their mothers bore them, and the women also . . . they were very well built, with very handsome bodies and very good faces. (1960, 22–24)

Columbus's first reaction was not to the lack of political organization of the island's inhabitants or to the geographical placing of these islands within the world scheme. Rather, by eroticizing the naked bodies of the inhabitants, he conjured up visions of Paradise, with Columbus receiving the Amerindians' awe and love. Columbus and his men felt themselves invited to penetrate this new erotic continent that offered herself without resistance.[8] These naked bodies and "empty" lands merged the sexual and the economic preoccupations of the would-be colonizers (Mason 1990, 170). Virgin land awaits insemination by man's seed of civilization. Women, symbolized by the land, are vanquished. Transforming this construction of the feminized Other and the virgin land contributes to a reconstruction that exposes the hidden transcripts of oppression in both Cubas and provides insight into one of the foundational tenets of *la lucha*. In continuing the task of teasing out the strands of *la lucha,* we must next address the issue of racism.

Racism

Webster's *Encyclopedic Dictionary* defines racism as "the *belief* that certain races, especially one's own, are inherently superior to others" (emphasis mine). With the exception of white supremacy groups like the Ku Klux

Klan Kubano (KKKK), few are willing to admit publicly a belief in the superiority of their race.[9] If no belief of superiority exists, then no racism exists. If traces of it are to be found, they are to be found either in a lingering bourgeoisie construct of the pre-Revolution period, as per Resident Cubans, or in a social ill of Euroamericans imposed on the Cuban culture, as per Exilic Cubans. Reducing racism to an outdated *belief* justifies the assertion that Cubans are not racist. The definition of racism, as used in this book, recognizes the three-pronged nature of racism, uniting prejudices (belief), power structures, and societal norms. Such a definition asserts that while an individual may not hold a *belief* of race superiority, he or she still contributes to racism by his or her complicity with the present power structures. The mere fact that their skin is lighter than that of other Cubans assures that they will enjoy more success in this country than Exilic Cubans who display Amerindian, African, or Asian features.

Race is not a biological factor differentiating humans; rather, it is a social construction whose function is the oppression of the Object-"I am not" for the benefit of the Subject-"I." Racism against the Cuban's Others (Amerindians, Africans, Chinese, and any combinations thereof) is normalized by the social structures of both Resident and Exilic Cubans. Because domination of a group of people by another is usually conducted by the males of the dominant culture, it becomes crucial to understand the construction of this domination as seen through the eyes of those who benefit from this oppression. The Cuban patriarchal structure projects onto the "darker" Other the position occupied by women, regardless of the Other's gender. For this reason, it is valid to explore how Cuban racism intersects with machismo. By examining the Spaniard's domestication of the Taínos (the Amerindians who first inhabited the island), I will expose the original typology of intra-Cuban oppression, moving on to an examination of the oppression of Africans and Asians throughout Cuban history.

AMERINDIANS

The macho subdues "virgin" land, relegating her inhabitants to landlessness. The gendering of Taíno men as nonmachos occurred early in the conquest of the so-called New World, providing a prototype for all subsequent forms of Cuban oppression. By 1535 Gonzalo Fernández de Oviedo, chronicler of the colonization venture, referred to the Amerindians as sodomites in the fifth book of his *Historia general y natural de las Indias* (General and natural history of the Indies). Although no hard evidence of attitudes toward homosexuality among the aborigines exists, de Oviedo claims that anal intercourse by men with members of both sexes was considered normal (Mason 1990, 56–57). In a report given to the Council of the Indies, Dominican friar Tomás Ortiz wrote, "The men from the mainland in the Indies eat human flesh and are more given to sodomy than all generations ever" (Gomara 1979, 309–10). Juan Suárez de Peralta, a resident of Mexico in the late sixteenth century, described, with obvious distaste, the inverted patriarchy of Amerindian society when he wrote, "The custom [of the Amerindians is] that the women do business and deal with trade and other public offices while the men remain at home and weave and embroider. They [the women] urinate standing while the men do so seated; and they have no reluctance to perform their natural deeds in public" (Pagden 1982, 174–75).[10]

By the eighteenth century, the prevalence of homosexuality among the Amerindians was assumed. Like other "primitives" of the world, Amerindians were regarded as homosexuals and onanists who also practiced cannibalism and bestiality. These sins against nature threatened the institution of the patriarchal family and, by extension, civilized society itself. The Europeans further demonstrated the supposed effeminacy of the Amerindians by emphasizing their lack of body hair and pictorially displaying their supposedly small genitals (Mason 1990, 67, 173). At the same time, the Amerindian woman was portrayed with excessively masculine features and exaggerated sexual traits, justifying the need for macho Spaniards to enter the land and restore a proper phallocentric social order. Such a divine order required vanquishing the supposed effeminate religiosity of the indigenous people by way of the Cross and the machismo of the conquistadors.

By constructing people of the periphery as nonmachos, machos naturalize their deserved servitude. In its domestication of the indigenous male Other as woman, colonization becomes a form of sexism. Ginés de Sepúlveda, the Spanish philosopher during the time of the conquest of the Americas who was the main defender of cultural evolution, illustrated the masculine inferiority of Amerindians to Spaniards by saying that they relate "as women to men" (Rivera Pagán 1992, 135). This feminine space was constructed for Amerindians through brutality. By linking sodomy to cannibalism and bestiality, the Spaniards justified their treatment of Amerindians, maintaining that the Amerindians violated both divine rule and the natural order of both men and animals. Their enslavement of the Amerindians was God's punishment for their crimes against nature.

Spaniards, seeing Taínos in the position of women, waged a ruthless war against *el vicio nefando,* the nefarious sin—a euphemism for sodomy

(Lovén 1935, 529). This crusade was waged with righteous indignation on the part of the colonizers, who had the Amerindians castrated and forced them to eat their own dirt-encrusted *cojones* (Iznaga 1986, xviii–xix). Conquistador Vasco Núnez de Valboa had forty Amerindians thrown to the dogs on charges of sodomy (Mason 1990, 56). Spanish machismo entailed contempt and rage toward the nonmacho, which displayed itself in many other barbarous acts. Bartolomé de las Casas, who sailed with Columbus on his second voyage, writes, "[The Spanish soldiers] would test their swords and their macho strength on captured Indians and place bets on slicing off heads or cutting of bodies in half with one blow" (1971, 94).[11] According to *licenciado* Gil Gregorio, the only hope for the Amerindians was acquiring civilization by working for the Spaniards and learning to live "like men" (Pagden 1982, 49). Meanwhile, the lack of machismo among Amerindian men allowed the Spaniards to take their wives and daughters by force without respect for or consideration of honor or matrimonial ties.

Spaniards were macho enough to be masters. If the Amerindians, and other slave groups, had possessed the virtue of the macho's courage, they would have preferred death to bondage, or so the reasoning went. Therefore slaves were thought of as having no honor, and no *cojones*. In other words, because the Taínos were not macho, they deserved their subjugation.

AFRICANS

The end of Amerindian enslavement in Cuba, caused by the decimation of the Amerindians, ushered in African slavery. Like the Taínos, Africans are at times constructed by elite Cubans as nonmachos and designated to serve those with power and privilege. By 1524, as Diego Columbus's term as viceroy came to an end, there were more African slaves in the Caribbean than there were Taínos. Before demonstrating how the engendering of black Cuban bodies constitutes machismo, I would first like briefly to review history from the underside of the African experience so as to expose the historical denial of Cuban racism. By exploring what was and is done to black and biracial Cubans, we will expose one aspect of the underlying tension existing in the Exilic Cuban religious expression of *la lucha*.

Initially, few African slaves inhabited the island, because of Cuba's lack of precious metals and a stagnant economy.[12] But by the 1640s, a sociopolitical change took place as semifeudal settlements in Cuba gave way to plantation agriculture. It was upon sugar that Cuba was created, hence the popular saying *sin azúcar no hay país* (without sugar there is no country). It was because of sugar that liberation was denied. The expansion of sugar production propelled the rapid growth of slave labor in the colony. By the 1830s, Cuba, the "jewel of the Spanish Crown," had become the largest single producer of cane sugar in the world.

Since Cuba's sugar-based economy was dependent on slaves, this ensured the loyalty of sugar oligarchies to the Crown, which protected the institution during the early wars for independence. Cuban racism was thus created in an atmosphere of fear and insecurity. Skillfully using the memory of the Haitian Revolution in 1791, in which slaves overthrew their brutal masters, Spain frightened white Cubans into loyalty. Every revolt against Spanish rule was presented as the start of a race war. "Remember Haiti" became an effective negrophobic rallying cry against Cuba's attempt to liberate herself from Spain. Independence would leave white Cuba unprotected from Africanization, threatening its property, security, and white women.

During La Guerra Chiquita (the Little War, the 1879 premature war for independence), Spain interpreted the conflict for white Cubans as the start of a race war led by black gangs of Haitian origins roving through Oriente (the eastern province). Whites feared a divided Cuba with a white west and a black east that would lead to civil war, culminating in a Haitian-style black dictatorship. The Spaniards' success in instilling fear of a "black peril" can be gauged by the remarks of Cuban freedom fighter Calixto García. During an interview in Spain after the close of the Guerra Chiquita, García confessed that the major obstacle to independence was white fear: "[Among] the whites . . . some eternally waver[ed] on account of the risks of the enterprise and others hesitat[ed] out of fear of a servile war with the negroes and mulattoes if Cuba became free" (Ferrer 1999, 93).

The final outbreak of the war for independence in 1895 was also labeled by Spain as a race war. Antonio Cánovas del Castillo, prime minister of Spain during Cuba's war for independence, said it best: "The fact that this insurrection threatens Cuba with all the evils of Haiti and Santo Domingo, and with the triumph of the colored people and perpetual wars of races, virtually obligates the whites in Cuba to side with Spain" (Helg 1995, 49–56, 80–89). These earlier wars for independence failed because of the revolutionaries' inability to overcome the privileged oligarchies, which remained militarily, psychologically, and economically dependent on Spain.

Legal slavery ended in the Caribbean when Cuba abolished it in 1886;

however, abolition of slavery did not mean an end to racism or exploitation. Racism continued as a salient feature of everyday life. In their "freedom" former slaves were hired only during peak seasons and left to themselves during *el tiempo muerto* ("the dead time," or off-season months, lasting from June through November). Slavery, the source of labor for sugar producers, was replaced with the rural proletarization of black Cubans. For Esteban Montejo, a former slave, life remained the same. He was still confined to the plantation, he still lived in abject poverty in the *barracón* (slave quarters), and he still submitted to a white master. Montejo wrote, "Some plantations were still the way they were under slavery; the owners still thought they owned the blacks" (1968, 96).

Throughout Cuban history, whenever the indigenous black population threatened to exceed the white population in numbers, a process known as *blanqueamiento* (whitening) occurred, whereby land was freely given to white Spanish families who would leave Spain and come to live in Cuba. During the early nineteenth century, a corporation called Junta de Población Blanca (Committee on the White Population) was organized to carry out *blanqueamiento*. They received their proceeds from a six-peso tax imposed on all male slaves (Corbitt 1971, 2). During the first decade after the end of the Spanish-American War, approximately three hundred thousand Spaniards emigrated to Cuba, while blacks were denied immigration rights.[13]

José Martí went further than any of his white contemporaries in affirming the equality of the races. As a white man he came to identify with the oppressed blacks. In a letter to Serafín Bello he wrote:

The man of color has a right to be treated according to his qualities as a man, with no reference whatsoever to his color; if some criterion is needed, it should be that of forgiving him for the faults for which we are responsible, and which we invited because of our unfair disdain. The worker is not an inferior being, nor must we tend to keep him in corrals and govern him with a stick. Brother to brother we must permit him to have the rights and considerations that assure people of peace and happiness. (1977, 308)

Martí attempted to give up his "whiteness" in order to create Cuba Libre, free from racist social structures, and his response to slavery was forceful; he fought racial injustice throughout his life. While in New York, he helped Rafael Serra, an Afro-Cuban, form La Liga, an organization dedicated to the education and advancement of Exilic black Cubans. Through this organization of so-called outcasts, and in many like it,

Martí attempted to create a revolution. His revolutionary work *Manifesto* is the only document of its kind in the western hemisphere mentioning blacks as a positive force in society.

In an era when most whites believed in and accepted the inferiority of blacks, Martí continually stated that "everything that divides men, everything that separates or herds men together in categories, is a sin against humanity" (1977, 311). He went so far as to insist that there is no such thing as race, viewing it as a social construction that allows one group to oppress another. Calling race categories *"razas de librería"* (bookstore races), he refused to make a connection between inferiority and slavery, for as he pointed out, "blue-eyed, blond-haired Gauls were sold as slaves in the Roman marketplace" (1977, 131). Martí believed that to be Cuban meant being *"más que blanco, más que mulato, más que negro"* (more than white, more than mulatto, more than black) (1977, 311–14). Unfortunately, this definition of being Cuban, based on "equality" between blacks and whites, only benefited whites.

For if there is no distinction between black Cubans and white Cubans, then the abuse and suffering caused by slavery ceases to be limited to black Cubans. Recounting a color-blind history makes all Cubans slaves, not just the black ones. Whites, as Cubans, can think of themselves as victims of slavery in a society that has moved beyond being white, being mulatto, and being black. This way of thinking makes whites and blacks, as Cubans, not only the victims of slavery but also its perpetrators. Hence, if racism exists, it is not institutional; rather, it is personal. Because all are simply Cubans, racism cannot exist as an inherent manifestation of social structures. Any exhibitions of racist actions must instead focus on the attitudes of the offending individual whose race-based actions indicate a personal rejection of the established color-blind society.

In his attempt to create this type of color-blind society, Martí blames blacks for being racist when they attempt to develop black consciousness. He asks, "What must whites think of the black who prides himself on his color?" Then he answers his own question by stating, "The black man who proclaims his race, even if mistakenly as a way to proclaim spiritual identity with all races, justifies and provokes white racism" (Pérez 1999, 91). Although Martí wrote poetically on combating racism, he undermined his own rhetoric. He maintained that an integrated liberation army will forge a single Cuban consciousness that will rise above the pettiness of racism. Obviously, his dream failed to materialize, even though later generations of Cuban whites would use *"más que blanco, más que mulato, más que negro"* to claim that no racism existed, for if there is no race then by definition there can be no racism (De La Torre 2002a, 49–50). A Cuban myth developed that racism vanished from the island during the Ten Years' War (1868–78) but was subsequently reintroduced by the end of the century with the U.S. military occupation (McGarrity and Cárdenas 1995, 77).

Although Martí attempted to create a color-blind society, his views included strains of social evolutionism. In his notes for a projected book, *La raza negra,* he insisted that blacks must rise to the levels of whites through both education and intermarriage. He spoke of a "savage element" in blacks that prevented them from fully participating in civilized culture. With time, Martí thought, blacks would embrace Western culture and reject their African heritage (Ortiz 1942, 346–47). Unfortunately, these comments were cited by the famed Cuban scholar Fernando Ortiz in an attempt to foster the very racism Martí fought so hard to eliminate.

Ortiz capitalized on Martí's comment on the black's "savage element" in his observations about the polarization of Cuban society. In his well-known work, *Contrapunteo cubano del tabaco y el azúcar (Cuban Counterpoint: Tobacco and Sugar),* he expresses the normative gaze of white Cuba. Ortiz refers to the existing polarity between whites and blacks as "the Cuban counterpoint," where "[t]obacco and sugar contradict each other in economics and in the social. Even rigid moralists have taken them under consideration in the course of their history, viewing one with mistrust and the other with favor" (1963, 1–2). According to Ortiz, sugar was introduced to the Americas by Christopher Columbus during his second voyage; Columbus likewise introduced tobacco to Europe.[14] Like sugar, half the Cuban island is sweet, refined, odorless, and white. Like tobacco, the other half is raw, pungent, bitter, aromatic, and dark. Tobacco requires constant care, whereas sugar can look after itself. Tobacco poisons, sugar nourishes. Within the spiraling smoke of a good Cuban cigar exists something revolutionary. The tobacco's consuming anarchic flames protest oppression. Sugar, on the other hand, contains neither rebellion nor resentment. It is calm, quiet, beyond suspicion. Sugar is the work of the gods, a scientific gift of civilization. Tobacco is of the devil, a magic gift of the savage world (1963, 5–15, 46).

Tobacco does not change color, it is born black and dies with the color of its race. Sugar changes color, it is born brown and whitens itself; it is syrupy mulatta that being blackish is abandoned to popular taste; later it is bleached and refined so that it can pass for white, travel the whole world, reach all mouths, and bring a better price, climbing to dominating categories of the social ladder. (1963, 7)

In short, Cuban racism manifested itself in two distinct forms during the early twentieth century. The most influential form was based on a theory of racial evolution that advocated the inferiority of Cubans who were not "pure" descendants of the evolved white Spaniards. The second, advocated by intellectuals like Martí and Ortiz, maintained that blacks had the potential of being equal to whites but were "stuck" in an earlier stage of cultural development.[15]

The backwardness of blacks was not biologically inherited; rather, it was culturally based. According to Ortiz, the black race characterized Cuba's low life, because it communicated its superstitions, its organizations, its languages, its dances, and so forth (1975b, 69–74). He believed, however, that the culture of blacks could be redeemed to the betterment of all Cubans. Ortiz reasoned, "Why should we lose [the African culture] when we can transform it, better it, and incorporate it, purify it, as our national folklore?" (1992, 24). The solution required assimilation to the "superior" white culture through a process of de-Africanization. *Blanqueamiento,* the whitening of Cuba, became a prerequisite for nationalistic advancement. While U.S. scientists and intellectuals understood racial mixing as degeneration and mongrelization, Cubans saw it as a way of advancing the savage races toward civilization and progress (De La Fuente 2001, 178).

Nevertheless, those with *cojones,* those who therefore write Cuban history, recast the story so that they could blame the numerous massacres of Africans on the Africans themselves. After the war for independence the Cuban African community made an attempt to reclaim their machismo. By 1910 black *mambises* (Cubans who fought for independence) were mobilizing to petition the government for their rightful share.[16] The creation of El Partido Independiente de Color (PIC, the Independent Party of Color) served as the political vehicle to force the government to consider seriously its rhetoric of racial equality. The PIC did not advocate black separatism; rather, it called for integration, specifically the elimination of racial discrimination, equal access to government jobs, and an end to the *blanqueamiento* policies. By the end of the Spanish-American War, 50 percent of the rebel army and 40 percent of the officers were of African descent. Most lost the little land they possessed to foreign investors and white *criollo* (born on the island) entrepreneurs. These former soldiers formed the PIC to pressure the government to establish justice. In effect, the PIC threatened hierarchical power structures based on race and class, and as such, was perceived as dangerous to the Republic. In 1910 PIC was outlawed by a bill presented by the only black senator of Congress, Martín Morúa Delgado. Blacks were indiscriminately rounded up, jailed, or killed. For a black person to question the white government was sufficient grounds for death. Even without this type of brutality, the knowledge that violence could arbitrarily occur pervaded the relationship between blacks and whites.

Blacks openly protested in 1912, which immediately led the white elite to label the protest as a "race war" between "white civilization" and "black barbarism." The 1912 "race war" is generally ignored in the official remembering called Cuban history. Yet thousands of black Cubans, mostly unarmed, were deliberately butchered by white Cubans, mostly for "resisting arrest" (a Latin American excuse for assassinating captured prisoners). Rather than using the term *race war,* it would be more accurate to label the conflict a race massacre. No trace of the rumored uprising could be found, no cache of arms was ever discovered, no demonstration occurred outside of Oriente, no white woman was ever raped or cannibalized (contrary to newspaper accounts), and no destruction of valuable property occurred. Yet thousands of white Cuban volunteers were given arms and paid by the government to rove across the nation putting down the revolt in any way possible (Helg 1995, 177–215). Bernardo Ruiz Suárez, a witness to the massacre, wrote:

All the bitterness, all the hatred, all the ancestral prejudice of the white race against the black, were let loose. While the machine guns of the government troops were mowing down thousands of colored men, not alone those in arms, but the peaceful inhabitants of towns and villages, . . . [in] the larger cities and even in the Capital of the Republic white men armed to the teeth went about ordering any and every black man to withdraw from the streets and public places on pain of death, and the mere color of his skin was sufficient reason to send a man to prison on the charge of rebellion. (1922: 43)

The "success" of the massacre settled the black question. The massacre of Afro-Cubans who challenged those with power and privilege limited future social protest by terrifying the surviving blacks into conformity. The Cuban worldview became white once again, because the black voice was effectively silenced.

Viewing history from the underside of Cuban society reveals racism to be an inherent part of Cuban history, existing before and after the 1959 Revolution. As such it is also an inherent part of Cuban religiosity, which is based on a reflection of this ethos. Yet Cuban (both Resident and Exilic) racism is rooted in the belief that Cubans are not racist, even though the primary criterion of social classification is color. And although Exilic Cubans are predominately white, they forcefully deny being racist, in spite of the fact that they live in one of the most racially tense cities in the United States. While white Cubans recognized the presence of non-whites, people of color had to shape their behavior according to white expectations, and were therefore unable to assert their own culture. As Fanon points out, "Not only must the black man be black; he must be black in relation to the white man" (1967, 110). Even when the terms *mulato, mestizaje, cosmic race, harmony of races,* or *racial miscegenation* are used, an assumption usually exists that the result of such mixtures will be an acceptable "whiter" ethnic group that, by definition, excludes Natives and Africans (Sathler and Nascimento 1997, 103). Among Cubans, the need to whiten Africans becomes the basis for developing racial reforms. The hidden agenda of those who talk up *mestizaje* or *mulatez* is to whiten the Africans.

According to José Elías Entralgo, sociologist, proponent of a Cuban version of eugenics, and chairperson of the 1959 Movimiento de Orientación e Integración Nacional (Movement of National Orientation and Integration), a cause-and-effect relationship exists between "mulattoization" and national integration. He applauds the "seduction" (that is, rape) of African women by their white masters as the necessary cause of bettering Africans, allowing white Cuba to be integrated:

The day . . . when a white slave master first had intercourse with a slave Negress in the bush or in the *barracoon* was the most luminous for mankind. . . . A vivifying transfusion took place that engendered a fertile and plastic symbiosis. From such miscegenation was to emerge new physical attributes and ascending psychic and moral virtues. (Moore 1988, 47)

Mulatez, as a process of whitening blacks, becomes a project of machismo, in which the seizing of the black female body by the white Cuban is celebrated as a fraternal embrace across color lines. The "savage" black female body willingly awaits insemination from the white Cuban's male seed of civilization.

Cuba's prized myth of racial equality persists on both sides of the Florida Straits. This myth contains two components. First, it credits the masters for the abolition of slavery. Manuel Sanguily, the lawyer-journalist-veteran of the earlier wars for independence celebrated the heroism of the wealthy whites who supposedly abolished slavery on the island. In 1893 he wrote:

[These Cubans] shed their blood and ruined themselves voluntarily to repair, at the cost of their treasures and their blood, of the fortunes and their lives, the errors and iniquities that others have committed, in order to purify with their sacrifice and to sanctify with their martyrdom the profaned soil of their nation. We have all suffered for the other: the black for the white, the Cuban for the slave. (Ferrer 1999, 122)

Sanguily concluded that the slave-insurgents gained their freedom, at the expense of the master-insurgents, who lost their lives and fortunes so that blacks could be free. In reality, Cuba's refusal to abolish slavery during the first war for independence was a calculated strategy to gain the political support of planters from the western part of the island whose livelihoods depended on slaves (Pérez 1988, 125).

Revolutionary fervor developed in areas where sugar and slavery were not significant; nonetheless, slave owners were somehow absolved of their participation in slavery, and the slaves were rendered dependent on their masters' generosity, even though 43 percent of the population were of African descent, while representing 70 percent of the military ranks.[17] As already mentioned, one of the main reasons the first war for independence failed was that whites were fearful about the ascendancy of black military leaders to positions of power in a postcolonial government (Mc-Garrity and Cárdenas 1995, 81–82).

The second component of the myth of racial equality is the assertion that equality was achieved in the military forces through fighting against Spain. Martí hoped the shared struggle of the liberating army would eliminate racial discrimination and serve as a catalyst for all of Cuban society. He wrote, "Facing death, barefoot all and naked all, blacks and whites became equal: they embraced and have not separated since" (*OC* I, 487–89). This embrace between men was to give birth to the nation through the macho act of war, which transcends whiteness and blackness. Racial union for Martí was less a product of miscegenation, which creates a *mestizo* Cuba, and more the product of machismo as heroism forged on the battlefield. Birthing a nation through the *machista* act of war rather than through the sexual union of mixed races eliminated women from the equation and relegated them to the role of birthing macho patriots. This new nation, born from the macho's embrace, transcended race and converted whites and blacks into Cubans (Ferrer 1999, 126–27).

This myth of racial equality was validated through the appointment of a few blacks to positions of prestige. During the war for independence, Maceo, Cuba's greatest general, became "proof" that racism had ceased to exist, even though the most prominent black freedom fighters were relatively absent from the public prose of independence. Regardless of Martí's rhetoric of a race-free Cuba, few biographical portraits of black insurgent leaders appear in his writings. Even when Martí is celebrating Maceo, most of his profile is devoted to Maceo's mother (Ferrer 1999, 230). Additionally, several veterans of African descent have suggested that General Maceo was forced to decline the role of general-in-chief (the post went to Máximo Gómez). Others insist that his death during an isolated skirmish was a result of a plot within the revolutionary ranks, which had him assassinated lest he become the first president of Cuba (McGarrity and Cárdenas 1995, 85).

Yet some black men who saw the future of Cuba through the eyes of white men were placed in positions of power. After the war, Juan Gualberto Gómez, a black politician (but never elected to Congress), became the advocate for the nation's views on race relations. He insisted that before claiming equal access to public employment, blacks needed first to become civilized through education. Additionally, Martín Morúa Delgado, the only black Cuban ever elected senator, was responsible for sponsoring legislation outlawing black political parties. Both men served in the Constituent Assembly, proving that civilized blacks could rise to national prominence. The end result of the myth of racial equality is that white Cubans excused themselves from restitution for slave exploitation, branded any organization protesting racial discrimination as racist, vilified black consciousness as a threat to national unity, and portrayed Cuban whites as superior to racist Anglos, living under the abomination of Jim Crow (Helg 1995, 16, 106).

Undergirding the construction of race is the perception that blacks are nonmachos.[18] Quoting anthropologists like Gustav Klemm from Dresden, Germany, Ortiz placed humans into two groups: active or masculine, and passive or feminine. Ortiz, like Klemm before him, reduced race to a polarity in which white Europeans were manly, while all others were womanly. Yet as in some marriages, a codependent relationship develops in which the stronger sex ultimately dominates the weaker sex. Likewise, Europeans, who have reached the apex of civilization, will through domestication save the entire world from savagery. Additionally, through the use of morphology, Ortiz supports this thesis by demonstrating that African skulls reveal feminine characteristics (Ortiz 1975a, 60, 88). Machismo manifested as racism can be observed in the comments of the nineteenth-century Cuban theologian José Augustín Caballero, who wrote, "In the absence of black females with whom to marry, *all* blacks [become] masturbators, sinners and sodomites" (Lumsden 1996, 50;

emphasis mine). Until emancipation, the plantation ratio of males to females was 2 to 1, with some plantation imbalances reaching 4 to 1 (Knight
1970, 76–78; Pérez 1988, 87). Usually, black women lived in the cities and
towns. Hence, slave quarters consisted solely of men, creating the reputation of the nonmacho roles of slaves, as voiced by Caballero.

Blacks, it was claimed, although they could be strong as mules, could
not be men, for they lacked the means of proving their manhood. The reality of Cuba's plantations made it impossible for black men to carry out
the "masculine" responsibility of providing for or protecting their families. Yet for the black man to place himself willingly in the female position was also unacceptable. In 1902 there was a wave of arrests of black
Cubans suspected of practicing African-based religions. For example,
several members from the Abakuá society were executed for alleged homosexual activities (Helg 1995, 108). Skewed gender ratios made black
males the targets of white masters, who as *bugarrones* could rape them.
The wives and children of male slaves were also understood as the master's playthings. It was even believed that white Cuban males contracted
an illness that could only be cured by having sex with a black woman. Esteban Montejo, the former slave, describes it thus: "There was one type
of sickness the whites picked up, a sickness of the veins and male organs.
It could only be got rid of with black women; if the man who had it slept
with a Negress he was cured immediately" (1968, 42).

Paradoxically, while the African man is constructed as a nonmacho, he
is feared for his potential machismo, particularly as asserted with white
Cuban women. White women who succumb to the black man, it was
thought, are not responsible for their actions because they were be-
witched by African black magic (Ortiz 1973, 325–30). Thus attraction becomes witchcraft and rape. Quoting Gunnar Myrdal, in *An American
Dilemma*, Ortiz shows how the myth of the black man's overly extended
penis (when compared to the white man's) and the white woman's small
clitoris (when compared to the black woman's) creates a need for pre-
cautions lest the white woman be damaged as well as spoiled (1975,
87–88). In reality, the white woman who lay with the black man may very
well have been seeking her own emancipation from patriarchal structures.
Her rebellion, through her sexual encounter with the male black body, afforded the white woman the means by which to take control of her own
sexuality.

Likewise, the seductive *negra* (black woman) is held responsible for
compromising the virtues of the white man. A popular Cuban saying was
"There is no sweet tamarind fruit, nor a virgin mulatto girl." The func-

tion of *la mulata*, specifically the exotic light-skinned *mulata* known as *amarilla* (high yellow), was to act as a sexual partner to white men, who did not have to worry about pregnancy, for in their minds, she was solely a sexual object, hence transforming her womb into a perpetual tomb (Kutzinski 1993, 20, 31).

Fanon captured the white Caribbean's sentiments about black sexuality:

As for the Negroes, they have tremendous sexual powers. What do you expect, with all the freedom they have in their jungles! They copulate at all times and in all places. They are really genital. They have so many children that they cannot even count them. *Be careful, or they will flood us with little mulattoes.* . . . One is no longer aware of the Negro but only of a penis; the Negro is eclipsed. He is turned into a penis. *He is a penis.* (1967, 157–59, 170; emphasis mine)

This construction of black Cubans as sex objects is best demonstrated by their overrepresentation in numerous La Habana tourist guidebooks published between 1930 and 1959, which directed the uninhibited Euroamerican to the nightly sex shows, predominately featuring blacks (Fox 1973, 278).

The African Cuban may be a walking penis, as per Fanon, but a penis that lacks *cojones*. White Cubans project their own fears and forbidden desires onto the African Cuban through a fixation on the black penis, which threatens white civilization. Yet the black penis is kept separate from the power and privilege that come only through one's *cojones*. Lourdes Casal documents this white Cuban fixation on the black penis in recounting the oral history of blacks being hung on lampposts by their genitals in the central plazas throughout Cuba during the 1912 massacre of blacks (1989, 472). The massacre was fueled by news reports of so-called black revolts leading to the rape of white women.

Important to the concept of *la lucha* is the fear among Resident Cuban blacks that national reconciliation with Exilic Cubans might lead to silence being reimposed. They fear any attempt by Exilic Cubans to change radically the present government in La Habana, lest it once again create a one-way empowerment of white Cubans. The danger of the religious expression of *la lucha* is that any post-Castro Cuba involving Exilic Cubans may lead to a type of "reconciliation" among white Cubans on both sides of the Florida Straits, to the exclusion of black Cubans. In contrast to *la lucha*, *ajiaco* Christianity calls for the dismantling of systemic white racism and elitism constructed to oppress the descendants of Amerindians, Africans, and Asians (De La Torre 1999b, 59–74).

ASIANS

A thorough investigation of intra-Cuban structures of oppression known as machismo would be incomplete without examining the social position of Cuban Asians. Asian laborers were brought to Cuba as "indentured" servants, an alternative to African slaves. Landowners were not necessarily interested in obtaining new slaves. Their concern was to procure domesticated workers. Although coolies were technically "free," their conditions were as horrific as, if not worse than, those of the slaves.[19] Many died during their long voyage to Cuba, ironically on the same ships previously used to transport Africans. As in the slave ships, an iron grating kept coolies separated from the quarterdeck. Cannons were positioned to dominate the decks in the event of a rebellion. A Pacific Middle Passage was thus created.[20] In some instances, almost half the coolies perished in transport. A shipment of coolies by Waldrop and Company sailed from Amoy on February 7, 1853, with 803 Chinese men and arrived in La Habana with only 480. In 1859, the Spanish frigate *Gravina* embarked with 352 coolies and arrived with eighty-two (Corbitt 1971, 16, 54). In spite of this great loss of human life, by 1874 the Chinese represented 3 percent of the Cuban population (Leng 1999, 249).

For many who survived the journey, suicide became a better alternative to slave work on Cuba's plantations. From 1850 to 1860, Cuba had the highest suicide rates in the world, 340 per million people, of which 92.5 percent were committed by Chinese. This suicide rate, when compared to Spain's fifteen per million, reveals the desperation of the Chinese in Cuba (Guanche 1983, 319–20). Others attempted to run away from the estates, only to be hunted down by *rancheadores,* or professional slave-catchers (Leng 1999, 249).

The opening of China to European penetration in the 1840s created a new potential source of labor as Asians were loaded at Macao (the Cuban recruitment center) for the deadly journey eastward. As early as 1806, the first coolie laborers arrived in the Caribbean (in Trinidad).[21] In 1847 the first 206 Coolies were brought to Cuba, a number that increased to one hundred forty thousand during the next two decades, surging in 1939 to more than three hundred thousand. According to an 1817 treaty, they were not to be regarded as slaves; however, the distinction between slave and indentured servant lay in semantics. Although coolies usually arrived in Cuba with an eight-year labor contract, their procurement was at times similar to that of Africans. According to a January 1859 report by the Spanish Consul at Amoy to the First Secretary of State in Madrid:

Of each hundred Chinamen that have embarked for Havana recently, I can assure Your Excellency that ninety were hunted like wild beasts and carried on board the vessels . . . , or they were seduced by deceitful promises and were deceived about the Country to which they were being transported and the kind of work for which they were being recruited. This criminal conduct quickly spread alarm throughout these extensive coasts, increasing the complaints of mothers who asked for husbands and sons that had been carried off by force. (Corbitt 1971, 28)

In many cases, the overseers of Asians where black, who were held in supreme contempt. The Chinese, most of whom were literate, saw Cuban blacks as their intellectual inferiors because of their illiteracy. In some cases, they revolted against the blacks, whom they accused of harsh treatment. At times their revolt led to the overseer's death (1971, 63, 78, 113).

For all intents and purposes, coolies were slaves. A Cuban landlord on his way to the *barracón* to contract field hands would be more likely to say, "I'm going to buy a *chino*" than, "I'm going to hire a *chino*." In fact, because they possessed no economic value after eight years, these servants tended to be treated worse than slaves. If the coolie disobeyed his "superior," he was corrected with more than twelve lashes and/or the stocks. They were usually paid four to ten pesos per month, although under a host of pretenses, substantial portions of their wage were extracted. Technically they were provided with clothes, food, medical treatment, and quarters. At the end of their contract, the laborer theoretically could become a tenant farmer or pay for return passage to his native land. Few lived long enough to exercise either choice. An estimated 75 percent died during their eight years of servitude (1971, 1–5, 8; de Quesada 1925, 4–6).

Cuban structures of white supremacy constructed the Chinese laborer as similar to the African slave.[22] As with Africans, few Chinese women were transported to Cuba. Market demand dictated the need for young men, not women, to work the sugar fields. Yet social and legal regulations forbade Africans (or whites) and Asians to intermarry (Corbitt 1971, 114–15; Guanche 1983, 319–20). And as with Africans, the lack of women led to the construction of the Chinese sexual identity as homosexual.

Fernando Ortiz credits the Chinese for introducing homosexuality (as well as opium) to Cuba (1973, 19). The consequence of the proscription against Chinese marrying white and black woman led society to conclude that they succumbed to "unspeakable vices," a euphemism for sodomy (Martinez-Alier 1974, 79). Early during Castro's regime, China exported to Cuba a shipment of "socialist" condoms. Machos refused to use them, claiming they were "too small," thus contributing both to the myth of the

Chinese's small penis and to a national rise in pregnancy (Franqui 1984, 146). With more objectivity, Hugh Thomas, a historian of Cuba, writes, "The Spaniards accused the Chinese as they had once the Arawak Indians; they were thieves, rebels, suicides and *homosexuals*—the last scarcely fair, even if true, since the traders in Chinamen introduced almost no women" (1971, 188; emphasis mine).

The Cuban Asian, African, and Amerindian share a sacred bond. These three ingredients of the Cuban *ajiaco* represent the underside of Cuban history as it has been incorporated into the expansion and development of capitalism. The close alliance between the establishment of *la lucha* and the socioeconomic arena where it evolved requires us to focus now on another component of machismo, classism.

Classism

An economic analysis of Cuban history is required to highlight the primary role it plays in shaping the oppression inherent in *la lucha*. Generally speaking, if Amerindians, Africans, and Asians represent the oppressed elements of the Cuban *ajiaco,* then Spaniards and Euroamericans represent the oppressive elements. Classism among Cubans can be understood as a manifestation of machismo in which a dialectic is created between the subject (Spanish and Euroamerican men) and the object (Amerindian, African, and Asian men and women), consisting of the continuous progressive subordination of the object for the purposes of the subject. When those with *cojones* narrate history, they construct non-Europeans as a secondary race needing civilization to be mediated through the paternal white hands of the macho.

The macho subject sees himself in the mirror of commodity purchasing as one able to provide for family, thus strengthening the patriarchal system. For example, when Exilic Cubans began to revisit Cuba in the 1970s, they demonstrated their "conspicuous consumption" á la Thorstein Veblen, the social theorist. The *gusanos* (worms) who left returned as *gusanos de seda* (silk worms). A popular pun at the time was that these *traidores* (traitors) were now *traedólares* (dollar-bringers). During the early 1990s, a Resident Cuban caught with U.S. dollars could have been jailed. Now the Cuban government encourages the influx of U.S. hard currency. More than half the population has access to greenbacks, contributing, according to the government, to a modest economic recovery of 2.5 percent in 1997. Yet the introduction of U.S.

dollars has had other profound effects on the Cuban economy. The popular joke in La Habana is of a man screaming to passersby: "I am a bellboy at the Riviera Hotel!" Concerned, his wife takes him to a psychiatrist, who tells the woman, "Madame, your husband is suffering from delusions of grandeur. He fails to realize he is only a brain surgeon." This joke illustrates the inequalities created when a government worker earns two hundred pesos a month ($10.50), the same amount a bellboy can earn in tips in a few hours.

Cuba's socioeconomic structure has been turned upside down, with highly trained and skilled professionals making less money then unskilled laborers working in tourist-related jobs. Three hundred thousand annual tourists prior to the collapse of the Soviet Union increased to 1.4 million in 1998 and to about two million by 2000. Tourism has become the engine of the country. But its effects go beyond economics; it also revolutionizes Cuban society. Dollar wealth is spreading, capitalist practices are developing, Resident Cubans have unprecedented contact with foreigners, prostitution is increasing, and an apartheid increasingly separates those who do and those who do not have U.S. dollars.[23]

For Exilic Cubans, Cuba's economic difficulties have proven Castro's inability to provide, forfeiting his role as *el macho,* as the head of the family. Exilic Cubans take great pride in their accomplishments since first arriving in Miami. Since 1980 the combined purchasing power of Exilic Cubans (who at that time represented 10 percent of the island's population) exceeded the total purchasing power of all Resident Cubans, allowing them to prove Castro wrong in labeling them *gusanos* (Levine and Moisés 2000, 101). Further, remembering *la Cuba de ayer* as economically advanced, like the United States, justifies *la lucha*'s moral need to reeducate Resident Cubans in a post-Castro Cuba in order to return the island to her former glory. Their inability to provide demonstrates the Resident Cubans' lack of manhood, and like children they require instruction in the ways of freedom and capitalism. The relationship Exilic Cubans hope to reestablish is one in which Miami positions itself "on top of" La Habana.

Yet *la lucha* for Cuba conceals some profound concerns. Who will own the means of production and who will profit in a post-Castro Cuba are questions requiring serious consideration. Millions of Resident Cubans fear losing their government-sponsored jobs, their houses, and their healthcare benefits to incoming Exilic Cubans advocating a libertarian economic state. For our analysis of intra-Cuban oppression to be complete, we must examine how classism, like sexism and racism, constructed the economic spaces now occupied by Resident and Exilic

Cubans. In examining classism as a form of machismo, I will now briefly review how Cuban class divisions (which are also racial) developed.

Sugar transformed Cuba from an underdeveloped, underpopulated island into a community of large sugar plantations dependent on imported capital, imported labor, and imported skills. The resulting economic boom caused by the late expansion of the sugar industry shaped an allegiance to colonial status. Here, then, is the colonial equation: classism plus racism. Sugar is what made Cuba valuable as a colony. The volume of sugar production escalated in direct proportion to the increase of the slave population. The money required to entice a white indentured servant who expected land at the end of a ten-year term was greater than the cost of a black slave.

This colonial equation is best expressed in the popular saying "White is a career, mulatto is an illusion, black is coal that you find anywhere." Nonetheless, in spite of the "cheapness" of slave labor, the slave remained the largest single "investment" on the plantation, representing up to 40 percent of initial costs. By 1838 the island was converted into a one-crop economy able by the 1860s to satisfy the world's cane-sugar market demand. For the first time, Cuba's commerce became an intrinsic part of global capitalism. The economy's dependence on sugar as a cash crop created the inability of one of the richest agricultural countries in the world to feed itself. Martí would later warn that a people commit suicide by basing its existence on a single crop.

With the development of the artificially constructed plantation complex, two societies took form (black and white) along with two economies (external and internal). The procurement of African slaves was not based on any theory of their inferiority: that came later. Slavery simply provided a solution to Cuba's labor problem. It is estimated that in 1834, three out of every five Africans leaving the Gulf of Benin were bound for Cuba. No other Spanish colony had a local economy so dependent on slavery, had African slaves constituting so large a bulk of the population, or had people of color representing the majority of the population.

The demand for sugar in the late seventeenth century triggered a demographic revolution, as Africans were brought to the island to work the emerging sugar plantations. These slaves worked an eighteen-hour day and a six-day week. Life expectancy for a slave arriving in Cuba was seven years. Slave deaths exceeded births, necessitating new "acquisitions." It was considered more cost effective to work a slave to death and to purchase a new one than to expend the resources needed for adequate slave healthcare.[24]

Spain's position in the global development of capitalism mandated that Cuba be part of its colonial social structure, where oppression crystallized in class domination. Class domination became synonymous with race and ethnic domination. In Miami, as in La Habana, then and now, class division roughly falls along racial lines. The darker the Cuban's skin, the more likely he or she is to occupy a place on the bottom strata. David Grillo Sáez, a black Cuban journalist in the 1950s, understood the solution to the "Cuban black problem" to be a change in economic status for all oppressed groups. For him, racism was basically a class problem. Still, while class-color correlations in Cuban social structures were and continue to be pervasive, they are not exclusive, creating a tension in preserving a carefully delineated hierarchy.

Historically, the top of Cuba's social hierarchy was occupied by whites, divided into a variety of stratified economic classes. Regardless of their degree of whiteness, all enjoyed equal political privileges: namely, the right to own as many slaves as desired and the right to acquire wealth in any manner whatsoever. The apex consisted of whites born in Spain, called *peninsulares,* who dominated the property market. They also dominated the commercial sector and held the majority of colonial, provincial, and municipal posts. More than 80 percent of the *peninsular* population was qualified to vote, compared to 24 percent of the entire Cuban population (Knight 1970, 88–89; Pérez 1988, 135, 152). The *peninsulares* saw themselves in the mirror as machos, while viewing the white *criollos* as effeminate and culturally backward. A frequent *peninsular* charge against the *criollos* was their effeminacy, their nonmacho position (Paquette 1988, 48, 91).

Below the *peninsulares* in the social hierarchy were the *criollos.* Antagonism between them and the *peninsulares* was checked by a shared racial fear. Being born in the Americas meant exile from the top echelons of social power. A popular joke of the time was that a *peninsular* could have anything he desired, except a Spanish son (1988, 43). At the bottom stratum of the hierarchy were the *monteros* or *guajiros* (country bumpkins) who lived in the shadows of the white elite. They labored as herdsman, teamsters, migrant farmers, slave drivers and hunters, sharecroppers, and dirt farmers. While their economic status differed little from that of the slaves, *peninsulares* and white *criollos* conferred on the *monteros* the distinction of being superior to all the nonwhites.[25] Valuing their elevation above blacks, they served as vigilantes during "slave revolts," showing intense viciousness in their suppression of blacks (Knight 1970, 177; Paquette 1988, 43). Under the *monteros* were Africans and their descendants.

In every circumstance, white skin prevailed over darker. However, unlike in the United States, the racial boundaries were never solidified. The subtle and fluid nature of Cuban racism allowed for a minimum crossing of racial boundaries (Paquette 1988, 111). The success of Cuba's interweaving of oppression is best summarized in the Cuban slaveholder's saying *"Es preciso tiranizar o correr el riesgo de ser tiranizado"* (One must tyrannize or run the risk of being tyrannized).

In short, classism is as indigenous to Miami as it is to La Habana. As part of the Exilic Cuban ethos, these structures of sexism, racism, and classism have become inherent in the religious expression of *la lucha*. Gender, race, and class oppression, as interconnecting components of machismo, the placing of one group of men above all others, becomes the not-so-well-hidden foundation of *la lucha,* at times manifesting themselves as moral imperatives on the streets of Miami, as demonstrated during the Elían saga. If Cuba is inhabited mostly by blacks, and if its economic structures are socialist, then *la lucha,* by definition, becomes the struggle to make Cuba white and capitalist again. To achieve this goal, the image in the mirror of the white male elite is projected on the desired post-Castro future of the island. Yet hidden under the sacred fervor of the religious crusade of *la lucha* is how machismo, as intra-Cuban gender, race, and class oppression, is obscured by *el exilio's* rhetoric of return.

CHAPTER 5

The End of the Elián Saga

The Continuation of La Lucha

On Sunday, October 21, 2001, the small home in Little Havana where Elián González had stayed during his international custody battle was opened as a shrine to his memory. Unidos en Casa Elián (United in Elián's House) attracted nearly five hundred people on its first day. Visitors were greeted with a picture hanging on the wall of Elián's mother, Elizabeth Brotons, who died during their trip to the United States. A poster on another wall bears a picture of the boy with the caption "The Miracle Child." Visitors can view hundreds of photographs of a happy Elián playing in the house. One of the displays includes a picture of Elián in a toy boat next to a statue of La Virgen de la Caridad (the Virgin of Charity, Cuba's patron saint). All the normal trappings of childhood— bicycle, stuffed Barney doll, toys, swing set, race-car-shaped bed, and Spiderman pajamas—become sacred relics as they are reverently displayed throughout the museum. Outside the house a large sign simply states, "Remember Elián—Vote Republican." This house, still owned by Delfín González, the boy's great-uncle, became a sacred space—a holy land—a place to contemplate, pray, and become spiritually fortified.

To comprehend thoroughly the Miami ethos that gave rise to the religious passions surrounding the Elián saga, we have examined *la lucha* as a religious expression indigenous to Exilic Cubans, and how this religious expression attempts to mask a *machismo* that encompasses race, class, and gender oppression. To understand further how Exilic Cubans' rise to power influences their ethnic construction, specifically when they fail to dismantle the societal structures once used to oppress them, in this

Elián's home as museum: On November 27, 2000, Elián's former home was converted into a museum. The banner in front of the house reads "I only want to live in freedom." On the mailbox are bumper stickers that read "Christ Saves Me," and "In Christ There's Liberty." A poster of Elián with Christ appears on the walkway leading to the front door stating "Elián knew Jesus while others denied Him." On the front door is a poster of Elián with the Virgin. On the right side of the building, mounted on the wall, is a five-foot-tall cross, and numerous rosaries are hung on the fence. One is not sure if one is visiting a museum, a shrine, or both. Photograph © Roberto Koltun/*The Miami Herald.*

final chapter we will examine the relationship between this small immigrant group and the dominant Euroamerican culture. By surmounting, rather than dismantling, oppressive power structures, Exilic Cubans are in peril of imitating their former oppressors while justifying machismo in the name of the holy war of *la lucha.*

The U.S. Colony of Cuba

The first colonizer to visit what would eventually be called the United States was the Spanish explorer Juan Ponce de Leon. Arriving in Florida in 1513, he named the region Florida ("feast of flowers"), either because he saw a profusion of flowers or because it was Easter week (Pascua florida, literally "florid Easter"). By 1565, prior to the establishment of Jamestown or Plymouth Rock, the first permanent European settlement in what would become the continental United States was established by the Spaniards in Saint Augustine, Florida. This land originally fell under the jurisdiction of the bishop of Santiago de Cuba. From the Chesapeake Bay to the San Francisco Bay, colonies, cities, and missions dotted the landscape. As Anglos began to invade "Spanish" territories, many of the original Spanish settlers left, finding themselves refugees in Cuba. The decline of the Spanish Empire, and the consequent rise of the U.S. Empire, contributed to a reversal in the colonial venture. The goal of making the Americas Spanish and Catholic gave way to Manifest Destiny.

As early as 1823, with the assertion of the Monroe Doctrine, the western hemisphere became the private preserve of the United States, which expressed opposition to any "outside" (read European) intervention, even though at that time the United States lacked the military credibility to enforce the doctrine. The relationship that eventually developed between the United States and Cuba, after Cuba's war for independence, can best be described by the title of Leland Jenks's 1928 book, *Our Cuban Colony,* or by Charles Morris's book title *Our Island Empire.* The proximity of Cuba to the United States created a relationship in which neither could be ignored by the other (this continues to be true in spite of the embargo, or perhaps because of it). Throughout its history, the United States has gazed on the island with covetous eyes, as voiced by John Quincy Adams, who saw Cuba as "a natural appendage" to the United States, which like an apple falling from the tree of Spain, "and incapable of self-support, can gravitate only toward the North American Union" (1917, 372–73). Thomas Jefferson advised then-president Monroe that subduing Cuba would provide control of the whole Gulf of Mexico (1944, 708–10). During the Revolutionary War, British troops used ports in La Habana to attack North America, a fact the strategic-minded New Republic never forgot. On at least seven documented occasions, the United States attempted to appropriate the island.[1]

On the safe domain of Cuban land, the United States launched its first venture into world imperialism. Earlier conquests of Texas and northern Mexico represented the expansionist ideology of extending U.S. boundaries and physically possessing and repopulating the new lands. Cuba represented a shift toward imperialism. By the 1880s, the former ideology of Manifest Destiny was revised to adjust to the new world context. The late nineteenth century saw a transition in the United States from competitive capitalism to monopoly capitalism. This new stage of capitalism merged with imperialism and found its first expression in Cuba. Maturing as an empire, the United States was less interested in acquiring territory than in controlling peripheral economies for the purpose of obtaining financial benefits. Industrial leaders, producing an ever-increasing surplus of goods, demanded a foreign policy that would create new overseas markets and protect those already in existence. The United States could either evolve as a new competing empire, or it could remain an isolated nation with a stagnating economy. It chose to join the existing global imperial race among the industrial European nations for raw materials, new markets, and national prestige. The Spanish-American War served as its baptism into this new global role.

The Reverend Josiah Strong, in 1885, best expressed the new imperialist ideology of Manifest Destiny, masked in Christian language:

It seems to me that God, with infinite wisdom and skill, is training the Anglo-Saxon race for an hour sure to come in the world's future. . . . If I read not amiss, this powerful race will move down upon Mexico, down upon Central and South America, out upon the islands of the sea, over upon Africa and beyond. And can any one doubt that the result of this competition of races will be the "survival of the fittest"? (Smith 1963, 85–87)

Political leaders of the United States, like Theodore Roosevelt and Henry Cabot Lodge, seemed to believe that the duty of the Anglo-Saxon race was to civilize and Christianize the backward areas of the world, a task begun in earnest in Cuba, thanks to the Spanish-American War. In fact, Cuba became a model for how the United States crafted its relationship with other Caribbean and Central American countries as its hegemony was imposed. Indeed, the United States learned, in the words of Theodore Roosevelt, to "speak softly but carry a big stick" as gunboat diplomacy developed. Prophetically, the first Anglo-Protestant communion service in Cuba (excluding the brief English occupation in the 1700s) was held on a United States gunboat in the 1871, officiated by Bishop Henry Whipple, an Episcopalian.

With the entry of the United States into what Roosevelt called "the splendid little war," Spain was quickly defeated. The Cuban freedom fighters were upstaged, and the insurgent leaders were prevented from being present when the Spanish forces capitulated. When the Cuban army requested to participate in the ceremonies witnessing Spain's departure from the island, the United States rejected the request. Thus on January 1, 1899, at noon, the Spanish flag was lowered and the U.S. flag was raised. It was the United States, not Cuba, who bid Spain farewell and was present during the symbolic "transfer of power." José Martí's concerns materialized:

We need to know the position held by this avaricious neighbor who admittedly has designs on us before we rush into a war that appears to be inevitable, and might be futile, because of that neighbor's quiet determination to oppose it as a means of leaving the island in a state enabling it to lay hands on Cuba at a later date. . . . And once the United States is in Cuba, who will drive it out? (1977, 244–46)

During the four years of U.S. military occupation (1898–1902), all facets of Cuban government, along with foreign trade and investment, were under U.S. supervision. Even with the military departure of the United States, subservient puppet officials were chosen to serve as leaders of the new Cuban Republic. Roosevelt's "splendid little war" reduced Cuba to a wasteland, yet a new generation of North American carpet-baggers saw Cuba as virgin territory. By 1905 they acquired title to 60 percent of all rural property (Pérez 1988, 195–96). While Cuba was under military occupation, the Cuban army was disbanded and an U.S.-style education system was imposed. Flying the U.S. flag (alongside the Cuban flag) from public buildings became common, as the restoration of the local economy was organized though U.S. hegemonic establishment. In effect, a pseudo-Republic was created.

United States military presence ensured that the first "presidents" of the Republic were more concerned with protecting U.S. interests than Cuban interests.[2] Cuba was forced to add the Platt Amendment to its constitution as a prerequisite for having U.S. military leave the island.[3] This amendment ended Cuban sovereignty before it even began. Leonard Wood, the head of the U.S. occupation government, best summarized the importance and purpose of the Platt Amendment when he said:

The Platt Amendment has left very little, if any, independence in Cuba, and the only reasonable course now is to seek annexation. This process will, of course, take time, during which it is desirable that Cuba will have its own government. . . . They will not be able to sign certain treaties without our consent, nor will they be able to obtain loans above certain limits . . . [A]ll of which should prove . . . that Cuba is clearly in the palm of our hands. . . . The control that we have over Cuba, a control that will soon be transformed into possession, will enable us to eventually exercise total control over the world sugar market. (McGarrity and Cárdenas 1995, 86)

In short, the Plattist client-patron relationship deprived Cuba of its autonomy. The right of the United States to intervene militarily at will emasculated Cubans, creating collective shame, humiliation, and alienation. Political parties became irrelevant, creating both an ideological vacuum and crises of legitimacy. Even after 1934, when the United States abrogated the Platt Amendment, Plattism remained the norm. The amendment was no longer needed, since the oppressive structures of clientage had become thoroughly indigenous.

While the U.S.-Cuban relationship was detrimental to most Cubans, it did benefit a small, yet privileged group that had developed a desire for a Eurocentric way of life. Succeeding economically required an ability to speak English (during the early military occupations by the United States, English was the primary language taught in schools). Hand-picked financial advisors were needed to manage the assets of absent Euroamericans. These Cubans were mostly white, educated in the States, and pro–North American. Their collaboration, instead of confrontation, provided opportunities for exploitation within their own population, specifically of the Cuban rural periphery. The Cuban elite, although an integral part of global capitalism, lacked sufficient economic power to foster a nationalistic response to U.S. colonialism.

The rise of Cuban nationalism during the 1920s directly related to the emasculation caused by Plattism. The political elite was reviled for willingly placing themselves in the "feminine" position before the United States. Fervor for national independence fanned anti-imperialist fires and began to play a central role in Cuban politics. Disgust at the emasculation of Cuba meant that the Revolution that took place in the 1950s would be basically anticapitalist and anti–North American. A frustrated United States, hoping to bring Castro's Cuba into line, resorted to the 1933 tactic of suspending Cuba's sugar import quota. Such a move normally would have stifled Cuba's attempt to implement nationalist economic policies; however, a new factor was added to the old equation. The Soviet Union offered an alternative market for Cuban sugar and a way to resist the hegemonic power of the United States.[4] Hence Cuba's revolution was more a product of Third World nationalism than of Marxism.

A New World Order

For those who left Cuba immediately after the Revolution, many of whom represented the upper echelons of La Habana society, a new ideology for *el exilio* was required. As we have seen, *la lucha* served as both a religious and a political worldview. As *la lucha* developed, Exilic Cuban theologians attempted to introduce their own interpretations of events based on the overall Latino/a experience. Adhering to what is termed Hispanic theology (or *mulato* theology), they found few converts to their theological perspectives in Dade County. Instead, many in Miami familiar with Hispanic theology criticized it as being either too leftist or too communist. While these Exilic Cuban theologians claimed to be expounding a theology of the people developed in the grassroots of the Latina/o community, they seldom consulted the grassroots in Dade County, mainly because it exhibits a very different reality from that of other U.S. Hispanic groups. As a result, Exilic Cuban Latino/a theologians contribute to the alienation of Exilic Cubans when they attempt to project on them their own theological perspectives based on the experiences of other U.S. Latina/o communities.

Although the loss of status and financial resources affected most migrating Cubans, with the rapid development of an economic enclave a financial elite soon developed. Analyzing this emerging space can shed light on the relationship between politics and religion as practiced in Miami. Generally speaking, Latin American liberation theologies have emphasized the economic and political position of those who are marginalized. While such an emphasis is valuable, U.S. Hispanic theologians have usually ignored the economic and political position of Exilic Cubans residing in Miami. The recently emerged Miami landscape of power has created new forms of economic oppression that some Hispanic theologians fail to address. For those theologians who are Exilic Cubans, such an omission masks the hierarchies established in Dade County, where some Exilic Cubans have ceased to be among the poor, as the condition was originally defined by liberation theologians. As we shall see, the failure of the exilic Cuban theologians to recenter both the economic and political reality of Exilic Cubans in Miami ignores the Exilics' complicity with the dominant culture that re-creates them as the new oppressors.

Marginalizing newly arrived Cubans, specifically those arriving since the Mariel exodus, produced in Miami a new power-based relationship. For the overall U.S. economy to function, an industrial "reserve army" must always exist. For example, Park Avenue profits from the surplus extracted from Spanish Harlem; Los Angeles subsists by using undocumented immigrants. Likewise, Miami developed itself by exploiting the reserve army of laborers located in *el solá* (the Cuban barrio in Little Havana's downtown section and portions of Hialeah) mostly through paying them substandard wages. The luxury houses of Coral Gables, Kendall, and Cocoplum establish their privileged space safe from the menace of *el solá*, while simultaneously capitalizing on this marginalized space.

While dependency continues to be a valid economic paradigm, it is also important to supplement this rubric with an understanding of the systematic barring from economic opportunities by elite Exilic Cubans of those whom they consider their Other. Exclusion as well as exploitation contribute to the conditions of *el solá*. With the development of the ethnic enclave, the first two waves of Exilic Cubans eventually resettled in the more exclusive neighborhoods, replacing the Euroamericans who departed during what has been termed the "white flight." The Exilic Cubans of *el solá* were thus replaced by a relative surplus population willing to occupy this satellite space. These were mostly *Marielitos,* Nicaraguans, Central Americans, and those Exilic Cubans "not macho enough" to succeed economically: in short, the collective Others of the emerging Exilic Cuban elite. Those who occupy *el solá* serve as a constant depressant on Miami's wages by providing cheap labor that prevents the inhabitants of *el solá* from improving their situation in the workplace.

The initial arrival of Cubans during the first two waves of immigration relegated them to an economically expendable periphery whose function was to provide a cheap labor pool. Since then, with the development of an economic enclave and the establishment of an Exilic elite, a socioeconomic apartheid has developed in Miami, as it has elsewhere in Latin America. The rich elite among Exilic Cubans isolate themselves from their poorer compatriots, moving to the exclusive suburbs of Dade County and hiring security for protection. While exclusion is not a new phenomenon among Exilic Cubans, what is new is their abandonment of the lower middle classes, who remain trapped in *el solá,* along with the incoming poor.

The new rich are unlike the old bourgeoisie *patrones* of *la Cuba de ayer* who may have felt paternalistic toward those under them. The new elite are the "executives" who accumulated wealth mostly through profitable sales instead of production. Since this new elite has no feelings of obligation to the poor, the poor are unable to take advantage of their client relations. Miami has become divided into two Cuban groups, reproducing in Miami a paradigm that has existed since the days of colonial Cuba but that now has become aggravated by the globalization of capitalism. The majority of Exilic Cubans is lower-middle-class or poor, while the minority is located behind walled-off sections of the city, enjoying their luxurious private clubs.

Middle-class Exilic Cubans can best be understood as members of the professional-managerial class, composed mainly of technical workers, managerial workers, "culture" producers, and so forth, occupying a distinct class within advanced capitalist society (Ehrenreich and Ehrenreich

1972, 8–11). This Exilic Cuban professional-managerial class becomes the buffer zone between those living in *el solá* and the elite living in the exclusive suburbs of Miami. It consists of salaried workers who do not own the means of production and who function as the reproducers of capitalist culture and of capitalist class relations. Hence the relationship between the Exilic Cuban professional-managerial class and the working class is antagonistic. If we compare the Exilic Cuban professional managerial class to socialist Resident Cubans, we can begin to comprehend their mutual hatred, a hatred based on class difference.

The professional-managerial class presents a paradox. On the one hand, those in this class are similar to the poor in that they are excluded from owning the means of production. Yet on the other their interests are opposed to those of the workers because of their managerial positions within corporate organizations. They occupy conflicting positions within an exploitative relationship. Although materially comfortable, they remain bound to property relations and to the associated processes of exploitation (Wright 1985, 285–86). The excessive profits of the Exilic Cuban elite make it possible for them to "bribe" this contradictory class into maintaining the status quo, thus strengthening the marginalization of the Exilic Cuban Other.

Yet maintaining the status quo comes at a cost for this class as well. The restructuring of global capitalism makes them ever more susceptible to unemployment, underemployment, and low wages. Individuals denied employment in Miami or losing jobs because of downsizing are not just those who are usually disenfranchised. These are also the predominantly middle-class Cubans with college degrees, years of experience, and seemingly impeccable credentials. This downwardly mobile professional-managerial class feels in grave danger of the barriers separating them from their Others becoming blurred. Not surprisingly, fury soon replaces the hope of those who were once upwardly mobile and are now doomed. They blame *Marielitos, eso indios de Sur America* (those Indians from South America), or *los negros* of Liberty City for their economic woes. The psychological function of *el solá* in Miami is to accentuate the separation of the professional-managerial class from the Other. The managerial class can take comfort in knowing "things may be economically bad, but at least we don't live in *el solá*."

Paradoxically, those living in *el solá* do not necessarily see themselves as economically oppressed. On the contrary, they view their new space in Miami as one of freedom and contrast it to the slavery they knew "under the tyranny of Castro's Cuba." While no one questions the severity of life in Miami and the struggle to survive, these new Exilic Cubans find pride in the fact that they live in the United States. The idea of building a new just society in Miami appears abstract and unreal. In their own minds, they have already crossed over to freedom and opportunity.

As long as the disenfranchised are oppressed, a religious response to that oppression will exist. In this respect, theologies of liberation remain eternal. The question is not whether Hispanic theology will survive into the twenty-first century or if it will ever be relevant to the Exilic Cuban community; rather, the question is, *How* will it reflect these new conditions in Miami? For worn-out themes of liberation simply do not meet the challenges of Miami's new reality. If theology is a second act, a reflection on the social context, then this "new world order" requires a new theological interpretation and response. Because the elite have escaped to their walled-in communities, abandoning the cities to the poor, the new task of any theological expression of liberation requires a social liberation that can transform these cities, specifically Miami.

Liberation continues to be a religious motif with political ramifications. However, to be relevant, this theology must embrace the realization that yesterday's economic oppression appears differently today as society continues to evolve. In Miami, the new face of oppression is sometimes Cuban. For this reason, it becomes crucial to unmask Miami's structures of oppression, particularly as we strove to do in the last chapter. With this done, it becomes possible to understand Exilic Cubans and the passion they expressed over a small boy named Elián.

Understanding Exilic Cubans

Non-Cuban Hispanics in the United States shook their heads in bewilderment over the Elían drama. They, like the rest of the nation, have difficulty understanding the passions permeating Miami. As we have seen, part of this misunderstanding is based on the social position of Exilic Cubans, which is radically different from that of any other Latino/a group in the United States. Miami Cubans are whiter and more economically, politically, and educationally established, mostly owing to the enclave they have carved out for themselves. These pronounced differences between Exilic Cubans and other U.S. Hispanics have created misinterpretations, and at times, mistrust. In this final section, I will briefly attempt to explain the disconnection existing among Latino/as, a disconnection masked by pan-Hispanic theological perspectives.

Unless these differences between Exilic Cubans and other Hispanics are uncovered, the religious and political underpinnings of *la lucha* will remain unchallenged. The temptation of any marginalized group that surmounts the very power structures that were used to oppress them is the refusal to dismantle those structures. By continuing to use the Euroamerican model, which has successfully privileged one group over all others, the former marginalized group runs the risk of becoming the new oppressors. The rise of Exilic Cubans in Miami serves as a prototype of what can occur as other marginalized groups attempt to wrestle control from their former oppressors without designing new structures geared toward a more just social order.

ECONOMICS

Most Exilic Cuban children are taught by their parents and by the overall Exilic community that they are somehow different from other Hispanics, specifically Puerto Ricans and Mexicans. As they are instilled with pride for their heritage, these children are unconsciously taught never to allow anyone to confuse them with those other Latinos/as. In fact, Cubans learn to regard themselves as equal to, if not more advanced than, the North Americans in intelligence, business acumen, and common sense. Regardless of the fact that Cuba's history is fraught with political repression, the original generation that settled in Miami claimed that prior to Castro, Cuba was as advanced as (if not more advanced than) the United States, and that it was certainly the most beautiful country in the world. A deep sense of cultural pride, understood as arrogance by other Latino/a groups, infuses the Exilic identity.

An important component of the Exilic Cuban ethnic construction, different from that of other minority groups, including other Latinos/as, is the economic achievements of Exilic Cubans. Mentioning these achievements is not meant to minimize the fact that the early refugees were exploited as cheap labor. In fact, the 1970 Census Bureau showed that one out of every five Exilic Cubans lived in a "low-income" area. By the early 1980s, a racial and ethnic economic structure existed in Miami, where Euroamericans dominated the more prestigious and higher-paying jobs. Although Exilic Cubans were beginning to make modest inroads, most African Americans and Exilic Cubans tended to hold lower-status jobs. Until 1980, the socioeconomic profiles of African Americans and Exilic Cubans were more alike than different, especially when compared to those of Euroamericans. But during the late 1980s and the 1990s,

Exilic Cubans made substantial gains in having high-status occupations, outdistancing local African Americans and other Hispanic groups. The 1980s served as a transition period as the economic enclave facilitated the acceptance of Exilic Cubans into mainstream economic sectors.

Yet many members of the Exilic Cuban community still find themselves in lower-paying service jobs. Thus the story of the "golden exile" appears to have applied only to the emerging Exilic Cuban elite, many of whom previously belonged to the pro-Euroamerican Cuban elite of the first wave of immigrants. The real "success stories" were those of the Euroamericans who did not participate in the "white flight." During four decades of Exilic Cuban presence, these Euroamericans were able to make the occupational shifts concomitant with the changing Miami economic structure, becoming the principal economic beneficiaries of Miami's economic transformation (Pérez-Stable and Uriarte 1993, 141–58).

POLITICS

Although differentiating economic levels between Exilic Cubans and other Latinos/as elucidate the disconnection between the Miami community and U.S. Hispanics in general, the dividing line primarily remains one of ideology, specifically, the theology of *la lucha*. To understand the Exilic Cuban mind-set, the reader must realize that for the Miami Cubans, the universe is conceived and perceived in its relationship to one person, Fidel Castro. Castro is an omnipresent figure central to the construction of every opinion, action, and resolution that may originate in Miami. Castro, as the incarnation of Satan, informs the daily experience of the Exilic community. *La lucha,* the very struggle of life, is fought against this incarnation.

Jaime Suchlicki, director of the Institute of Cuba and Cuban-American Studies (ICCAS) at the University of Miami, speaking of the Elián saga, reminds us that the fight was not so much about Elián as it was about Fidel.[5] This sentiment is expressed by Isaura Felipe, eighty-six, at the Buena Vista Social Club, a Little Havana center for the elderly. While clutching the gold crucifix around her neck she exclaimed, "[If Elián is returned] I will cry, because that would be giving Fidel Castro pleasure, and he will be making fun of us."[6] Sonia Ruiz, thirty-six, while keeping an all-night vigil in front of Elián's home, echoed these feelings: "Why are they going to give [Elián] to that communist dad? Our government has betrayed us again. Why are they letting Castro win?"[7]

Max Castro, of the North-South Center at the University of Miami, captures the underlining consequences of Elián's return to Castro when he states, "[Exilic Cubans feel] that if this child is returned to Cuba, it means that *el exilio* image of Cuba as the ultimate, absolute hell is not valid. One doesn't send anyone back to a concentration camp, to a slave plantation, and that is the image in which Cuban-Americans tend to portray and view the Cuban situation—in stark, black-verses-white, absolute Manichaean terms" (Bikel 2001). In short, the Elián saga has more to do with Castro and the construction of Cuba as a "hellhole" then it does with Elián.

Studies conducted by Alejandro Portes and Rubén Rumbaut suggest that Cuban émigrés differ from other Latino/a émigrés because their immigration was rooted in the changing political situation in the homeland (1996, 133). Thus the Exilic Cuban interest in politics focuses on U.S. foreign policies toward Cuba. Other U.S. Latina/o groups pursue a political agenda with a variety of issues, including bilingual education, immigration, affirmative action, improving social services in *los barrios,* and police brutality, to mention just a few. Exilic Cubans, conversely, are politically focused, with their focus on one thing: the elimination of Castro. As one local bumper sticker succinctly put it, No Castro—No Problem. Consequently, unlike in any other metropolitan area in the United States, Dade County's cities routinely pass resolutions concerning foreign policy. (In fact, a common joke is that Miami is the only local municipality with a foreign policy.) Candidates running for either Congress or the local school board are elected or defeated based on their anti-Castro credentials. According to a 1997 poll conducted in Dade County, 70 percent of Exilic Cubans said that in local elections the candidate's position on Cuba was an important factor in determining how they would vote (Grenier and Gladwin 1997, 28).

The religious expression of *la lucha* has its own eschatology, revolving around the conquest of evil, personified by Fidel Castro. The common joke is that whenever Fidel sneezes, Exilic Cubans chill their champagne bottles, anticipating the celebration of his demise. This was most evident on June 23, 2001, when a seventy-four-year-old Castro, wearing his traditional long-sleeved military uniform over what is believed to be a bullet-proof vest, fainted while giving one of his loquacious speeches under a sweltering summer sun. In response Miami-Dade Mayor Alex Penelas huddled with advisors to discuss the city's readiness in the event of Castro's death.

Even though most of the planning revolves around maintaining order and safety in what is expected to be spontaneous celebration on the streets of Miami, some of those plans are secret, dealing with the transition of power. Contingency plans are in place, based on numerous rumors of Castro's impending death, for how the United States will manage the first days of a post-Castro Cuba. While the White House has declined to comment on such plans, Exilic Cuban U.S. Congresswoman Ileana Ros-Lehtinen, who has attended intelligence briefings on the subject, has mentioned the possibility of a naval blockade, mostly to prevent a wave of immigration from the island. Additionally, at the behest of the Florida Legislature, the state's economic development agency has studied business opportunities in Cuba. Enterprise Florida has commissioned studies to help with marketing and investment on the island for Exilic Cubans.[8]

The Elián saga was not the first occasion for the Exilic community to take actions based on how the community perceives they would affect Castro. In just one year (1982–1983), the Miami City Commission passed twenty-eight ordinances and resolutions dealing with international issues, specifically issues concerning Cuba. For example, in the summer of 1990, a hero's welcome was being planned for Nelson Mandela's Miami visit by the African American community. But before arriving in Miami, Mandela acknowledged, during an ABC television interview, his friendship with Fidel Castro, causing the Miami commission to withdraw their official welcome. When the black community objected, by declaring a boycott of their own city and asking outside conventioneers not to choose Miami, those in the Cuban political power structure declared that the African American community was insensitive to Cubans. Similarly, in 1991 permission for Miami's Haitian community to celebrate Jean Bertrand Aristide's inauguration as president was contingent on Castro not being invited to the inauguration in Haiti.

In short, Miami becomes its own country, in which the needs and interests of the dominant Cuban power structure in maintaining fever-pitch hostility toward Castro outweigh the needs and interests of any other constituency, even to the point of enforcing censorship and violating basic civil rights. During the prayer vigils held outside Elián's Miami house, Exilic Cubans were not seen by the dominant culture as American citizens protesting but as Cubans protesting America. This perspective contributes to their being dismissed as "right-wing extremists" living in a "banana republic."[9] The failure of other Hispanic groups, as well as of the overall U.S. dominant culture, to understand the inaccuracy of this view is perceived by the Exilic community as a form of repression. The Reverend Alberto Cutie of St. Patrick's Church in Miami Beach believes that the underlying problem is a lack of compassion among non-Cubans.

Closing the Port of Miami: Elderly Exilic Cubans such as Ramon Verdes took to the streets yelling their protest against Elián's return to Cuba by blocking the Port of Miami on January 2, 2000. Several protesters were arrested. Photograph © Tim Chapman/*The Miami Herald*.

He states, "Not only the media, but our neighbors here, don't understand the pain of the Cuban-American community. We can't ignore the Holocaust, it happened. We can't ignore prejudice and bias in any form to any group in our community, and we shouldn't ignore the historical process of a communist regime ninety miles from our shores. That is part of what is happening. A lack of compassion, of understanding."[10] Henry Cuik, a thirty-one-year-old construction worker, tries to explain Exilic Cubans' passion over Elián: "If you are Cuban, you know what I mean. If Cuban blood does not flow in your veins you have no idea of what it is like to be us—all of our memories of what it is like under Castro and what it means to be separated from your homeland. For us, we can express ourselves with all our emotion in this city we helped build for 30 and 40 years. This is our little bit of Cuba, here in Miami, where we can be ourselves."[11]

The unsympathetic attitude expressed by most non-Cubans in Miami over the Elián saga has convinced several influential Exilic Cubans that the forty-plus-year *lucha* for Cuba has become counterproductive. With this in mind, they lobbied to have the 2001 Latin Grammy Awards held in Miami. Originally courted by civic and political leaders to improve the city's image after Elián was sent back to Cuba, the Latin Grammys was also expected to generate $35 million locally and to be watched by more than eight hundred million people worldwide. CANF's new chairman, Jorge Mas Santos, was one of those who lobbied to bring the show to Miami to demonstrate to the world the community's capacity for tolerance after the negative images of Miami that surfaced after Elián's seizure by the U.S. government. "This was [to be] an image of a different generation," said Juan Carlos Espinosa, director of St. Thomas University's Center for Cuban Studies. Nevertheless, the events surrounding the second annual Latin Grammys only appeared to have shattered any illusions of a cohesive *lucha* while reinforcing negative images of the community's intolerance.

Although Miami was eventually chosen as the 2001 site for the Latin Grammys, the threat of Exilic protest led organizers to move the event to Los Angeles.[12] Some Exilic Cubans, encouraged by local radio commentators, wanted to protest the nomination of several Resident Cuban artists, even though none were scheduled to perform, and it was unclear if any would attend. The controversy revolved around the sites chosen for protest of the international show by a coalition of more than one hundred Exilic groups. These sites were close to the arena where the Latin Grammy Awards was to be hosted, well within sight of news cameras, invited guests, and spectators. The proximity of the protestors to the event raised concerns among Latin Grammy officials, concerns that appeared to be legitimate. Two years earlier, on October 9, 1999, about 3,500 protestors demonstrated outside the Miami Arena during a concert put on by Los Van Van (a Resident Cuban musical group). Some protestors pelted concert-goers with eggs, rocks, soda cans, and at least one large battery. One of the Latin Grammy protest leaders, Emilio Izuierdo Jr., fifty-three, a former UMAP labor camp prisoner in Cuba, jumped a barricade during the concert, and charged up the stairs of the Miami Arena, Cuban flag in hand.[13]

Days after the Latin Grammys pulled out of Miami, a full page ad, titled "Declaration of Principles," appeared in *The Miami Herald* urging the Exilic Cuban community to remain strong in their opposition to Fidel Castro and to those associated with his regime. The ad, according to some who appended their names to it, served as a warning to Exilic Cubans who had endorsed bringing the Latin Grammys to Miami. Diego Suárez, a former senior official of CANF, said, "It is a message that

Los Van Van protest: On October 9, 1999, Miami police apprehended anti–Van Van protestors who broke through the police barricades outside the Miami Arena, where the Resident Cuban band performed. Several protesters were arrested. Photograph © Pedro Portal/*The Miami Herald*.

fixes our view that there should not be any kind of deviation in the exile community from the position of never compromising with the Castro regime or any other type of alternative of toleration that only serves to send mixed signals to the Communist regime."[14]

Armando Codina, a real estate developer whose former business partner is Governor Jeb Bush, might very well be among those who are beginning to view *la lucha* as counterproductive. Commenting on the Latin Grammy fiasco, he said, "This is a terrible embarrassment to this community and to Cubans in particular. [The Latin Grammy Awards] had been invited here. Then for us to cause them to pull out because of a small group that I don't think represents the Cuban community—and to see politicians playing into the issue—that's a disgrace." Darío Moreno, a political scientist at Florida International University, provides a perceptive interpretation of these events: "We're in a very interesting moment in exile Cuban politics. There has been a rethinking, and it began because of Elián, which was such a public relations disaster for the exiles. You're seeing a debate between those who want to keep the purity of the old exile politics, the intransigent line if you will, and those taking a more PR-savvy line that Miami must seem to be the reasonable one in this debate."[15]

A poll conducted by Bendixen and Associates two years after Elián's return to Cuba demonstrated a shifting away from hard-line positions among Exilic Cubans in Miami.[16] The poll revealed a statistical tie on the question of whether the Bush administration should lift restrictions on travel to Cuba by Euroamericans. While 61 percent continue to support the embargo, 52 percent believe it should cease being the focus of U.S. policy. In addition, the majority (79 percent) of those polled supports a peaceful and gradual transition toward democracy for the island, including an amnesty for Resident Cubans serving as governmental officials. Only a few (16 percent) continue to call for an "abrupt and violent" change in the government. Additionally, the poll revealed that about half the Exilic-Cubans surveyed send money to their family members on the island, pumping $600 to $950 million a year into the Cuban economy, making this a top source of the island's income. These revelations appear to indicate a softening in attitudes among Exilic Cubans since the Elián saga. Even Pepe Hernandez, president of CANF, was not surprised by the poll's findings, since their own internal polls have arrived at similar conclusions. According to Hernandez, "Over the past few years, but especially since the Elián González episode, there has been a change. Growing numbers of exiles no longer look at the situation in Cuba in terms of confrontation, but in terms of reconciliation, in the sense of looking for a common destiny, and not one in which there will be winners and losers."[17]

The ability to manipulate a constituency of voters over fifty-five through the fervor of *la lucha* will, with time, dissipate. As time goes by, the older, more intractable adherents to *la lucha* will be replaced by a younger generation of Exilic Cubans born in this country with no memory of the Cuba of their parents (or grandparents). Additionally, since the early 1990s, more than two hundred and fifty thousand Cubans emigrated to the United States. These new immigrants still have and maintain relationships with parents, siblings, and friends on the island. For these new Exilic Cubans, Resident Cubans are not the enemy; rather, they are still very much part of *la familia*.

Yet using *la lucha* to manipulate the Cuban voting bloc is not limited to local politics. Officials in both the national Republican and Democratic parties agree that the Miami Cuban voting bloc made a difference in the 2000 presidential election. The perception that the Exilic Cuban community can make or break a national election is very real.[18] According to Miami City Commissioner Tomás Regalado, "Who can dispute that the Cuban vote elected President Bush?"[19] An attempt to keep the fervor alive can best be noted in the recent creation of the Cuban Liberty Council. About two months before the Latin Grammys, former CANF spokesperson Ninoska Pérez Castellón and others left CANF to form a more hard-line rival organization, mainly because they felt CANF was moving toward the political center.

In spite of these recent political developments, no doubt the time will come to speak in terms of a post–Exilic Cuban identity. Or maybe the time has already come, even though the danger of a postexilic perspective is that it might negate the exile. As the "old guard" who left Cuba as adults become fewer in number, a newer U.S.-bred generation may remain faithful to the religion of their elders, while evangelizing the message of *la lucha* to make it more palpable to mainstream U.S. audiences who have moved beyond the Cold War.

A Post-Exilic Cuban?

A common joke among Exilic Cubans revolves around a pair of tortoises that were given to Fidel Castro for his seventy-fifth birthday. *El jefe* asks about their life expectancy. An aid informs Castro that they have been known to live in excess of 150 years, to which Castro responds, "That's the trouble with pets. You become attached to them and then they die on you." For the past twenty years, I, along with the rest of the Exilic Cuban community, have been reading Castro's premature obituaries. In fact, it appears that the foreign policy of both the Exilic Cuban community and of the United States government consists solely of waiting for Castro to die. Ironically, Castro has now outlived most of his opponents, even those who were younger than he. Although he appears to be in good health (mostly maintaining a vegetarian diet and daily exercising on a stationary bicycle) and that he can easily live a few more decades (longevity seems to be a family trait—his grandmother recently celebrated her one hundred and fifth birthday), the fact remains that Castro will one day die.

If the glue that appears to hold the Exilic Cuban community together, contributing to the definition of its cultural identity, is a mutual hatred of this one man (and to a lesser degree of his brother, Raul), what will happen when the object of this hatred ceases to exist? After Miami erupts in spontaneous celebration, and its political and business leaders scramble to influence a post-Castro Cuba, how will Exilic Cubans begin to see and define themselves? With each passing year, the number of people who remember a pre-Castro Cuba continues to dwindle. Can one still be an Exilic Cuban when one was born and raised in the United States, never having laid eyes on the mystical island of one's parents (or grandparents)? Throughout this book, I have used the term Exilic Cuban to define all individuals who were born in Cuba, regardless of where they live in the diaspora, and those who were born on foreign land but remain culturally Cuban. As this book comes to a close, it is crucial now to question whether it will continue to be appropriate to use the term Exilic for individuals of Cuban descent who are born in this country and who will live in a post-Castro world. When do we begin a conversation, if ever, about a postexilic Cuban?

All religions change with each generation. Any faith practiced by the devotees of today's generation will differ from the faith their parents, or grandparents, practiced. While the religious message may not necessarily change, the way the message is heard and put into practice usually does, as the younger generations replace the older ones. And it is no different with *la lucha*. How will *la lucha* be understood if there is no Castro to wage *la lucha* against? How will *la lucha* evolve to reflect the ideologies and beliefs of the next generation of Exilic(?) Cubans?

The current generation of Exilic Cubans refers to itself as Generation Ñ. Although this term has also been used to refer to the current generation of U.S. Latinos/as, it appears that among Hispanics, Exilic Cubans who came of age in the United States have embraced this term more so than other groups. Generation Ñ is currently the name of a glossy magazine marketed to young Latinas/os. Among Hispanic youth the moniker Generation Ñ serves as a counterpart to the Euroamerican Generation X. What differentiates Generation Ñ from Generation X is its attempt to live simultaneously in two worlds, one Cuban and the other Euroamerican. As members of Generation Ñ, these Exilic Cubans are bicultural in the fullest sense of the word, largely bilingual, most often fluent in English. Most are well educated and possess clout in the marketplace. Predominately in their twenties and thirties, they are younger than the aging Euroamerican baby boomers. They have learned how to "be" American when necessary but can easily revert to being Cuban when desired. In effect, they are flaunting, not hiding, their Cuban roots, telling the dominant culture that they will live and succeed in Miami on their own terms.

Because these Ñ's are predominately light skinned and middle-class, possessing cultural capital, they are more easily accepted by Euroamerican institutions. Greater opportunities exist for these "acceptable" Latinas/os than for other "less acceptable" ones. Generation Ñ is one manifestation of a new cultural identity that is neither fully Latina/o nor fully Euroamerican. In some respects, it has become a space for Cubans, and other Latinas/os who are neither "too dark" nor "too poor" (De La Torre and Aponte 2001, 142–45). As these "successful" Cubans rise within community structures, intra-Hispanic power struggles develop between them and those Latinos/as who still suffer economically because of their pronounced African and/or Amerindian features.

The disparity between the children of Exilic Cubans and other U.S. Latino/a groups is evident. The children of Exilic Cubans regard becoming "American" as highly desirable. To become an "American" is a choice made by the individual but also accepted by the national community, if the child is "white" enough and has sufficient middle-class status. Therefore, Miami's Cuban children face an entirely different set of circumstances than do children of other Hispanic groups, contributing to their rapid assimilation into the dominant culture. Portes and Rubén's 1992 study on segmented assimilation showed that while Exilic Cubans share the exile experience with other Hispanics, the next generation of Exilics will have little or nothing in common with other Latinas/os. Their study indicated that children of middle-class Exilic Cubans who attend bilingual private schools are effectively insulated from discrimination and other influences of barrio life. The screening of negative outside messages protects these children from the low self-esteem reported in other ethnic groups. Cuban children are ethnically isolated (94 percent report that most of their friends are other Exilic Cubans), are enthusiastic about this country (55 percent insist the United States is "the best country in the world"), are more likely to identify themselves as "Americans" (discarding the term Cuban American), and score higher than other ethnic groups in reading, English, and mathematics (1996, 232–68).

In a more recent survey done by Rumbaut and Perez, it was found that Cuban youth preferred speaking English and were least likely to identify themselves by national origin, that is, as Cuban. Only 3 to 6 percent of youths in private schools thought of themselves as Cuban, as opposed to 17 percent of those in public schools. Rubén Rumbaut and Lisandro Perez concluded that those with greater socioeconomic advantages and ambitions adopted a more mainstream identity, while those with fewer advantages continued to identify themselves as Cuban. Not surprisingly, Cuban youths are the least likely to report experiencing discrimination, even less likely than European or Canadian whites (1998, 5). How then can these children identify with a second-class "Hispanic Other" when their "honorary whiteness" and class privilege allow easy assimilation into the dominant culture?

Take the example of George P. Bush, nephew of president George W. and son of Florida governor Jeb Bush. Even though he is not of Cuban descent (his mother, Columba, is Mexican born), he fully demonstrates what occurs when Hispanics are exposed to economic privilege and insulated from the discriminatory influences of barrio life. Although once referred to as the "little brown ones" when then–vice president George Bush Sr. introduced the grandchildren to President Reagan, George P., according to fellow classmates at Rice University, did not seem interested in Latino/a issues or causes. His absence in the Hispanic Association for Cultural Enrichment at Rice (HACER) has led the director of Multicultural Affairs to name him the "invisible man" of multicultural events. Yet during his uncle's 2000 presidential campaign, when it was advantageous to be Latino, George P. ran political commercials geared to Hispanics where he proclaimed, "I am a young Latino in the United States and very proud of my bloodline."[20] Although a tendency to be seen as "American" exists, Latino-ness is flaunted when it is fortuitous to be seen as Hispanic, and at that point a cross-dressing of identity occurs.

As the death of Castro, the personification of all that is evil, approaches, and as the latest generation of post-Exilic Cubans typified as Generation Ñ arises, *la lucha* as the religious expression of *el exilio* either will evolve to meet the challenges of a post-Castro Miami or will come to an end. Perhaps the inability of Exilic Cubans to keep Elián in Miami, in spite of the political clout amassed by *el exilio,* signals a new stage in the evolution of *la lucha*. Perhaps this indigenous Exilic Cuban religion is taking on a new form with the changing identity of Miami's Cuban population. Whatever shape *la lucha* may eventually take, it would be a mistake to think that the repatriation of Elián signals the demise of the Exilic Cuban resolve to view the world through an anti-Castro lens. The November 13, 2001, mayoral election of Manny Diaz, a political no-name in Miami politics but a central figure in the Elián episode (he was the legal representative for Elián's Miami family) clearly indicates that *la lucha* continues. The Miami community's determination to maintain fever-pitched hostility toward anything that might appear pro-Castro is only stiffened as right-wing hardliners (as in the case of defeated mayor Carollo) are accused of and punished for not standing firmer in their defense of Elián. The Elián custody battle is but the latest example of how the Miami community formulates its actions, cloaked in the religiosity of *la lucha,* based on the supposed impact it will have on Castro. Nothing else, for now, matters.

Notes

Chapter 1. An *Ajiaco* Christianity

1. The term *Cuban American,* which refers to Cubans residing in the United States, is an artificial designation amalgamating "who they are" and "where they live." It is the name given to Cubans in the United States by the dominant culture, not a name they choose. Most simply refer to themselves as Cubans. The term attempts to reconcile two distinct cultures into one, creating within the Cuban a dichotomous existence. As "Cuban Americans" they are too Cuban to be accepted by this country and too Americanized to be accepted by their native compatriots. Because self-naming is a powerful and liberating praxis, in this book Cubans are defined as all individuals who were born in Cuba, regardless of where they live now, or all those who were born on foreign land but choose to identify culturally with being Cuban. *Resident Cubans* refers to those who inhabit the island of Cuba; *Exilic Cubans* refers to those in the diaspora who reside mainly within the United States, specifically in Miami, Florida. Because exile spans generations, *Exilic Cubans* also includes those who were neither born nor raised on the island yet whose identity was forged by their parents' act of (re)membering Cuba from the social location of exile. Although Exilic Cubans are not a monolithic group, they are united, no matter how loosely, by the experience of being separated from the island that defines them.

2. Eunice Ponce and Elaine de Valle, "Mania over Elián Rising," *Miami Herald,* January 10, 2000.

3. Wilfredo Cancio Isla, "Los Reyes Mago a los pies de Elián," *El Nuevo Herald,* January 10, 2000.

4. Alejandra Matus, "El fevor religioso aumenta entre los manifestantes frente a la casa de Elián," *El Nuevo Herald,* April 22, 2000.

5. Joaquim Utset, "Devotos de la Virgen dicen ver una señal contra el regreso del niño," *El Nuevo Herald,* March 26, 2000.

6. Matus, "El fevor religioso."

7. Meg Laughlin, "Prayer Vigil Lifts Elián Fervor to New High," *Miami Herald,* March 31, 2000.

8. "Ceremony Set to Honor Elián's Mom," *Miami Herald,* May 14, 2000.

9. Amy Driscoll and Sandra Marquez-Garcia, "Thousand Join Glowing Prayer Vigil," *Miami Herald,* March 30, 2000.

10. D. Aileen Dodd, "Catholic Leaders Low-Profile," *Miami Herald,* April 15, 2000.

11. D. Aileen Dodd, "Elián a Bridge Linking Rival Faiths," *Miami Herald,* April 10, 2000.

12. Rui Ferreira, "Vigilia permanente en casa de Elián," *El Nuevo Herald,* April 5, 2000.

13. Dodd, "Elián a Bridge."

14. Joaquin Utset, "Miles de personas participan en virilia en Miami," *El Nuevo Herald,* April 11, 2000.

15. Laughlin, "Prayer Vigil."

16. Maria Travierso and Charles Cotayo, "Elián, un niño 'milagroso' hecho símbolo," *El Nuevo Herald,* March 6, 2000.

17. Edward Wasserman, "Elian, the Unifier?" *Broward Daily Business Review,* April 24, 2000.

18. Paul Brinkley-Rogers, "Protestors from Abroad Flock to Home," *Miami Herald,* April 19, 2000.

19. Daniel Shoer Roth, "Los cubanos se ven reflejados en el niño balsero," *El Nuevo Herald,* January 7, 2000.

20. "Elián's Lawyer: Why an Observant Jew Is Fighting to Keep Him Here," *Chicago Jewish News,* January 28, 2000.

21. Travierso and Cotayo, "Elián, un niño 'milagroso.'"

22. Travierso and Cotayo, "Elián, un niño 'milagroso.'"

23. Ponce and de Valle, "Mania over Elián."

24. J. Utset and R. Ferreira, "De la protesta cívica al júbilo popular," *El Nuevo Herald,* January 9, 2000.

25. Roth, "Los cubanos."

26. Karen Branch, "Adult Exiles Recall Cuban Childhoods," *Miami Herald,* April 15, 2000.

27. Roth, "Los cubanos."

28. Daniel A. Grech, "Pastors Join Criticism, but Appeal for Calm," *Miami Herald,* April 23, 2000.

29. Andrea Robinson, "A Community Looks to Heal," *Miami Herald,* April 24, 2000.

30. "Little Cousin's Dream Strengthens Exiles' Faith Boy Will Stay in U.S.," *Miami Herald,* April 24, 2000.

31. Concilio Cubano is an umbrella organization representing numerous dissident factions that present the most significant political challenge to the Castro regime. It is interesting to note that they do not call for the overthrow of the government; rather, they are demanding freedom of expression, which remains a violation of the present penal code, punishable by up to seven years in prison.

32. Cuba has many competing dissident groups. Some advocate a free-market economy; others are socialist and are disenchanted with present conditions; some are religious groups; some are composed of independent journalists; still others are former prisoners of conscience, human right advocates, and unrecognized political party leaders. Probably the most critical challenge to Castro's political power is the Varela Project, spotlighted on the island during former president Jimmy Carter's 2002 visit. The Varela Project gathered 11,020 signatures for a petition requesting that the National Assembly (in accord with Articles 63 and 88 of the Cuban constitution) hold a referendum asking voters if they favor human rights, amnesty for political prisoners, the right to own a business, and electoral reforms.

33. It is important to note that criticizing the Exilic Cuban sociopolitical ethos does not automatically mean defending present Resident Cuban political structures. Existing intra-Cuban hostility rests on the fallacy of this dichotomy. Cubans are forced to choose between two options only: Miami's capitalism and La Habana's Fidelismo. Criticizing one side leads to the risk of being labeled a supporter of the other. Because the focus of this book is on the Miami Exilic community, little will be written about the present Resident Cuban position or any other Cuban position outside of Dade County.

34. I recognize that Christianity is not, nor should it be, the only model through which Cuban spirituality can be understood. As previously mentioned, religions like Santería, Judaism, and Islam are also practiced by many Cubans and are crucial in any understanding of *cubanidad*. This book concentrates on Christianity because it has remained the "official" religious expression of Exilic Cubans and, as such, has been most prone to influencing political views.

35. Fernando Ortiz was the first to use *ajiaco* as a metaphor for the Cuban experience. He used this term within the context of a Cuba composed of immigrants who, unlike those of the United States, reached the island on their way to someplace else. His usage of *ajiaco* did not indicate his belief that Cuban culture achieved complete integration; rather, the *ajiaco* is still simmering on the Caribbean stove and has not yet become fully blended (1940, 165–69). Rather than accenting the immigrants, I use this term to refer to the distinctive nexus of the Cuban's heredity, specifically their Amerindian, African, Spaniard, Asian, and Euroamerican roots. While I portray the *ajiaco* metaphor as positive, Ortiz included a racist element in his ethnology. This is evident when he described the negative aspects of the *ajiaco*. He wrote:

The white race influenced the Cuban underworld through European vices, modified and aggravated under certain aspects by the social factor of the children of the ambient. The black race provided its superstitions, its sensualism, its impulsiveness, in short, its African psyche. The yellow race brought the addiction of opium, its homosexual vices, and other refined corruptions of its secular civilization. (1973, 19)

Furthermore, Ortiz advocated that immigration solely from northern Europe in order to "sow among us the germs of energy, progress, life." To continue accepting other races, according to Ortiz, only increased criminality on the island (1906, 55–57).

36. *Cubanidad* is more than just Cubanness. For Ortiz, *cubanidad* is a "condition of the soul, a complexity of sentiments, ideas and attitudes" (1939, 3).

José Martí (1853–1895), Cuban journalist, revolutionary philosopher, and patriot, is credited with organizing the physical invasion of Cuba to bring about its independence from Spain. A prolific writer (whose *Obras Completas* consists of seventy-three volumes) and precursor of *modernismo,* Martí is regarded as the father of Cuba by both Resident and Exilic Cubans. He was killed a month after landing in Cuba during a skirmish with Spanish troops at Dos Ríos (May 19, 1895). His death made him a martyr and a symbol of Cuban liberation.

37. The *ajiaco* metaphor is not intended to represent Cubans exclusively. Obviously, cultural mixtures also occurred within other Latin American countries, and Cubans are no more or less a product of cultural blends. Yet the term *ajiaco* may not be the best word to represent other Hispanic groups; Central Americans might use the term *sancocho* Christianity to refer to their own perspective, since *sancocho* is their term for their indigenous stew.

38. Etymologically, *mulato* is believed to be a derivative from the Arabic *mulwállad* (pronounced *muélled*). *Muwállad* is defined as "one born of an Arab father and a foreign mother," a possible passive participle of the second conjugation of *wálada,* "he begot." However, *mulato,* literally "mule, young or without domesticity," was influenced in form by a folk-etymological association with the Spanish word *mulo,* "mule," from the Latin *mulus.* Adding the diminutive suffix *-at* to the word *mulo* creates a general hybrid comparison. Dozy, in his monumental work on the Arabic language, insists the word *mulato* is actually a Portuguese word of contempt signifying mule. See *Supplément aux dictionnaires Arabes,* 3rd ed., s.v. "Begot," by Reinhart Dozy. Fernando Ortiz concurs with this etymological definition of *mulato* to the nature of a mule (1975a, 40).

39. José Vasconcelos (1882–1959), Mexican philosopher and statesman, is credited with constructing the utopian concept of the cosmic race as a way of combating the prevalent positivism of his time, which advocated the destruction of Mexican culture because it was believed Anglos were evolutionarily superior. Although we can celebrate the defense of Latin American culture against Eurocentrism, we need to recognize that philosophers like Vasconcelos still upheld positivism's hierarchical view of race.

40. Just as a Middle Passage exists in the Atlantic, so does one exist in the Pacific for Cubans. With the abolition of slavery and the sugar industry's need for laborers, Cubans imported Chinese to replace the emancipated blacks. Although these Chinese were not official slaves, their journey to the island and their existence on Cuban soil were similar to those of slaves.

Cuba's European roots are not necessarily in Spain alone but also in the United States. For most central Europeans, Spain is spiritually and ethnically more aligned with Africa than it is with Europe. Even though the Crescent was vanquished from Spain by the Cross, they believe that eight hundred years of Islamic rule have imprinted a Moorish soul upon the Spaniards.

41. To reduce the Amerindian ingredient to just Taínos is problematic. As more laborers were needed on the island, they were imported (kidnapped or

brought as prisoners of war) from surrounding territories, including but not limited to the Yucatán Peninsula.

Andalusians, Basques, Castilians, Catalonians, Galicians, *isleños* (Canary Islanders), and Portuguese are some of the diverse cultures of the Iberian Peninsula who came to Cuba. Hence the term Spaniard cannot be limited to one ethnically homogeneous Iberian population. Also, on the Iberian Peninsula a series of peoples culturally and genetically merged with one another. They include, but are not limited to, Arabs, Berbers, Carthaginians, Celts, Greeks, Gypsies, Jews, Romans, Phoenicians, and Visigoths. Additionally, after Latin American wars for independence, royalists throughout the hemisphere found a haven in Cuba, as did the French before them, who fled the Haitian Revolution. Hence, the word Spaniard reflects an *ajiaco* in and of itself.

Under the label "African" exists another *ajiaco*. Ortiz provides a brief ethnological sketch of ninety-nine different African nations represented in Cuba. African has become a homogeneous term signifying the mixture of different peoples, traditions, and cultures (1975b, 40–56). More recent studies by the Cuban Academy of Sciences show more than two thousand African names in Cuba (Barnet 1986, 8). Further complications occurred over the definition of African, as black Haitians, Bahamians, Jamaicans, and other islanders settled in Cuba during the past two centuries, having found employment harvesting sugar.

Like the other elements of the Cuban *ajiaco*, immigrants from the Pacific regions cannot be simply categorized as Asian. They came from Swatow, Amoy, Canton, Hong Kong, Saigon, and Manila. They came from different districts of China and other countries with differing customs, traditions, languages, and dialects.

42. In 1980 the Dade County legislative delegation to Tallahassee included only one Republican and no Cubans. Additionally, all three Miami congresspersons were Euroamerican Democrats. By the 1988 election, out of the twenty-eight state legislative seats from Dade County, eleven were held by Republicans, ten of them Exilic Cubans. Also, two of the three congressional seats were held by Republican Exilic Cubans. When the Miami Hispanic vote is compared with the rest of the nation's Latino population, it is easy to see the strong loyalty Exilic Cubans have for the Republican Party.

43. For example: Miguel H. Díaz, *On Being Human: U.S. Hispanic and Rahnerian Perspectives* (2001); Orlando O. Espín, *The Faith of the People: Theological Reflections on Popular Catholicism* (1997); Alexandro García-Rivera, *St. Martín de Porres: The "Little Stories" and the Semiotics of Culture* (1995); Roberto S. Goizueta, *Caminemos con Jesús: Toward a Hispanic/Latino Theology of Accompaniment* (1995); Justo L. González, *Mañana: Christian Theology from a Hispanic Perspective* (1990); Ada María Isasi-Díaz, *En la Lucha: A Hispanic Women's Liberation Theology* (1993); Luis G. Pedraja, *Jesus Is My Uncle: Christology from a Hispanic Perspective* (1999); and Fernando Segovia, *Decolonizing Biblical Studies* (2001).

44. Liberation theologians like Gustavo Gutiérrez expressed concern that revolution theology has the tendency to "baptize" the revolution by placing it beyond criticism. Castro's well-known phrase, "Everything within the Revolution,

nothing outside of the Revolution," fixes limits of acceptability on all discourse, including Christian. Gutiérrez accuses theologies of revolution of "reductionism," in which the gospel is reduced to sociology, economics, or politics. Faith becomes a justification for Christians to participate in achieving the goals of the Revolution (1984, xiii, 44). Similarly, Clodovis Boff states that the overall process of revolution tends to be confused with just one of its moments, the moment of breakage in which the people are dragged by the yoke through "vanguardism." Fulfilling basic needs is not the end but the means to a full realization of humanity (1990, 101). While José Míguez Bonino admits that the Cuban Revolution was an inspiration in providing an example for overcoming the United States imperialist system in this hemisphere, he insists that the Cuban model is not ideal for reproducing elsewhere (1975, 33).

45. Postmodernity is defined by Jean-François Lyotard as an "incredulity toward metanarratives," in which the great heroes, dangers, voyages, and goals of the narrative function are lost (1984, xxiv). I aver that postmodernity, like liberation theology, is a neomodernist movement, an heir of the Eurocentric Enlightenment. To describe postmodernity as a theology or philosophy instead of a theory contradicts Fredric Jameson's assertion that postmodernity "marks the end of philosophy" (1983, 112). Latin American theologians have taught us to speak of theology and philosophy as a "second act," a reflecting praxis that struggles for basic human rights. Thus, metanarratives can be understood as transcendental categories invented by modernity to interpret and normalize reality, a reality comprehended philosophically as postmodernity. My use of the term *postmodernity* does not indicate a systematic engagement with or exclusive academic reflection of its paradigms. Rather, following Gustavo Gutiérrez's methodological example, I use whatever tools of human thought are available that illuminate the Exilic Cuban social position.

46. It could be argued that from 1962 to the fall of the Soviet Union, Cuba existed on the periphery of the Soviet Union.

Chapter 2. *La Lucha*

1. The 26 of July Movement was an underground operation designed to overthrow the dictatorship of Batista. The movement has been growing in Cuban cities since 1953 and was named after the date when Castro led a bloody attack on the Moncada barracks in Santiago. Once caught, Castro, who had conceived of the attack, spent twenty-one months in Batista's prison.

2. Karen Branch, "Crowds Target Reno's Home," *Miami Herald,* April 6, 2000.

3. Meg Laughlin, "Prayer Vigil," *Miami Herald,* March 31, 2000.

4. Carolyn Salazar and Manny Garcia, "Federal Agents Seize Elián in Predawn Raid," *Miami Herald,* April 22, 2000.

5. For a complete review of this type of Latina feminism, see Isasi-Díaz.

6. By the 1920s United States capitalists controlled all the infrastructures,

banks, and major sugar mills and 60 percent of the rural lands. By 1958 the U. S. dollar and the Cuban peso were interchangeable on the island as the Cuban economy dissolved into the U.S. economy. Even the currency of Cuba was printed in England and the United States. By the time Castro entered La Habana, Cuba had no national economy. Instead, it existed as an extension of the U.S. economy (Huberman and Sweezy 1989, 5–7).

7. Although scholars classify the clusters of arriving refugees differently, for purposes of understanding the overall creation of *la lucha,* I have constructed the flow of migration into four discernable waves, recognizing that the parameters are not absolute.

8. After the CIA-sponsored Playa Girón (Bay of Pigs) fiasco, the Castro government announced in June 1961 that anyone leaving the country could leave only with bare necessities. All other properties, including bank accounts, were confiscated. At most, they could carry five U.S. dollars, a suit of clothing, and a few changes of underwear. With time, the five U.S. dollars were replaced with worthless pesos.

9. Between the end, with the suspension of the airlift in April 1973, of the second wave and the start, with the Mariel boat lift of 1980, of the third wave were seven years in which substantially fewer Cubans entered the United States. During this time, 34,541 immigrants eventually made it to the States. Most had to fly first to Spain and wait for a long time for visas to be granted (Azicri 1988, 67).

10. Joel Russell, "1997 Hispanic Business Rich List," *Hispanic Business* 20 (March, 1997): 16–17.

11. Cathy Booth, "The Capital of Latin America: Miami," *Time* 142, no. 21 (1993): 84.

12. Christopher Marquis, "A Second Plan to Oust Castro Hatched After Bay of Pigs," *Philadelphia Inquirer,* November 19, 1997; and Laura Myers, "CIA Offered Crime Boss $150,000 to Assassinate Castro, Memo Shows," *Philadelphia Inquirer,* July 2, 1997.

13. William R. Amlong, "How the CIA Operated in Dade," *Miami Herald,* March 9, 1975; William R. Amlong, "CIA Sold Airline Cheap," *Miami Herald,* March 10, 1975; Martin Merzer, "Airline Does Job—Quietly," *Miami Herald,* December 10, 1986.

14. Gail Epstein Nieves, "Militant Exile Tells of Plot to Kill Castro: Group's Plan Detailed at Cuban Spy Trial," *Miami Herald,* March 28, 2001.

15. Elaine de Valle, "Cuba Again Links Dade Man to Plot," *Miami Herald,* June 22, 2001.

16. The two other cofounders were Raúl Masvidal, businessman and former candidate for the mayorship of Miami, and Carlos Salman, a Miami realtor and former chair of the Dade County Republican Party (Skoug 1996, 71, 80).

17. Ann Louise Bardach and Larry Rohter, "Key Cuba Foe Claims Exiles' Backing," *New York Times,* July 12, 1998; and "Alleged Castro Murder Plot Foiled," Associated Press, August 10, 1998. CANF denies any financial relationship with Posada and is suing the *New York Times* for libel on account of this story.

18. Frances Robles, "Imprisoned Castro Foe Rejects Use of Terror; Posada Denies He Bombed Airline," *Miami Herald,* July 24, 2001.

19. Gail Epstein Neives, "Spy Testimony Heated," *Miami Herald,* March 14, 2001.

20. Roberto Suro, "Exile Group Leader and 6 Others Are Accused of Plotting to Kill Castro," *Philadelphia Inquirer,* August 26, 1998; and Chris Hawley, "Three Plead Innocent to Castro Plot," Associated Press, September 2, 1998.

21. María Cristina García has documented more than eighty-four independent *periodiquitos.* Her description of these *periodiquitos* best illustrates their ethos. She writes:

> The rhetoric and symbolism in the *periodiquitos* were powerful. With names like *Conciencia* (Conscience), *El Clarín* (The bugle), *Centinela de la Libertad* (Sentinel of liberty), and even *El Gusano,* the *periodiquitos* referred to Cuba as *la patria sangrienta* (the bleeding nation) and *nuestra patria esclava* (our enslaved homeland); the exile community was referred to as *el pueblo libre de Cuba* (the free people of Cuba). Their mottos were battlecries: *¡Con Cuba, contra los traidores!* (With Cuba, against the traitors!); *¡En defensa de nuestros valores tradicionales!* (In defense of our traditional values!); *¡Sin unidad no hay regreso!* (Without unity there will be no return!) One editor always ended his essays with the dateline *"Miami, año ____ de la entrega de Cuba a los Rusos"* (Miami, year ____ of Cuba's deliverance to the Russians). (1996, 102–3)

Some *periodiquitos* provided serious news coverage relying on respectable journalism, but most consisted of "yellow journalism." For many of these journalists, their work is a religio-political calling that keeps *la causa sagrada* in the public consciousness, creating uniformity in thought among the Exilic Cuban community and exposing those who betray *la lucha.*

22. William R. Long and Guillermo Martínez, "Castro invita al exilio a un diálogo," *El Herald,* September 7, 1978.

23. *La Crónica,* October 15, 1979, 23.

24. Luisa Yáñez, "Brigade Ousts 2 for Trip to Cuba: Taunts, Threats Made; No One Hurt," *Miami Herald,* April 9, 2001; and Elaine De Valle, "40 Years After Bay of Pigs, Veterans Face New Battle: Men Who Fought in 1961 Invasion Fighting Fidel Castro, Each Other," *Miami Herald,* April 15, 2001.

Chapter 3. Psalm 137

1. All scriptural quotes have been translated by the author from the original Hebrew (the Hebrew Bible) and the Greek (the New Testament).

2. The Lieberson and Silverman study's findings on the causes of U.S. race riots were amply matched in Miami. Specifically, the causes were found to be (1) too few black police officers, (2) too few black entrepreneurs and store owners, and (3) an electoral system constructed to prevent blacks from participating in local representative government (1965, 887–98).

3. "Cuba's New Refugees Get Jobs Fast," *Business Week,* 12 March 1966; "Those Amazing Cubans," *Fortune,* October 1966; and "Cuban Success Story in the United States," *U.S. News and World Report,* 20 March 1967.

4. In spite of the tremendous political clout enjoyed by CANF today, the Ex-

ilic Cuban community of the 1960s through the 1980s stood impotent before a Soviet Union that supported Castro and a United States that prevented military action against Cuba, per the 1962 Kennedy-Khrushchev accord.

5. The last time African swine fever appeared in Cuba it was introduced by the CIA to destabilize the country, according to U.S. Senate investigations. See Peter Winn, "Is the Cuban Revolution in Trouble?" *Nation,* June 7, 1980, 682–85.

6. In spite of the extreme repression in Haiti, Haitian refugees were classified as fleeing the island because of economic difficulties, while Exilic Cubans were thought to be fleeing for political reasons. The latter gained entrance into the United States, while the former were repatriated.

7. Alfonso Chardy, " 'Invisible Exiles': Black Cubans Don't Find Their Niche in Miami," *Houston Chronicle,* September 12, 1993.

8. Unlike most cities in the United States, Miami has historically suffered from a power vacuum. Because of Miami's history as a tourist town, an elite with "old" money was never established. The *Miami Herald* was able to fill this power vacuum by becoming the voice of the Euroamerican establishment. From this position, Cubans could be kept "in their place" and used as scapegoats for the city's ills. While the rest of the national media portrayed the lives of Exilic Cubans as a "success story" during the first two waves of migration, the local media maintained a critical stance toward the federal government for allowing the arrival of so many Cubans. By 1971, as the Exilic Cuban economic enclave was becoming established, the CEO of the *Herald* formed the "nongroup" composed of thirty-eight members of the Euroamerican elite who headed different governmental, political, business, and social structures of powers (for example, owners or top managers of Eastern Airlines, Burdines, Miami Dolphins, Knight-Ridder, major banks, and the utility companies). They were called the nongroup because its existence was always denied. Once a month they met for dinner at one another's houses and essentially served as the shadow government of Dade County. Through this group, along with the "voice" of the *Herald,* a campaign was launched during the Mariel boat lift to portray these refugees as criminals.

Speaking for the Miami Euroamerican establishment, the *Miami Herald,* through its editorials and letters to the editor, sought to prevent the Mariel immigration by discrediting the arrivals. For the first two months of the exodus, the *Miami Herald* coverage was 90 percent negative. Their highly negative stereotyping of *Marielitos* affected all Exilic Cubans, regardless of their year of immigration (Portes and Stepick 1993, 27). Ironically, as the decade progressed, many Euroamericans left Miami, in a development known as "white flight," causing substantial declines in newspaper readerships. In 1960, as Cubans were beginning to arrive in Miami, 79 percent of all households in the county received the *Miami Herald.* By 1985 only 40 percent received the paper (Soruco 1996, 41–42). For the first time in U.S. history, an English paper was translated into another language and given away for free with a subscription to the English paper. Also in 1986 Cuban-born lawyer Angel Castillo became the paper's first Hispanic managing editor, initiating an emphasis on covering Cuban issues and hiring Cuban personnel. However, on November 21, 1987, Luis Botifol, chairman of Miami's Republic National Bank and trustee of CANF, ran a full-page ad in the *Miami Herald* charging "over the years the *Herald* has exhibited a pattern of neglect, manipulation, and censorship of Cuban and Cuban-American news. . . . It refuses to understand how anyone can feel such passion against communism without being right-wing kooks on the fringe of society." With this opening charge, a successful boycott of the *Herald* led by CANF forced the *Herald* to change its position. By the late 1980s, two Exilic Cubans of the Cuban elite were included in the nongroup. Five years after Mariel, the *Herald* wrote of our moral obligation in accepting Nicaraguans fleeing communism during the Sandinista years. Even so, when the *Herald* ran an editorial in 1992 opposing the Torricelli bill, which tightened the embargo on Cuba, CANF placed ads on buses and printed bumper stickers that read, "I Don't Believe the *Miami Herald*." Newspaper vending boxes were vandalized, several smeared with human feces, and publishers of the paper received death threats. This relationship between Exilic Cubans and the city's newspaper illustrates how the exilic community successfully transcended its representation in the local media.

9. When Orlando "El Duque" Hernandez (half-brother to then–Florida Marlins pitcher Livan Hernandez and catcher Alberto Hernandez) arrived on a raft in the Bahamas with six other *balseros,* then–attorney general Reno quickly offered "humanitarian visas" for him and his common-law wife (and not to the other five on the raft). She cited humanitarian reasons based on the fact that Orlando Hernandez is considered Cuba's finest pitcher, throwing a ninety-miles-per-hour fastball and holding the Cuban national tournament record for games won. Ironically, Orlando Hernandez turned down Reno's offer and migrated instead to Costa Rica, allowing him the opportunity to sign as a free agent with a major league team and avoiding the major league draft, which would have forced him to negotiate only with the team choosing him. By not seeking asylum in the United States, he became eligible for the free-agent bonus worth several million dollars over and above any multimillion-dollar contract he would sign with a major league team. His decision proved profitable when he landed a $6.6 million contract with (ironically) the New York Yankees. Basically, wealth, or the potential to earn it, qualifies as a reason to grant asylum. What makes this case interesting is the reconstruction of El Duque's escape from communism. Hernandez's story, as he told it to the Associated Press and NBC, contributes to the Exilic Cuban self-identity of fleeing on a sinking raft, through shark-infested waters. Yet Juan Carlos Romero, the captain of the "raft," tells a different story. He says the raft was in fact a twenty-foot craft with a cabin and diesel motor and that El Duque spent the majority of the voyage in the cabin because of seasickness. The boat never took to the water, nor did it sink off the shores of the Bahamas. Rather, it returned to Cuba after dropping off El Duque. No leaky raft, no rowing, no sharks, calm seas, plenty of drinking water, and four cans of Spam are the details the captain remembers about the journey—but such details are unimportant in the construction of *la lucha.* See "Fact or Fiction? Travel Mate Says El Duque's Story Not Accurate," *Chicago Sun-Times,* December 6, 1998.

10. The name of the returning Jew who led emancipated compatriots to the

homeland (Ezra 2:2), directed the building of the altar and temple (Hag. 1:12–14), and appointed Levites to inaugurate the finished Temple was Zerubbabel, which literally means the "shoot of Babylon." Regardless of any role our children may play in a post-Castro Cuba, they will always be the "shoots of the United States."

11. The biblical account tells us that Nebuchadnezzar carried off "*all* Jerusalem into exile." *All* is defined as the officers, the mighty men of valor, craftsmen, and the blacksmiths. Those left behind were the "poorest of the land" (2 Kings 24:14).

12. Three such tomb markers in Miami's Woodlawn Park Cemetery bear the names of Cuba's former "presidents." They are Gerardo Machado, who was deposed in 1933 and died in exile on a Miami Beach operating table; Carlos Prío, who led the country from 1938 to 1952 and shot himself in Miami Beach in 1977; and Carlos Hevia, who was "president" for a day in 1933 but was deposed when the true ruling junta changed its mind.

13. The cupbearer did more than taste the king's wine to thwart assassination attempts; he was also a confidant of the royal entourage who influenced the king's policies, as was the case with Nehemiah.

14. Yuca, named by the Amerindians, is an indigenous Cuban plant with pointed, stiff leaves and white, waxy flowers. It is often tall with a stout stem. The fruit is brown on the outside and white on the inside and looks like potatoes. It is boiled or fried and serves as a standard part of most Cuban meals—Cubans eat them as frequently as North Americans eat potatoes. YUCA also stands for Young Upwardly Mobile Cuban Americans. Usually YUCAs are part of the one-and-half generation described earlier.

Generation Ñ are usually the children of YUCAs coming of age in Miami. They are counterparts to the Euroamerican Generation Xers.

15. Tere Figueras, "Love of Country: Cuba's Centennial," *Miami Herald,* May 17, 2002.

16. Along with Exilic Cubans, sugar growers in Florida, Louisiana, and Hawaii and the citrus industries of Florida, Texas, and California oppose normalization, fearing competition from Resident Cubans.

17. Jose De Cordoba and Carla Anne Robbins, "Pope's Cuban Visit Creates Ripples in U.S.: Officials Debate Modifying Trade Embargo, Improving Ties," the *Wall Street Journal,* January 30, 1998.

18. "Food Program Starts Cuba Appeal," Associated Press, September 2, 1998.

19. Frank Davies, "Bush Backs Proposal to Fund Activities of Dissidents in Cuba," *Miami Herald,* May 19, 2001.

20. Associated Press, "Bush Refuses to Lift Embargo on Cuban Trade Until Castro Meets Tough Conditions," *Miami Herald,* May 20, 2002.

21. Fernando Remirez de Estenoz, "Cuba: Past History, Present Realities, Future Possibilities" (paper presented at NAFSA: Association of International Educators' workshop, Stanford University, February 9, 2001).

22. Frank Davies and Nancy San Martin, "Aid for Cuba Dissidents Doomed to Fail, Critics Say," *Miami Herald,* May 17, 2001; "Cuba 'Endorses' Bill to Aid Island's Dissidents," *Miami Herald,* May 24, 2001; and Lesley Clark, "Lieberman Meets with CANF," *Miami Herald,* June 25, 2001.

23. Luisa Yanez, "Cuban Spies Put in Prison 'Hole': Their Lawyers Protest Isolation," *Miami Herald,* July 2, 2001.

24. CANF is not the only organization vying for the Exilic Cubans' hearts and souls. Other groups exist to combat the normalized Exilic Cuban perceptions, such as the Cuban Committee for Democracy, composed mostly of academic scholars. Outside the United States, based in Madrid, is the Plataforma Democrática Cubana (Cuban Democratic Platform), a pluralistic coalition relying on international efforts to pressure Castro into moving toward democratic reform. But such groups are usually located outside Dade County, existing at the margins of the Miami community. They possess too few resources and adherents to provide a viable alternative.

25. Peter Slevin, "60 Minutes Examines Mas Canosa," *Miami Herald,* October 19, 1992.

26. A popular joke in Miami is that if Exilic Cubans owned as much land as they claim to have owned before the Revolution, then Cuba would have been the size of the Soviet Union.

27. Ana Arana, "United States Firms Making Cuban Land Claims," *Ft. Lauderdale Sun Sentinel,* May 16, 1993.

28. Cuban Liberty and Democratic Solidarity Act of 1996, Title III.

29. Ezra was appalled by marriages between Jewish men and non-Jewish women, specifically the intermingling of the community's leaders. This was a clear violation of the Pentateuchal law, which forbade the union of Canaanites with Jews, lest "their daughters, prostituting themselves to their own gods, may induce [Israel's] sons to do the same" (Exod. 34:14–16). Ezra's solution was for the men to divorce their foreign wives. It is interesting to note that the biblical book of Ruth, written during this period, provides an alternative voice to the mandate laid down by Ezra, thus capturing the spirit of Second Isaiah. In the story of Ruth, God uses a "foreign wife," a Moabite, of the type put away by Ezra, to represent society's most vulnerable members. Ruth is saved because of the egalitarian laws that Ezra tries to abort, and through her King David arises to save Israel (De La Torre 2000, 278).

Chapter 4. Machismo

1. For Martí, *patria* meant the reconciliation of all Cubans, a reconciliation achieved by consciousness-raising. Martí envisioned an egalitarian Cuba established through education and based on social equality instead of on the social tensions and inequalities existing in the United States. He called for a balancing (not elimination) of classes. He had no problem with the capitalist who paid fair wages and made an honest profit. He also fought in words and deeds for racial equality. During a time when racism was the norm, if not a virtue, Martí constantly argued that it was immoral and evil, linking a liberated Cuba to a liberated black community. He called for a *patria* void of the Catholic Church's influence. Although anticlerical, he insisted on total freedom in religious practices and be-

lief. As an Exilic Cuban, he held as paramount the unification of Exilic and Resident Cubans. Martí provided a Christian call for the unification of those oppressed and those oppressing, seeking liberation not from any particular group but from institutionalized structures.

2. Sexism names social structures and systems in which the "actions, practices, and use of laws, rules and customs limit certain activities of one sex, but do not limit those same activities of other people of the other sex" (Shute 1981, 27).

3. The Latin legal concept known as *patria potestad* maintained the authority of the male as the head of the family. It was instituted in Spain during the mid-1200s and became law in Cuba (as well as in the rest of Latin America) in 1680. This concept was reinforced by the 1809 Napoleonic Code and the 1886 Spanish Civil Code (Stoner 1991, 202).

4. Queen Isabella ruled Spain during the first war for independence, the Ten Years' War.

5. Throughout the world, Cuba is renowned for its cigars, the ultimate phallic symbol. According to Fernando Ortiz's study of tobacco:

Among people, like the Cuban Indians, given to phallic cults, erotic ceremonies, and sexual propitiation, the tobacco or cigar, by its form, can also have a priapic symbol, and the smoked and shredded cigar have a figuration of seminal potency which penetrates, fecundates, and animates life in all its manifestations. (1963, 114)

Cuban machismo seeks world recognition for the potency of Cuban cigars, even if it means bringing the world to the brink of a nuclear conflagration, as in 1962.

6. In short, women, gays, nonwhites, and the poor are not macho enough to construct *patria*. Between 1965 and 1968, thousands of artists, intellectuals, hippies, university students, Jehovah's Witnesses, and homosexuals were abducted by the State Secret Police and interned, without trial, in Military Units for Assistance to Production (UMAP) reeducation labor camps. Because they were dissidents under the normative gaze, they were constructed as homosexuals, as illustrated by the slogan posted at the camp's entrance: "Work will make men of you."

7. This is not to assert that homosexuals do not face violence on both sides of the Florida Straits. Just as the Cuban poet Reinaldo Arenas faced persecution by the Castro government, so too have gay Exilic Cubans experienced violence at the hands of the Exilic community. For example, Manolo Gomez, who tried to create an organization countering Anita Bryant's mid-1970s crusade against homosexuals, found himself fired from his job at *Vanidades,* a monthly periodical, and suffered a severe beating from unknown assailants. He eventually left Miami, fearing for his life (Arguelles and Rich 1985, 127).

8. Columbus recorded indigenous reports of an island called Matino believed to be entirely populated by women (1960, 50–51). Rather then visiting it, Columbus returned to Spain, possibly indicating that he and his crew had had their fill of native, "erotic" women.

9. In 1928 the U.S. Ku Klux Klan created a chapter in Cuba.

10. Anthony Pagden also quotes Cieza de León, who wrote, "Many of them

(as I have been reliably informed) publicly and openly practiced the nefarious sin of sodomy." Also, he quotes Gonzalo Fernández de Oviedo as stating, "[They even wore jewels depicting] the diabolical and nefarious act of sodomy" (1982, 176).

11. Las Casas's accounts of the barbarism inflicted on the indigenous people led to the construction of the Black Legend, which justified the superiority of Protestantism to Catholicism for Euroamericans, diverting attention from the treatment of the indigenous population of North America. Regardless of how the Black Legend was constructed for Euroamerican consumption, it cannot be denied that within one lifetime, an entire culture developed on the islands of the Caribbean was exterminated. Those few Taínos who survived were assimilated into the dominant Spanish culture.

12. The African influence on the Cuban ethos can be traced to 711 C.E. with the Moorish invasion of Spain by both East and North Africans; however, its greatest impact was felt when slavery was introduced to Cuba.

13. Other proposals to eliminate blacks from the Cuban social setting included the policy of dividing black from biracial Cubans by according privileges to the latter and assimilating them (up to a point) as allies. This policy in part explains the desire of some blacks to become whiter (McGarrity and Cárdenas 1995, 80).

14. In reality, it was not until 1523 when la Casa de la Contratación of Seville provided the financial backing needed to transplant the sugar industry from its base in the Canary Islands to Cuba.

15. Fernando Ortiz, in his early studies of African culture, held the ulterior motive of identifying the traditions of Afrocubans so that such customs could be effectively eradicated. Ironically, toward the end of his intellectual career, Ortiz's views about Afro-Cuban culture changed, as he fought against racism and sought to validate aspects of Afrocubanismo as folkloric by establishing the Society of Afrocuban Studies.

16. *Mambises,* from the African word *mambí,* are the offspring of an ape and a vulture. It is a derogatory term given to revolutionaries (regardless of skin color) by the Spaniards. Yet this slur has become a name of honor. Today in Miami one of the most ultraconservative radio stations, owned and operated by whites, is called *Radio Mambí.*

17. A larger number of black Cubans died in the struggle for independence than did whites. If they were equal in military services, then overrepresentation in fighting for Cuba Libre could be ignored and the proportional rewards of military victory denied. After the war they believed they earned sociopolitical recognition and a right to participate in constructing *patria.* Black Cuban general Quintín Banderas, who bravely fought for independence, attempted to get employment in a "free" Cuba. His white counterparts won government jobs and positions as rural officers. He was denied a government job as a janitor. When his money expired he solicited help from President Estrada Palma. The president denied him an audience. He eventually joined a group to protest the fraudulent reelection of Estrada Palma. He was murdered by the rural guard, who mutilated his body (Helg 1995, 16, 105–6, 120).

18. In spite of machismo placing the black man in the position of a woman, it must be noted that within Cuban African culture, sexism is also prevalent. For example, Ibos girls are taught to obey and serve men, while boys learn to look down on their mothers. The *machista* ethos of the *abakuá* allows intercourse only if the man is on top and is the only one who is active (Lumsden, 1996, 47, 221–22). The *bantú* use the word *man* only in referring to members of their nation. All other Africans are not men (Ortiz 1975a, 37).

19. No disrespect is meant by the usage of the word *coolie,* which historically has been used as a derogatory term. I use the word to refer to the Chinese laborer because it best describes their social location of oppression. The word *coolie* is composed of two Chinese characters, *coo* and *lie. Coo* is defined as "suffering with pain"; *lie* means "laborer." Hence the coolie is the "laborer who suffers with pain," a definition that well describes their situation in Cuba.

20. The Middle Passage was the route slave trading ships took across the Atlantic; however, this voyage signifies more than just the transporting of African slaves. The Middle Passage was the most dangerous period in the lives of captured Africans. The African human cargo was tightly packed in the galleys of the slave ships, hence facilitating the spread of infectious diseases and death. Although profitable for traders, the Middle Passage has come to represent the ultimate evil caused by slavery. I maintain that a similar Pacific Middle Passage was created in the transport of Asians to Cuba. Like the Africans before them, Asians endured extreme misery and suffering during their journey to Cuba.

21. In reality, since the late-sixteenth and early-seventeenth centuries, Chinese laborers began arriving in New Spain and Peru, as a by-product of the Manila-Acapulco trade connection initiated after 1565 (Leng 1999, 248).

22. A popular Cuban saying is *"Vale más un muerto que un chino"* (A corpse is worth more than a Chinaman). Cuban sinophobia has led Carlos Franqui, Castro's friend and biographer, to conclude it was the reason for the intensity of the Sino-Cuban feud (Moore 1988, 264).

23. Andrew Cawthorne, "Feature—Tourism Boom Shakes Up Cuban Society," Associated Press, September 8, 1998.

24. Commenting on the short life span of slaves, the eighteenth-century Cuban poet and slave Juan Francisco Manzano wrote:

> But where, you ask me, are the poor old slaves?
> Where should they be, of course, but in their graves!
> We do not send them there before their time,
> But let them die, when they are past their prime.
> Men who are worked by night as well as day,
> Somehow or other, live not to be gray
> Sink from exhaustion—sicken—droop and die,
> And leave the Count another batch to buy;
> There's stock abundant in the slave bazaars,
> Thanks to the banner of the stripes and stars!
> You cannot think, how soon the want of sleep
> Breaks down their strength,'tis well they are so cheap,

Four hours for rest—in time of crop—for five
Or six long months, and few indeed will thrive.
With twenty hours of unremitting toil,
Twelve in the field, and eight in doors, to boil
Or grind the cane—believe me few grow old,
But life is cheap, and sugar, sir,—is gold.
You think our interest is to use our blacks
As careful owners use their costly hacks;
Our interest is to make the most we can
Of every Negro in the shortest span. (1981, 71–72)

25. The lyrics of a slow rumba called "En el año '44" (In the year '44, the year
of a preemptive violent repression of a supposed slave revolt), sung in Matanzas
by slaves, serve as a hidden transcript describing the economic reality of both
blacks and the poor whites:

yo 'taba en el ingenio
En el año '44, negra,
yo 'taba en el ingenio
Ahora, ahora
negro con blanco
chapea cañaverá

        (Scott 1985, 255)

I was on the sugar mill
In the year '44, *negra,*
I was on the sugar mill
Now, now,
black with white
weeding in the canefields

Chapter 5. The End of the Elián Saga

1. These attempts were as follows: (1) Concerned about Cuba falling into
British or French hands, Jefferson proposed to James Madison in 1809 an ex-
change with Napoleon (who supposedly controlled Spain and its empire): Cuba
in return for a free hand elsewhere in Spanish America. (2) President Madison
tried to negotiate Cuba's annexation with the elite rich Cuban landowners; however, negotiations fell through because of Cuban fears of a British invasion if annexation were to take place. By 1822 talks had resumed, but to no avail. (3) During Latin America wars for independence (1823–1825), Bolívar intended to include
Cuba but was foiled by then–secretary of state Henry Clay, who assumed a future
annexation of the island by the United States. (4) After annexing Texas, then-
president James Polk made a $100 million offer to purchase Cuba from Spain in
1848. (5) When the talks to purchase Cuba failed, Narciso López, a nemesis of
Bolívar, set up an expedition force from New Orleans. Euroamerican veterans

took part in the venture attracted by the offer of $1,000, plus 160 acres of Cuban land. The 1848 expedition did not sail, mostly because the newly elected president and Mexican War hero, Zachary Taylor, preferred to buy Cuba. By 1850 a second expedition force was developed with the assistance of Mississippi governor John Quitman, who wanted to absorb both Cuba and the rest of Mexico. A six-hundred-man force landed, but the locals refused to join it, perceiving it to be part of a U.S. invasion. (6) In 1854 then-president Franklin Pierce raised his offer to $130 million. Retaliating against Spain's rejection of it, the United States signed the Ostend Manifesto, maintaining that Spain's refusal to sell justified (by human and divine laws) U.S. seizure of Cuba. (7) Before declaring war, President William McKinley offered $300 million for Cuba, with $6 million more going directly to the Spanish mediators.

2. Tomás Estrada Palma, Cuba's first president, rested comfortably in the United States during the war for independence. A U.S. citizen, he was well-known for his pro-annexation ideas and his racism.

3. The Platt Amendment required approval from the United States before entering into any treaty with another foreign power; the right of the United States to acquire land for the purpose of lodging the U.S. Navy, for example, at the Guantánamo Naval Base; and the right of the United States to intervene in the Cuban government for the "preservation of Cuban independence," translated to mean protection of U.S. interests.

4. After a century of a United States–oriented economy, the blockade would have meant the eventual downfall of Castro, if it had not been for the intervention of the Soviet Union. Yet admission into the Soviet bloc meant exchanging one hegemonic power for another. Different organizational principles and economic paradigms were required to ensure Cuba's survival and to construct an indigenous form of socialism. The rapid reorganization of Cuba's economy, the external pressure of the United States, the legacy of centuries of colonialism, the development of unrealistic economic goals, the mismanagement caused by inexperienced personnel in turn caused by departing high management–level Cubans, the constant flow of administrative improvisations, and the switch in priority to industrialization over the island's economic dynamo, sugar, created economic failures during the attempt to build socialism. The economic disappointments of the 1960s led Cuba to forsake an alternative model to socialism, succumbing to the European model constructed by the Soviet Union. Submitting to the Soviet Union hegemony and becoming the sugar bowl of the Eastern bloc resulted in economic growth measured by sustained rise in productivity. During the 1970s and early 1980s Cuba's economy enjoyed respectable rates of growth because the Soviet Union decided to allow Cuba to sell any Soviet oil not domestically consumed on the free market; Cuba improved its planning techniques; and Cuba began to grant material incentives for laborers rather than expecting an increase in production based on moral obligation. The rejection of Marxism as symbolized by the crumbling of the Berlin Wall sent Cuba into an economic tailspin, as the foundation of the "socialist paradise" ended. The end of Soviet subsidies, euphemistically called the "special period," is characterized by the abrupt end of

about 85 percent of foreign trade with the Soviet Union and the Eastern European community, causing imports to drop by 75 percent and the GNP to drop by 60 percent. Sugar production dropped to less than 4 million tons (the lowest since 1963), while factories ran at 30 percent capacity. The "new world order" forced Cuba to abolish the central planning board responsible for piloting the state-directed economy. By the end of 1994 Cuba signed joint ventures with 185 foreign corporations causing an increase in tourism (17 percent between 1991 and 1993) and the introduction of Western consumer products. These measures have contributed to the island turning a crucial financial corner since the economic collapse of 1993. While the economic free fall has been stopped by cracking a window to the economic breeze of the free market, inequalities caused by these latest initiatives threaten to undermine Cuba's boast of providing the most equal distribution of wealth among Latin American countries. Recent events have weakened some of the basic healthcare and educational accomplishments of the Revolution. The dollarization of the economy has increased the inequalities between the races. Because whites have access to diaspora capital on account of family connections, their ability to survive the "special period" has been enhanced. With an estimated $600–950 million from Exilic Cubans making its way across the island annually, a two-tier society has developed, one with dollars and one without. Usually those without dollars are not white (Bulmer-Thomas 1994, 12, 321, 347; Donghi 1993, 305–7, 373; and Fedarko 1998, 181–83). Additionally, tourism (with an industry growth of 12 percent in 2001) has provided a steady source of hard currency, increasing the living standards of those living in La Habana, which has undertaken major construction project to modernize the city; see Nancy San Martin, "Cafes, ATMs, Luxury Cars Dot City," *Miami Herald,* May 27, 2001.

5. Paul Brinkley-Rogers, Curtis Morgan, Elaine de Valle, and Audra D. S. Burch, "Case Provokes Harsh Feelings, Hope," *Miami Herald,* April 5, 2000.

6. Paul Brinkley-Rogers, "Exiles Tearful Over Boy's Future," *Miami Herald,* April 8, 2000.

7. Paul Brinkley-Rogers and Eunice Ponce, "For Most in Miami, Ruling Draws Restrained Reaction," *Miami Herald,* June 2, 2000.

8. Marika Lynch and Luisa Yanez, "Leaders Dust Off a Post-Castro Plan for South Florida," *Miami Herald,* July 9, 2001.

9. Paul Brinkley-Rogers, "Case Provokes Harsh Feelings," *Miami Herald,* April 5, 2000.

10. "I'm Tired of Not Being Proud of Miami," *Miami Herald,* May 21, 2000.

11. Paul Brinkley-Rogers, "Emotional Bond Compels Protesters," *Miami Herald,* January 8, 2000.

12. The event was scheduled for September 11, but the tragic events in New York, Pennsylvania, and Washington, D.C., led to the show's cancellation. Nevertheless, the playing out of *la lucha* before September 11 deserves analysis.

13. Cynthia Corzo, Daniel Chang, Charles Rabin, and Martin Merzer, "Miami May Lose Latin Grammys," *Miami Herald,* August 18, 2001; Elaine de Valle and Luisa Yanez, "Exiles Accept Plan for Protest Site at Latin Grammys," *Miami Her-*

ald, August 20, 2001; Marika Lynch, "In Grammy Flap, an Unlikely Face," *Miami Herald,* August 21, 2001; John Dorschner, "Miami Suffers Blow Over Grammys," *Miami Herald,* August 22, 2001.

14. Alfonso Chardy, "Exile Ad Exhorts Anti-Castro Hard Line," *Miami Herald,* August 23, 2001.

15. Andres Viglucci, Jordan Levin and Charles Rabin, "Protests Jeopardize Safety at Event, Show Chief Says," *Miami Herald,* August 21, 2001; Andres Viglucci, "Grammy Flap Exposes Split Among Exiles," *Miami Herald,* September 2, 2001.

16. The poll was conducted for the Cuba Study Group, an informal association of about a dozen wealthy Exilic Cubans. Some of the group's members include Carlos Saladigas of Premier American Bank, Carlos de la Cruz of Coca-Cola Puerto Rico Bottles, Paul L. Cejas of PLC Investments, and Alfonso Fanjul of Flo-Sun Inc.

17. Andres Oppenheimer, "Poll Says Exiles Shifting from Hard-Line Positions," *Miami Herald,* May 16, 2002.

18. Realizing the importance of the Exilic Cuban voting bloc in the 2004 presidential election, President George W. Bush attended the centennial celebration of the formation of the Cuban Republic in Miami on May 20, 2002. There he unveiled his "initiative for a new Cuba," which reaffirms the U.S. economic embargo on the island; upholds the ban on most U.S. travel to the island, a ban that is defied by tens of thousands of Euroamericans each year; provides direct assistance to Cubans through nongovernmental agencies; negotiates for direct mail service between the two countries; provides educational scholarships for family members of political prisoners and those wishing to establish independent civil institutions; and facilitates humanitarian assistance by U.S. religious and nongovernmental groups. See Tim Johnson, "President to Reveal New Plan to Help Cubans," *Miami Herald,* May 20, 2002.

Yet leading dissidents on the island have responded negatively to Bush's proposal. Vladimiro Roca, who served almost five years in prison for his political views, insists that "dialogue, negotiation, and reconciliation" would better serve the cause of freedom than the continued Cold War rhetoric. Dissidents worry that Bush's proposal to provide funding to Resident Cubans would only strengthen Castro's arguments that dissident groups on the island are bankrolled by the CIA. "Any kind of financial help from any government for our work is unacceptable," said human rights activist Elizardo Sanchez. "That's especially true of a government such as Washington which has such very bad relations with Cuba." See Anita Snow, "Cuban Officials Accuse Bush of Pandering to Miami Exiles, Dissidents Fear Continued U.S. Policies Will Hurt Their Cause," *Miami Herald,* May 21, 2002.

19. "Bush Visit Today Sign of Exiles Influence," *Miami Herald,* May 20, Carol Rosenberg, 2002.

20. Russell Contreras, "Everyone's Loco for the Latino Bush They Call "P": Gorgeous George," *Austin Chronicle,* August 11, 2000.

References

Abel, Christopher. 1986. "Martí, Latin America and Spain." In *José Martí: Revolutionary Democrat,* edited by Christopher Abel and Nissa Torrents. London: Athlone Press.

Adams, John Quincy. 1917. "Letter to Hugh Nelson, Minister in Madrid: April 23, 1823." In *Writing of John Quincy Adams,* vol. 7, edited by Worthington Chauncey Ford. New York: Macmillan.

Allman, T. D. 1987. *Miami: City of the Future.* New York: Atlantic Monthly Press.

Amaro, N. V., and A. Portes. 1972. "Una sociología del exilio: Situación de los grupos cubanos en los Estados Unidos." *Aportes,* no. 23: 6–24.

American Association for World Health. 1997. *Denial of Food and Medicine: The Impact of the United States Embargo on the Health and Nutrition in Cuba.* Available at www.usaengage.org/archives/studies/cuba.html.

Amnesty International. 1992. *Cuba: Silencing the Voices of Dissent.* New York: Amnesty International.

Arenas, Reinaldo. 1993. *Before Night Falls.* Translated by Dolores M. Koch. New York: Viking.

Arguelles, Lourdes, and B. Ruby Rich. 1984. "Homosexuality, Homophobia, and Revolution: Notes Toward an Understanding of the Cuban Lesbian and Gay Male Experience, Part 1." *Signs: Journal of Women in Culture and Society* 9, no. 4 (Summer): 683–99.

———. 1985. "Homosexuality, Homophobia, and Revolution: Notes Toward an Understanding of the Cuban Lesbian and Gay Male Experience, Part 2." *Signs: Journal of Women in Culture and Society* 11, no. 1 (Winter): 120–36.

Azicri, Max. 1988. *Cuba: Politics, Economics, and Society.* London: Pinter Publishers.

Baker, Christopher P. 1999. *Cuba.* Emeryville, Calif.: Avalon.

Barkin, David. 1973. "La redistribución del consumo." In *Cuba: Camino abierto,* edited by David Barkin and Nita R. Manitzas. Mexico City: Siglo XXI.

Barnet, Miguel. 1986. *The African Presence in Cuban Culture*. Warwick, U.K.: University of Warwick.

Behar, Ruth. 1995. Introduction to *Bridges to Cuba*, edited by Ruth Behar. Ann Arbor: University of Michigan Press.

Benjamin, Medea, Joseph Collins, and Michael Scott. 1984. *No Free Lunch: Food and Revolution in Cuba Today*. San Francisco: Food First Books.

Bethell, Leslie, ed. 1993. *Cuba: A Short History*. Cambridge: Cambridge University Press.

Bhabha, Homi K. 1994. *The Location of Culture*. New York: Routledge.

Bikel, Ofra. 2001. "Saving Elián." *Frontline*. Written, produced, and directed by Ofra Bikel. Aired on PBS, February 6, 2001.

Boff, Clodovis. 1990. *Feet-on-the-Ground Theology: A Brazilian Journey*. Translated by Phillip Berryman. Maryknoll, N.Y.: Orbis Books.

Bonino, José Míguez. 1975. *Doing Theology in a Revolutionary Situation*. Philadelphia: Fortress Press.

Booth, Cathy. 1993. "The Capital of Latin America: Miami." *Time* Special Issue: The New Face of America, How Immigrants are Shaping the World's First Multicultural Society, 142, no. 21 (Autumn): 82–85. Bourdieu, Pierre. 1977. *Outline of a Theory of Practice*. Translated by Richard Nice. Cambridge: Cambridge University Press.

Brubaker, Rogers. 1985. "Rethinking Classical Theory: The Sociological Vision of Pierre Bourdieu." *Theory and Society* 14: 745–75.

Bulmer-Thomas, Victor. 1994. *The Economic History of Latin America Since Independence*. Cambridge: Cambridge University Press.

Büntig, Aldo J. 1971. "The Church in Cuba: Toward a New Frontier." In *Religion in Cuba Today*, edited by Alice Hageman and Philip E. Weaton. New York: Association Press.

Casal, Lourdes. 1975. *Images of Cuban Society Among Pre- and Post-Revolutionary Novelists*. Ph.D. diss., New School for Social Research.

———. 1989. "Race Relations in Contemporary Cuba." In *The Cuban Reader: The Making of a Revolutionary Society*, edited by Philip Brenner, William M. LeoGrande, Donna Rich, and Daniel Siegel. New York: Grove Press.

Clifford, James. 1988. *The Predicament of Culture: Twentieth-Century Ethnography, Literature and Art*. Cambridge, Mass.: Harvard University Press.

Columbus, Christopher. 1960. *The Journal of Christopher Columbus*. Translated by Cecil Jane. New York: Clarkson N. Potter.

Comblin, José. 1996. *Cristãos rumo ao século XXI: Nova caminada de libertação*. São Paulo: Paulus.

Corbitt, Duvon Clough. 1971. *A Study of the Chinese in Cuba, 1847–1947*. Wilmore, Ky.: Asbury College.

Croucher, Sheila L. 1997. *Imagining Miami: Ethnic Politics in a Postmodern World*. Charlottesville: University Press of Virginia.

de Caturla, Brú. 1945. *La mujer en la independencia de America*. La Habana: Jesus Montero.

de la Fuente, Alejandro. 2001. *A Nation for All: Race, Inequality, and Politics in Twentieth-Century Cuba*. Chapel Hill: University of North Carolina Press.

de las Casas, Bartolomé. 1971. *History of the Indies.* Edited and translated by An-
dree Collard. New York: Harper & Row.

De La Torre, Miguel A. 1999a. "Beyond Machismo: A Cuban Case Study." *Annual of the Society of Christian Ethics* 19: 213–33.

———. 1999b. "Masking Hispanic Racism: A Cuban Case Study." *Journal of His-
panic/Latino Theology* 6, no. 4 (May): 57–74.

———. 2000. "Miami and the Babylonian Captivity." In *Sacred Texts, Secular
Times: The Hebrew Bible in the Modern World,* edited by Leonard Jay Green-
spoon and Bryan F. Le Beau. Bronx, N.Y.: Fordham University Press.

———. 2001. "Constructing Our Cuban Ethnic Identity While in Babylon." In
A Dream Unfinished: Theological Reflections on America from the Margins, edited
by Eleazar S. Fernandez and Fernando F. Segovia. Maryknoll, N.Y.: Orbis
Books.

———. 2002a. *The Quest for the Cuban Christ: A Historical Search.* Gainesville:
University Press of Florida.

———. 2002b. *Reading the Bible from the Margins.* New York: Orbis Books.

De La Torre, Miguel A., and Edwin Aponte. 2001. *Introducing Latino/a Theology.*
New York: Orbis Press.

de los Angeles, Torres. 1995. "Encuentros y Encontronazos: Homeland in the
Politics and Identity of the Cuban Diaspora." *Diaspora* 4, no. 2: 211–38.

de Quesada, Gonzalo. 1925. *The Chinese and Cuban Independence.* Leipzig: Bre-
itkopf & Hartel.

de Varona, Adolfo Leyva. 1996. *Propaganda and Reality: A Look at the U.S. Embargo Against Castro's Cuba.* Miami: Cuban American National Foundation.

Dickason, Olive Patricia. 1980. "The Concept of *L'Homme Sauvage.*" In *Manlike
Monsters on Trail: Early Records and Modern Evidence,* edited by Marjorie M.
Halpin and Michael M. Ames. Vancouver: University of British Columbia
Press.

Didion, Joan. 1987. *Miami.* New York: Simon and Schuster.

Donghi, Tulio Halperín. 1993. *The Contemporary History of Latin America.* Edited
and translated by John Charles Chasteen. Durham: Duke University Press.

Eckstein, Susan Eva. 1994. *Back from the Future: Cuba Under Castro.* Princeton:
Princeton University Press.

Ehrenreich, Barbara, and John Ehrenreich. 1972. "The Professional-Managerial
Class." In *Between Labor and Capital,* edited by Pat Walker. Boston: South
End Press.

Eliade, Mircea. 1957. *The Sacred and the Profane: The Nature of Religion.* Translated by Willard R. Trask. New York: Harcourt, Brace & World.

———. 1963. *Patterns in Comparative Religion.* Translated by Rosemary Sheed.
New York: Meridian Books.

Elizondo, Virgilio. 1988. *The Future Is Mestizo: Life Where Cultures Meet.* Oak
Park, Ill.: Meyer-Stone.

Fagan, Richard R., Richard A. Brody, and Thomas J. O'Leary. 1968. *Cubans in
Exile: Disaffection and the Revolution.* Stanford: Stanford University Press.

Fanon, Frantz. 1963. *The Wretched of the Earth.* Translated by Constance Far-
rington. New York: Grove Press.

————. 1967. *Black Skin, White Masks.* Translated by Charles Lam Markmann. New York: Grove Press.

Fedarko, Kevin. 1998. "Open for Business." In *Developing World 97/98,* edited by Robert J. Griffiths. Guilford, Conn.: Dushkin Publishing Group/Brown & Benchmark Publishers.

Ferrer, Ada. 1999. *Insurgent Cuba: Race, Nation, and Revolution, 1868–1898.* Chapel Hill: University of North Carolina Press.

Firmat, Gustavo Pérez. 1994. *Life on the Hyphen: The Cuban-American Way.* Austin: University of Texas Press.

Fischer, Michael M. J. 1986. "Ethnicity and the Post-Modern Arts of Memory." In *Writing Culture: The Poetics and Politics of Ethnography,* edited by James Clifford and George E. Marcus. Berkeley and Los Angeles: University of California Press.

Foner, Philip S. 1972. *The Spanish-Cuban-American War and the Birth of American Imperialism, 1898–1902.* Vol. 2. New York: Monthly Review Press.

————. 1977. *Antonio Maceo: The "Bronze Titan" of Cuba's Struggle for Independence.* New York: Monthly Review Press.

Forment, Carlos A. 1989. "Political Practice and the Rise of an Economic Enclave: The Cuban-American Case, 1959–1979." *Theory and Society* 18 (January): 47–81.

Foucault, Michel. 1973. *Madness and Civilization: A History of Insanity in the Age of Reason.* New York: Random House.

————. 1978a. *Religion and Culture.* Edited by Jeremy R. Carrette. New York: Routledge.

————. 1978b. *The History of Sexuality.* Vol. 1, *An Introduction.* Translated by Robert Hurley. New York: Vintage Books.

————. 1984. *The Foucault Reader.* Edited by Paul Rabinow. New York: Pantheon Books.

————. 1988. *Technologies of the Self: A Seminar with Michel Foucault.* Edited by Luther H. Martin, Huck Gutman, and Patrick H. Hutton. Amherst, Mass.: University of Massachusetts Press.

————. 1995. *Discipline and Punish: The Birth of the Prison.* Translated by Alan Sheridan. New York: Vintage Books.

Fox, Geoffrey. 1973. "Honor, Shame, and Women's Liberation in Cuba." In *Female and Male in Latin America: Essays,* edited by Ann Pescatello. Pittsburgh: University of Pittsburgh Press.

Frank, Andre Gunder. 1969. *Capitalism and Underdevelopment in Latin America: Historical Studies of Chile and Brazil.* Middlesex: Penguin Books.

Franqui, Carlos. 1984. *Family Portrait with Fidel: A Memoir.* Translated by Alfred MacAdam. New York: Random House.

Frederick, Howard H. 1986. *Cuban-American Radio Wars: Ideology in International Telecommunications.* Norwood, N.J.: Ablex Publishing Corporation.

Freire, Paulo. 1994. *Pedagogy of the Oppressed.* Translated by Myra Bergman Ramos. New York: Continuum.

García, María Cristina. 1996. *Havana USA: Cuban Exiles and Cuban Americans in South Florida, 1959–1994.* Berkeley and Los Angeles: University of California.

Geertz, Clifford. 1973. *The Interpretation of Cultures: Selected Essays.* New York: Basic Books.

Gomara, Francisco López de. 1979. "Historia general de las Indias y vida de Hernán Cortés (1552)." *Biblioteca Ayacucho,* vol. 1. Edited by Jorge Gurria Lacroix. Caracas, Venezuela: Biblioteca Ayacucho.

Gonzalez-Pando, Miguel. 1998. *The Cuban Americans.* Westport, Conn.: Greenwood Press.

Gonzalez-Wippler, Migene. 1989. *Santería: The Religion.* New York: Harmony Books.

Grenier, Guillermo J., and Hugh Gladwin. 1977. *FIU 1997 Cuba Poll.* Institute of Public Opinon Research (IPOR) of Florida International University and the *Miami Herald.* Available at www.fiu.edu/orgs/ipor/cubapoll/index.html.

Guanche, Jesús. 1983. *Procesos etnoculturales de Cuba.* La Habana: Editorial Letras Cubanas.

Gutiérrez, Gustavo. 1984. *The Power of the Poor in History.* Translated by Robert R. Barr. Maryknoll, N.Y.: Orbis Books.

Hamm, Mark S. 1995. *The Abandoned Ones: The Imprisonment and Uprising of the Mariel Boat People.* Boston: Northeastern University.

Helg, Aline. 1995. *Our Rightful Share: The Afro-Cuban Struggle for Equality, 1886–1912.* Chapel Hill: University of North Carolina Press.

Hewitt, Nancy A. 1995. "Engendering Independence: Las Patriotas of Tampa and the Social Vision of José Martí." In *José Martí in the United States: The Florida Experience,* edited by Louis A. Pérez Jr. Tempe: Arizona State University Center for Latino American Studies.

Huberman, Leo, and Paul M. Sweezy. 1989. "The Revolutionary Heritage." In *The Cuba Reader: The Making of a Revolutionary Society,* edited by Philip Brenner et al. New York: Grove Press.

Isasi-Díaz, Ada María. 1993. *En la Lucha: A Hispanic Women's Liberation Theology.* Minneapolis: Fortress Press.

Iznaga, Diana. 1986. Introduction to *Los negros curros* by Fernando Ortiz. La Habana: Editorial de Ciencias Sociales.

Jameson, Fredric. 1983. "Postmodernism and Consumer Society." In *The Anti-Aesthetic Essays on Postmodern Culture,* edited by Hal Foster. Port Townsend, Wash.: Bay Press.

Jefferson, Thomas. 1944. "Letter to President James Monroe: October 24, 1823." In *The Life and Selected Writings of Thomas Jefferson,* edited by Adrienne Kock and William Peden. New York: Random House.

Jenks, Leland H. 1928. *Our Cuban Colony: A Study in Sugar.* New York: Vanguard Press.

Jorge, Antonio, Jaime Suchlicki, and Adolfo Leyva de Varona, eds. 1991. *Cuban Exiles in Florida: Their Presence and Contribution.* Coral Gables, Fla.: University of Miami.

Kiger, Patrick J. 1996. *Squeeze Play: The United States, Cuba, and the Helms-Burton Act.* Washington, D.C.: Center for Public Integrity.

Kirk, John M. 1988. *Between God and the Party: Religion and Politics in Revolutionary Cuba.* Tampa: University Presses of Florida.

Knight, Franklin W. 1970. *Slave Society in Cuba During the Nineteenth Century*. Madison: University of Wisconsin Press.

———. 1990. *The Caribbean: The Genesis of a Fragmented Nationalism*. 2nd edition. New York: Oxford University Press.

Kunz, Egon F. 1981. "Exile and Resettlement: Refugee Theory." *International Migration Review* 15: 42–51.

Kutzinski, Vera M. 1993. *Sugar's Secrets: Race and the Erotics of Cuban Nationalism*. Charlottesville: University Press of Virginia.

Lacan, Jacques. 1977. *Écrits: A Selection*. Translated by Alan Sheridan. New York: Norton.

Leiner, Marvin. 1994. *Sexual Politics in Cuba: Machismo, Homosexuality, and AIDS*. Boulder, Colo.: Westview Press.

Leng, Lim Bee. 1999. "The Caribbean." In *The Encyclopedia of the Chinese Overseas,* edited by Lynn Pan. Cambridge: Harvard University Press.

Levine, Robert M., and Asís Moisés. 2000. *Cuban Miami*. New Brunswick, N.J.: Rutgers University Press.

Lieberson, Stanley, and Arnold R. Silverman. 1965. "The Precipitants and Underlying Conditions of Race Riots." *American Sociological Review* 30 (December): 887–98.

Lovén, Sven. 1935. *Origins of the Tainan Culture, West Indies*. Göteborg: Elanders Boktryckeri Aktiebolag.

Lumsden, Ian. 1996. *Machos, Maricones and Gays: Cuba and Homosexuality*. Philadelphia: Temple University Press.

Lyotard, Jean-François. 1984. *The Postmodern Condition: A Report on Knowledge*. Translated by Geoff Bennington and Brian Massumi. Minneapolis: University of Minnesota Press.

Manzano, Juan Francisco. 1981. *The Life and Poems of a Cuban Slave: Juan Francisco Manzano, 1797–1854*. Edited by Edward J. Mullen and translated by R. R. Madden. Hamden, Conn.: Archon Books.

Martí, José. 1963–1973. *Obras Completas*. 27 vols. La Habana: Editorial Nacional de Cuba.

———. 1975. *Inside the Monster: Writings on the United States and American Imperialism*. Edited by Philip S. Foner and translated by Elinor Randall, Luis A. Baralt, Juan de Onís, and Roslyn Held Foner. New York: Monthly Review Press.

———. 1977. *Our America: Writings on Latin America and the Struggle for Cuban Independence*. Edited by Philip S. Foner and translated by Elinor Randall, Juan de Onís, and Roslyn Held Foner. New York: Monthly Review Press.

Martinez-Alier, Verena. 1974. *Marriage, Class, and Color in Nineteenth-Century Cuba: A Study of Racial Attitudes and Sexual Values in a Slave Society*. London: Cambridge University Press.

Mason, Peter. 1990. *Deconstructing America: Representations of the Other*. London: Routledge.

Masud-Piloto, Felix Roberto. 1988. *With Open Arms: Cuban Migration to the United States*. Totowa, N.J.: Rowman & Littlefield.

Maza, Manuel P. 1982. *The Cuban Catholic Church: True Struggles and False Dilemmas*. M.A. thesis, Georgetown University.

McClintock, Anne. 1995. *Imperial Leather: Race, Gender, and Sexuality in the Colonial Conquest*. New York: Routledge.

McGarrity, Gayle, and Osvaldo Cárdenas. 1995. "Cuba." In *No Longer Invisible: Afro-Latin Americans Today*, edited by Minority Rights Group. London: Minority Rights Publications.

Montejo, Esteban. 1968. *The Autobiography of a Runaway Slave*, edited by Miguel Barnet and translated by Jocasta Innes. New York: Pantheon Books.

Moore, Carlos. 1988. *Castro, the Blacks, and Africa*. Los Angeles: Center for Afro-American Studies, University of California.

Mörner, Magnus. 1967. *Race Mixture in the History of Latin America*. Boston: Little, Brown.

Morris, Charles. 1899. *Our Island Empire*. New York: Lippincott.

Newman, Philip C. 1965. *Cuba Before Castro: An Economic Appraisal*. New Delhi, India: Prentice-Hall.

Nietzsche, Friedrich. 1971. *The Portable Nietzsche*. Translated by Walter Kaufmann. London: Chatto & Windus.

Oboler, Suzanne. 1995. *Ethnic Labels, Latino Lives: Identity and the Politics of (Re)Presention in the United States*. Minneapolis: University of Minnesota Press.

Olson, James S., and Judith E. Olson. 1995. *Cuban Americans: From Trauma to Triumph*. New York: Twayne Publishers.

Ortiz, Fernando. 1906. "La inmigración desde el punto de vista criminológico." *Derecho Sociogía* 1 (May): 54–64.

———. 1939. "La cubanidad y los negros." *Estudio Afrocubanos* 3: 3–15.

———. 1940. "Los factores humanos de la cubanidad." *Revista Bimestre Cubana* 45, no. 2: 1–30.

———. 1942. "Martí y las razas." *Vida y pensamiento de Martí*, vol. 2. Edited by Emilio Roig de Leuchsenring. La Habana: Municipio de la Habana.

———. 1963. *Contrapunto cubano del tabaco y el azúcar*. La Habana: Dirección de Publicaciones Universidad Central de Las Villas.

———. 1973. *Los negros brujos: Apuntes para un estudio de etnología criminal*. Miami: New House Publishers.

———.1975a. *El engaño de las razas*. La Habana: Editorial de Ciencias Sociales.

———. 1975b. *Los negros esclavos*. La Habana: Editorial de Ciencias Sociales.

———. 1992. *Los cabildos y la fiesta afrocubanos del dia de reyes*. La Habana: Editorial de Ciencias Sociales.

Pagden, Anthony. 1982. *The Fall of Natural Man: The American Indian and the Origins of Comparative Ethnology*. Cambridge: Cambridge University Press.

Paquette, Robert L. 1988. *Sugar Is Made with Blood: The Conspiracy of La Escalera and the Conflict Between Empires over Slavery in Cuba*. Middletown, Conn.: Wesleyan University Press.

Pedraza, Silvia. 2001. "Cuba's Refugees: Manifold Migrations." In *Cuban Communism*, edited by Irving Louis Horowitz and Jaime Suchlicki. 10th ed. New Brunswick, N.J.: Transaction Publishers.

Pedraza-Bailey, Silvia. 1981. "Cubans and Mexicans in the United States: The Functions of Political and Economic Migration." *Cuban Studies/Estudios Cubanos* 11 (July): 79–97.

Pérez, Louis A., Jr. 1988. *Cuba: Between Reform and Revolution*. New York: Oxford University Press.

———. 1999. *On Becoming Cuban: Identity, Nationality, and Culture*. Chapel Hill: University of North Carolina Press.

Pérez-Stable, Marifeli ,and Miren Uriarte. 1993. "Cubans and the Changing Economy of Miami." In *Latinos in a Changing U.S. Economy: Comparative Perspectives on Growing Inequality*, edited by Rebecca Morales and Frank Bonilla. Newbury Park, Calif.: Sage Publications.

Peterson, Mark F. 1982. "The Flotilla Entrants: Social Psychological Perspectives on Their Employment." *Cuban Studies/Estusios Cubanos* 12 (July): 81–86.

Porter, Bruce, and Marvin Dunn. 1980. *The Miami Riot of 1980: Crossing the Bounds*. Lexington, Mass.: Lexington Books.

Portes, Alejandro, and Juan M. Clark. 1987. "Mariel Refugees: Six Years Later." *Migration World* 15 (Fall): 14–18.

Portes, Alejando, and Rubén G. Rumbaut. 1996. *Immigrant America: A Portrait*. 2nd ed. Berkeley and Los Angeles: University of California Press.

Portes, Alejandro, and Alex Stepick. 1993. *City on the Edge: The Transformation of Miami*. Berkeley and Los Angeles: University of California Press.

Poyo, Gerald E. 1975. "The Cuban Exile Tradition in the United States: Patterns of Political Development in the Nineteenth and Twentieth Centuries." In *Cuba: Cultura e identidad nacional*. La Habana: Ediciones Union.

Prohías, Rafael J., and Lourdes Casal. 1980. *The Cuban Minority in the United States: Preliminary Report on Need Identification and Program Evaluation Final Report for Fiscal Year 1973*. Vol. 1. New York: Arno Press.

Rieff, David. 1987. *Going to Miami: Exiles, Tourists, and Refugees in the New America*. Boston: Little, Brown.

Rivera, Luis N. 1992. *A Violent Evangelism: The Political and Religious Conquest of the Americas*. Louisville: Westminster/John Knox Press.

Rogg, Eleanor Meyer. 1974. *The Assimilation of Cuban Exiles: The Role of Community and Class*. New York: Aberdeen Press.

Rumbaut, Rubén G. 1991. "The Agony of Exile: A Study of the Migration and Adaptation of Indochinese Refugee Adults and Children." In *Refugee Children: Theory, Research, and Services*, edited by Frederick L. Ahearn Jr. and Jean L. Athey. Baltimore: John Hopkins University Press.

Rumbaut, Rubén G., and Lisandro Pérez. 1998. "Pinos Nuevos? Growing Up American in Cuban Miami." *Cuban Affairs: Asuntos Cubanos* 3–4 (Fall/Winter): 4–5.

Sáez, David Grillo. 1953. *El problema del negro cubano*. La Habana: n.p.

Sathler, Josué A., and Amós Nascrimento. 1997. "Black Masks on White Faces: Liberation Theology and the Quest for Syncretism in the Brazilian Context." In *Liberation Theologies, Postmodernity, and the Americas*, edited by David Batstone, Eduardo Mendieta, Lois Ann Lorentzen, and Dwight N. Hopkins. London: Routledge.

Sauer, Carl Ortwin. 1966. *The Early Spanish Main.* Berkeley and Los Angeles: University of California Press.

Segovia, Fernando F. 1996. "In the World but Not of It: Exile as Locus for a Theology of the Diaspora." In *Hispanic/Latino Theology: Challenge and Promise,* edited by Ada María Isasi-Díaz and Fernando F. Segovia. Minneapolis: Fortress Press.

Scott, James C. 1990. *Domination and the Arts of Resistance: Hidden Transcripts.* New Haven: Yale University Press.

Scott, Rebecca J. 1985. *Slave Emancipation in Cuba: The Transition to Free Labor, 1860–1899.* Princeton: Princeton University Press.

Shute, Sara. 1981. "Sexist Language and Sexism." In *Sexist Language: A Modern Philosophical Analysis,* edited by Mary Vetterling-Braggin. Totowa, N.J.: Littlefield, Adams.

Skoug, Kenneth N. 1996. *The United States and Cuba Under Reagan and Shultz: A Foreign Service Officer Reports.* Westport, Conn.: Praeger.

Smith, Robert F. 1963. *What Happened in Cuba? A Documentary History.* New York: Twayne Publishing.

Soruco, Gonzalo R. 1996. *Cubans and Mass Media in South Florida.* Gainesville: University Press of Florida.

Stoner, K. Lynn. 1991. *From the House to the Streets: The Cuban Woman's Movement for Legal Reform, 1898–1940.* Durham, N.C.: Duke University Press.

Strong, Josiah. 1891. *Our Country: Its Possible Future and Its Present Crisis.* Rev. ed. New York: Baker & Taylor.

Suárez, Bernardo Ruiz. 1922. *The Color Question in the Two Americas.* New York: Hunt Publishing.

Suárez, Virgil. 1999. *In the Republic of Longing: Poems by Virgil Suárez.* Tempe, Ariz.: Bilingual Press.

Thomas, Hugh. 1971. *Cuba: The Pursuit of Freedom.* New York: Harper & Row.

Todorov, Tzvetan. 1984. *The Conquest of America: The Question of the Other.* Translated by Richard Howard. New York: Harper & Row.

West, Alan. 1997. *Tropics of History: Cuba Imagined.* Westport: Bergin & Garvey.

Wright, Erik Olin. 1985. *Classes.* London: Verso.

Young, Allen. 1981. *Gays Under the Cuban Revolution.* San Francisco: Grey Fox Press.

Index

Abakuá society, 109, 155n18
Acción Cubana (Cuban Action), 43
Adams, John Quincy, 120
Aeroflot, 43
Africa, 8, 16, 17, 90, 97, 99–113, 115–16, 121,
    138, 143n35, 154n12, 155nn18,20
African Americans, 38–39, 57–61, 64, 126,
    128–29, 131
African swine fever, 63, 149n5
Aguiar, Margarita, 11
Aguile, Luis, 68
Air Cubana, 45
ajiaco, 15–17, 30, 113, 143n35, 144n37,
    144–45n41
ajiaco Christianity, xvii, 15–18, 21–26, 30,
    110
Albizu, Father Antonio, 28
Albright, Madeleine, 87
Alfonso, Angel Manuel, 45
Allen, Richard, 77
Allende, Salvador, 41
Almeida, Juan, 27
American Association for World Health,
    73
American Dilemma, An (book), 109
Americas Watch, 14
Amerindians, 16, 90, 94–99, 106, 110, 113,
    126, 138, 143n35, 144–45n41, 151n14,
    153n5, 153–54n10, 154n11
Amnesty International, 14–15
Andalusia. *See* Spain

Antonio Maceo Brigade, 13
Arabs, 144n38, 144–45n41
Aranegui, Santiago, 10
Arawakan. *See* Amerindians
Arenas, Reinaldo, 32, 55–56, 93, 153n7
Argentina, 68
Aristide, Jean Bertrand, 131
Artaxerxes, 70. *See also* Persia
Ashcroft, John, 76
Asia, 16–17, 75, 97, 110–13, 143n35,
    144–45n41, 155nn20,21
Avery Fisher Hall, 43

Babylonian captivity, xvii, 53, 67–71, 76–77,
    79–80. *See also* Judaism
Babylonian Talmud, 10
Bahamas, 144–45n41, 150n9
balseros (rafters), 12, 62, 66, 67, 150n9
Baltimore, Maryland, 52
Banderas, Quintín, 154n17
Barker, Bernard, 41
Basque. *See* Spain
Basulto, José, 45
Batista, Fulgencio, 25, 27–28, 30, 32–34, 58,
    69, 94, 146n1
Bay of Pigs. *See* Playa Girón
Behar, Ruth, 92
Bello, Serafín, 101
BellSouth Corporation, 78
Bendixen and Associates, 125
Benes, Bernardo, 49–50

Berbers, 144–45n41
Berlin Wall, 157–58n4
Betancourt, Ernesto, 11
Big Five (social club), 34
Black Legend, 154n11
blanqueamiento, 101–2, 104
Blaya, Joaquín, 35
Blue Ribbon Commission for the Eco-
    nomic Reconstruction of Cuba, 78
Boff, Clodovis, 145–46n44
Bolívar, Simon, 156–57n1
Bolivia, 53
Bonino, José Míguez, 145–46n44
Bonne, Felix, 14
Bosch, Orlando, 45
Botifol, Luis, 149–50n8
Brigade 2506 Veteran Association, 14,
    50–51
Britian, 53, 82, 121, 156–57n1
Bronx, New York. *See* New York City
Brothers to the Rescue, 45–46, 76, 87
Brotons, Elizabeth, 3, 5, 10, 30, 118
Bryant, Anita, 153n7
Buena Vista Social Club (elderly center), 129
Burdines, 149–50n8
Burger King, 78
Buró de Investigaciones (Bureau of Inves-
    tigations), 25
Bush, Columba, 139
Bush, George P., 139
Bush, George W., 74–76, 135–36, 139,
    159n18
Bush, Jeb, 134, 139
Bush Sr., George, 46, 139

Caballero, José Augustín, 108–9
Cabello, Mario, 50
California, 31, 151n16
Calle Ocho (Eighth Street), 7, 56
Calzón, Frank, 10
Camarioca boat lift, 34
Canaanites, 152n29
Canada, 138
Canary Islands. *See* Spain
Caney (restaurant), 31
Cánovas del Castillo, Antonio, 100
Canton. *See* China
capitalism, 13, 19, 36, 41–42, 58–62, 81,
    113–17, 120, 123–26, 143n33
Cardenas, Cuba, 3
Caribbean, 3, 16, 60, 62, 66, 70, 73, 91,
    99–100, 106, 110–11, 120–21, 143n35

Caridad del Cobre, 5, 29, 118. *See also* Vir-
    gin Mary
Carolle, Joe, 30, 139
Carreta, La (restaurant), 31
Carter, Jimmy, 14, 143n32
Carthaginian, 144–45n41
Casa de la Contratación (Contracting
    House), 154n14
Casal, Lourdes, 92, 110
casinos, 40, 56
Castilla. *See* Spain
Castillo, Angel, 149–50n8
Castro, Fidel: blame for Cuban exile, xv,
    39, 70; and dissidents, xv, 11, 14–15,
    74–75, 77, 87–88, 93, 142n31, 143n32;
    and Elián González, 7, 9; and Exilic
    Cubans, xv–xvi, 3, 9, 29, 34–35, 39,
    43–45, 70, 75, 77, 114, 126, 129–34,
    136–37, 139; as evil, xv–xvii, 3, 7–9,
    28–30, 42, 66, 129–30, 139; *la lucha*
    against, 9, 30–32, 42–45, 72, 77, 94;
    personal life, 8–9, 130, 136; post-
    Castro, 13, 55, 71–73, 77–80, 90, 110,
    114, 117, 130–31, 136–37, 139, 150–51n10;
    regime, xv, 7, 9, 27–29, 31, 40, 53, 58,
    62, 80, 90–91, 95, 112, 134, 143n33,
    145–46n44. *See also* Cuban Revolu-
    tion of 1959; July 26 Movement
Castro, Fidelito, 8–9
Castro, Max, 130
Castro, Raul, 136
Catalonia. *See* Spain
Catholic, 4–7, 11, 14, 17, 27–29, 85, 120,
    152–53n1, 154n11
caudillismo, 90–91
Celts, 144–45n41
Center for a Free Cuba, 10
Centinela de la Libertad (tabloid), 148n21.
    See also *periodiquitos*
Central America. *See* Latin America
Central Intelligence Agency (CIA), 39–42,
    44, 50, 75, 147n8, 149n5, 159n18
Chabebe, Father José, 28
Chelala, Father, 28
Chesapeake Bay, 120
Chicago, Illinois, 40
Chile, 41
China, 17, 75, 90, 97, 111–13, 144n40,
    144–45n41, 155nn19,22. *See also* Asia
Chirino, Willy, 10
Christianity, xvii, 1–6, 15–18, 29. See also
    ajiaco Christianity; diaspora theology;

ST OLAF COLLEGE BOOKSTORE

56 CASH-1   4105 0901 105

978052023852 NEW
DELATOR/LA LUCHA F   MDS IN   26.65
                 TOTAL   26.65

APPROVAL: 904540 SEQ NUM: 5662
TICKET# 111190000132
ACCOUNT NUMBER XXXXXXXXXXXX8290 XX/XX
    Visa/MasterCard   26.65

KEEP RECEIPT FOR RETURNS

                    4/29/11 9:00 AM

Hispanic theology; liberation theology; *mulato* Christianity; *mujerista* theology; revolution theology; *sancocho* Christianity
Christmas, 28
CIA. *See* Central Intelligence Agency
cigars. *See* tobacco
Citibank, 78
Civil Rights Movement, 13, 37, 60
Clarín, El (tabloid) 148n21. See also *periodiquitos*
classism, xvii–xviii, 15, 18, 64, 81, 84, 88–89, 104, 113–18, 152–53n1
Clay, Henry, 156–57n1
Clifford, James, 32
Clinton, Bill, 45, 56, 73, 77
Club Amnesia, 49
Coca-Cola, 35
Cocoplum, Florida, 124
Codina, Armando, 134
Cold War, 31, 37, 62, 66, 72
Colombia, 15, 27, 44
Columbus, Christopher, 96, 99, 103, 153n8
Columbus, Diego, 99
Comando Cero, 43–44
comité de los 75 (the committee of the 75), 48–49. See also *diálogo*
Commandos F-4, 42
communism. *See* Marxism
Conciencia, La (tabloid), 148n21. See also *periodiquitos*
Concilio Cubano (Cuban Assembly), 142n31
conquistadors, 90, 95, 98–99
Consejo Revolucionario Cubano (Cuban Revolutionary Council), 39
Constituent Assembly, 108
Continental Bank, 49–50
Contrapunteo cubano del tabaco y el azúcar (book), 103–4
coolies. *See* China
Coral Gables, Florida, 124
Cortés, Hernán, 62
Coser y cantar (theatrical play), 49
cosmic race, 17, 106, 144n39
Costa Rica, 150n9
Council of Indies, 98
Council of Trent, 95
criollo, 104, 116
Crónica, La (tabloid), 49. See also *periodiquitos*
Cruz, Celia, 68

Cruz, Humberto, 11
"Cuando salí de Cuba" (song), 68
Cuba: of African descent, 8, 16–17, 32, 64–65, 86–87, 89–90, 94, 97, 99–111, 113, 115, 144n40, 144–45n41, 152–53n1, 154nn13,17, 155n18, 155–56n24; Castro regime, xv, 7, 9, 22, 27–29, 31, 40, 53, 58, 62, 80, 90, 112, 134, 143n33, 145–46n44; definition of, 26, 67, 141n1; economics, 63–64, 113–17, 120–23, 135, 157–58n4; elite, 33–34, 38–39, 52, 69, 82, 85–88, 99–100, 103, 105, 113–17, 123, 131, 153n3, 156–57n1, 157–58n4; history of, xvii, 10, 14, 22, 26, 57, 59, 69, 71, 79, 81–82, 85, 90, 92, 95–96, 99–105, 113, 115–17, 119–23, 128; immigrants, 16–17, 95, 101, 111, 120, 143n35; National Assembly, 143n32; *patria,* 15, 22, 83, 91, 95, 148n21, 152–53n1, 153n6, 154n17; post-Castro, 13, 55, 71–73, 77–80, 90, 110, 114, 117, 130–31, 136–37, 139, 150–51n10; prisons, xv, 14, 74, 159n18; promised land, 9, 22, 30, 66, 71; relationship with China, 112, 155n22; relationship with Spain, 30, 82–84, 88–90, 92, 100–101, 107, 144n36, 153n4, 154n16; relationship with the Soviet Union, 82, 148–49n4; relationship with the United States, xviii, 11, 13, 17, 28, 30, 33, 52–53, 58–59, 62, 69, 71, 74–77, 81–83, 90, 92, 113–14, 119–23, 135–36, 145–46n44, 146–47n6, 148–49n4, 152–53n1, 156–57n1, 157n3, 157–58n4, 159n18; two Cubas, 13, 72–73. See also Castro, Fidel; *Cuba de ayer;* Cuban embargo; Cuban Revolution of 1959; Cuban Wars for Independence; *diálogo;* Habana, Cuba; Resident Cubans; slavery; sugar; tobacco
Cuba de ayer, 31–32, 67, 71, 73, 114, 125
Cuban Academy of Science, 144–45n41
Cuban American National Foundation (CANF), 5–6, 20, 30, 44–45, 65, 72–79, 133, 135–36 147n17, 148–49n4, 149–50n8
Cuban Americans. *See* Exilic Cubans
Cuban Commission on Human Rights, 14
Cuban Communist Party, 29. *See also* Marxism
Cuban embargo, 13, 73–75, 77, 81, 120, 135, 149–50n8, 157–58n4, 159n18
cubanidad, 30, 84, 16, 143n34, 144n36

Cuban Interest Section, 75
Cuban Liberty Council, 136
Cuban missile crisis, 33–34, 40
Cuban Museum of Art and Culture, 14
Cuban Refugee Program, 37
Cuban Research Institute, 70
Cuban Revolution of 1959, 13, 27–28, 35, 53, 58, 64, 69, 75, 80–81, 90, 92, 94, 105, 123, 152n26, 157–58n4
Cuban Solidarity Act, 76
Cuban State Secret Police, 153n6
Cuban Wars for Independence, 30, 52, 83, 88–90, 92, 100, 102–4, 106–7, 120–21, 144n36, 153n4, 154n17, 157n2
Cuik, Henry, 132
Cutie, Alberto, 131

Dade County AFL-CIO, 19
Dade County public schools, 19, 130
Dade County Republican Party. See Republicans
Dallas, Texas, 45
David (King), 152n29
de Cuneo, Miguel, 96
de las Casas, Bartolomé, 99, 154n11
De La Torre, Miguel A., xv–xvi, 19, 24–25, 67–68
de la Torre, Mirta Mulhare, 92
de la Torriente, José, 14
de León, Cieza, 153–54n10
de Lugo, Father Ismael, 29
Democrats, 41, 135, 145n42
dependency theory, 124–25
diálogo (dialogue), 13, 43, 48–50
Diario-La Prensa (newspaper), 43
diaspora theology, 22
Diaz, Manny, 139
Díaz, Miguel H., 145n43
Diaz-Balart, Lincoln, 9, 72–74
Diaz-Balart de Núñez, Mirta, 8–9
Didion, Joan, 51
Divini Redemptoris (encyclical), 27
Dominican order, 98
Dominican Republic, 44–45, 100
Donestevez, Ramón, 13
Dos Ríos, Cuba, 144n36
Dozy, Reinhart, 144n38
Dresden. See Germany
Durkheim, Emile, 21

Easter. See Holy Week
Eastern Airlines, 149–50n8

Echevarría, José Antonio, 28
Edom, 54
Egypt, 77
Eig, Spencer, 10
Eisenhower, Dwight, 74
Elegguá, 8. See also Santería
Elijah (prophet), 10
England. See Britian
Enlightenment, the, 146n45
Enterprise Florida, 131
Entralgo, José Elías, 106
Esperanza (yacht), 45
Espín, Orlando O., 145n43
Espinosa, Juan Carlos, 133
Espinosa, Manuel, 31
Estéfan, Gloria, 10, 35
Ethiopia, 74
Euroamerican. See United States
Europe, 17, 36, 39, 66, 113, 120–21, 138, 144n40, 157–58n4
Evangelical Church, 31
Exilic Cubans: capitalists, 13, 19, 36, 41–42, 58–62, 114, 124–27, 131, 143n33; cause of exile, xv, xvii, 29, 53, 58, 62–64, 70, 126–27; and CIA, 39–42; contrasts with other Hispanics, xviii, 17–18, 32, 35–36, 57–58, 86–87, 124–32, 137–38, 145n42; contrasts with Resident Cubans, xv–xvii, 7, 30, 53, 57–58, 62–63, 70, 72–76, 79–81, 95, 97, 110, 114, 126, 133, 145–46n44, 152–53n1; definition of, 136–37, 141n1; discrimination against, 18, 34; economic enclave, 25, 35, 38–39, 70, 86–87, 124–29, 149–50n8; economic statistics about, 18–19, 35, 64, 128; el exilio, xvi, 15, 17, 20–22, 24–25, 33–35, 37, 48–49, 51, 54, 56–70, 75, 81, 117, 123, 125, 129–30, 135, 139, 147nn7,9; ethnic identity, xvii, 15, 31–32, 36–37, 39, 54–66, 69–71, 81, 92, 128, 135–37, 150n9; and Fidel Castro, xv–xvi, 3, 9, 29, 34–35, 39, 43–45, 70, 75, 77, 114, 126, 129–34, 136–37, 139; gusano, 13, 35, 66, 92, 113–14; martyrs, 5, 30, 41, 45–46, 50–51; paramilitary, 14, 43–44; persecutions of dissenters, 13–14, 31, 43–44, 47–51, 77, 91; power and privilege, xvi, xvii, 1–2, 18–20, 25, 33–43, 51, 55, 57–63, 70, 80, 86–87, 91, 93, 124–27, 129, 131, 138–39, 149–50n8; pro-Castro, 13, 139; protest for Elián González, xvi–xviii, 1–13, 20–21,

24–27, 29–30, 54–55, 73, 117–19, 127, 129–35, 139; represented in Elián González, 10–11; Republicans, 19, 30, 145n42; scholars, 15, 17–20, 86, 123–24; structures of oppression, xvi–xviii, 31, 42–43, 51, 55–59, 61, 69, 80–117, 127–28, 131; and the United States, xvi–xvii, 2, 13, 18–19, 33–35, 53–55, 59, 61–62, 65–66, 68, 70–71, 78, 80, 92–93, 97, 124–28, 130, 135–37, 150–51n10, 152–53n1, 159n18. See also *diálogo; lucha, la;* machismo; Postexilic Cubans
Exodus (biblical book), 53
Ezekiel (prophet), 68–69
Ezra (prophet), 79–80, 152n29

Facts about Cuban Exiles (FACE), 19
Fanon, Frantz, 83, 93, 106, 110
Federal Bureau of Investigation (FBI), 14, 41, 44
Federal Communications Commission, 49
Feijoo, Samuel, 91
Felipe, Isaura, 129
Fernández, María Ester, 5
Fernández de Oviedo, Gonzalo, 97, 153–54n10
Ferre, Maurice, 64
First Annual Festival of Hispanic Theater, 49
Florida, 9, 12, 31, 33–34, 119, 151n16
Florida Democratic Party. See Democrats
Florida International University, 10, 19, 39, 70, 134
Florida Keys, 3
Florida Legislature, 25, 131, 145n42
Florida Marlins, 150n9
Forbes Jr., Malcom, 78
Fort Lauderdale, Florida, 1
Foucault, Michel, 46–47
Fox Family Channel, 10
France, 102, 144–45n41, 156–57n1; French Revolution, 23
Franco, Francisco, 27, 29, 41
Franqui, Carlos, 94, 155n22
Frente de Liberación Nacional (National Liberation Front), 43
Freud, Sigmund, 21
Frómeta, Rodolfo, 42
Fuentes, Carlos, 94

Galicia. See Spain
Garcia, Andy, 10

García, Calixto, 100
Garcia, Joe, 72
Garcia, María Cristina, 148n21
García-Rivera, Alexandro, 145n43
Garcia-Rodríguez, Félix, 43
Gaul. See France
General Cigar, 78
Generation Ñ, 71, 137–39, 151n14
Generation X, 137, 151n14
Germany, 10, 108
Giacana, Sam, 40
Glenn, John, 40
Gobierno Cubano Secreto (Secret Cuban Government), 43
Goizueta, Roberto, Sr., 35
Goizueta, Roberto S., 145n43
Gomez, Manolo, 153n7
Gómez Manzano, René, 14
González, Delfin, 118
González, Elián: and Catholic Church, 4–6; custody battle, xvi–xviii, 1–13, 20–21, 24–27, 29–30, 54–55, 73, 117–19, 127, 129–35, 139; as Elijah, 10; and Fidel Castro, 7, 9; as Jesus Christ, 1, 4–7, 10, 29–30; Miami home, 1–2, 9, 11, 118–19, 129; as miracle child, 1, 4, 7, 9, 118; as Moses, 9–10; prayer vigil for, 1, 4–5, 7, 11–12, 129, 131; protected by Virgin Mary, 5; representative of Exilic Cubans, 10–11; rescue at sea, 1, 3–4; and Santería, 8; as symbol, 3–5, 7, 10
González, Juan Miguel, 3, 7, 10
González, Justo L., 145n43
González, Lazaro, 3, 7, 9
González, Virgilio, 41
Graham, Bob, 78
Granma (yacht), 27
Gravina (ship), 111
Greater Miami Board of Realtors, 19
Greeks, 144–45n41
Gregorio, Gil, 99
Grenier, Guillermo, 39
Grillo Sáez, David, 116
guajiros (or *monteros*), 32, 116
Gualberto Gómez, Juan, 108
Guantánamo Bay Naval Base, 40, 77, 157n3
Guatemala, 44
Guevara, Che, 4, 43
Gulf of Benin, 115
Gusano, El (tabloid), 148n21. See also *perio- diquitos*
Gutiérrez, Gustavo, 145–46n44, 146n45

Gutierrez, Orlando, 46
Gutiérrez Menoyo, Eloy, 74
Gypsies, 144–45n41

Habana, Cuba, xv, 7, 9, 31, 34, 38–40, 44,
    49, 55, 64, 66–67, 75, 80, 92, 105,
    110–12, 114, 116–17, 120, 123, 146–47n6
habitus, 36–37, 70
Haiti, 64, 100, 131, 144–45n41, 149n6
Havana, Cuba. See Habana, Cuba
Havana Dock Company, 52
Hawaii, 151n16
Hebrews. See Judaism
Helms, Jesse, 73, 76–78
Helms-Burton Act, 78
Hernandez, Alberto, 150n9
Hernandez, Esteban, 27
Hernandez, Francisco "Pepe," 45, 135
Hernandez, Livan, 150n9
Hernandez, Orlando "El Duque," 150n9
Herod, 7–8
heterosexism, xviii, 49, 58, 64, 84, 87,
    91–95, 97–99, 109, 112–13, 153nn6,7
Hevia, Carlos, 151n12
Hialeah, Florida, 13, 31, 124
Hialeah Gardens, Florida, 5
Hispanic Association for Cultural Enrich-
    ment at Rice (HACER), 139
Hispanic Business Magazine, 35
Hispanic religious scholars, xvii, 16–17, 20,
    30, 86, 123–24
Hispanics, xvi, xvii, 18, 39, 53; contrasts with
    Exilic Cubans, xviii, 17–18, 32, 35–36,
    57–58, 86–87, 124–32, 137–38, 145n42
Hispanic theology, 20, 124, 127
Historia general y natural de las Indias
    (book), 97
Holguín, Cuba, 28
Holocaust, 132
Holy Week, 10–11, 119
homosexuality. See heterosexism
Honduras, 44
Hong Kong. See China
honor/shame, 85–86, 99
Hunt, E. Howard, 41
Hyatt Hotels Corporation, 78

Iberian Peninsula. See Spain
Ibo, 155n18
Immaculate Conception Church, 5
Immigration and Naturalization Service
    (INS), 2, 3

Institute of Cuba and Cuban-American
    Studies (ICCAS), 129
Iriondo, Silvia, 11
Isabella, Queen, 153n4
Isaiah (biblical book), 79–80, 152n29
Isasi-Díaz, Ada Maria, 145n43
Islam, 10, 17, 143n34, 144n40
Island of Margarita, Venezuela, 45
Israel. See Judaism
Italy, 44
Izuierdo Jr., Emilio, 133

Jamaica, 144–45n41
Jamestown, Virginia, 119
Jefferson, Thomas, 120, 156–57n1
Jehoiachin (King), 70
Jehovah's Witnesses, 153n6
Jenks, Leland, 120
Jeremiah (prophet), 70–71
Jerusalem, 11, 54, 68–69, 70–71, 151n11
Jerusalem Talmud, 10
Jesus Christ, 4–6, 10–11, 13, 28–31, 119
Jews. See Judaism
Jim Crow, 64, 108
JM/WAVE, 40–41
John-Paul II, Pope, 73
Johnson, Lyndon B., 59
Jones, Donald Wheeler, 59
Jóven Cuba (Young Cuba), 43
Judaism, 9–11, 17, 54, 67–71, 76–80, 143n34,
    144–45n41, 151n11, 152n29
Judd, Walter H., 37
July 26 Movement, 28, 146n1. See also
    Cuban Revolution of 1959
Junta de Población Blanca (White Popula-
    tion Board), 101

Kendall, Florida, 124
Kennedy, John F., 45, 74
Kennedy, Robert (Bobby), 40
Kennedy Airport, 43
Kennedy-Khrushchev accord, 148–49n4
Kings (biblical book), 70
Kirkpatrick, Jeane, 78
Klemm, Gustav, 108
Knight-Ridder. See *Miami Herald*
Ku Klux Klan Kubano, 96–97, 153n9
Kunz, Egon F., 72

Laffer, Arthur, 78
Langley, Virginia, 40
Las Vegas, Nevada, 56

Latin America, 16, 18, 20, 27, 33, 38–40, 45, 53, 57, 70, 80, 84, 90–91, 105, 121, 125–26, 144nn37,39, 144–45n41, 145–46n44, 146n45, 153n3, 156–57n1, 157–58n4
Latin Grammy Awards, 133–34
Latino/as. *See* Hispanics
Latino/a theology. *See* Hispanic theology
Letelier, Orlando, 41
Levites, 150–51n10. *See also* Judaism
liberation theology, xv, xvii, 20, 22–24, 27, 29, 53, 124, 127, 146n45
Libertad, Milena, 12
Liberty City, Florida, 60, 126
Lieberman, Joseph, 76
Liga, La (political club), 101
Lili (hurricane), 14
Lincoln Center, 43
Little Havana, Florida, 5, 7, 30, 124, 129
Llama, Jose Antonio, 45
Lodge, Henry Cabot, 121
López, Narciso, 156–57n1
Los Angeles, California, 124, 133
Los Van Van (music group), 133–34
Louisiana, 151n16
Louisville, Kentucky, 25
lucha, la, xvi–xviii, 9, 30–32, 35, 39, 42–43, 47–51, 55, 58–59, 69, 72–77, 81, 83–84, 95–96, 99, 110, 113–14, 117–19, 123, 128–30, 132–36, 137, 139, 147n7, 150n9, 158n12
Lyotard, Jean-François, 146n45

Maceo, Antonio, 88–89, 107–8
Maceo, Mariana Grajales, 88–89, 108
Machado, Gerardo, 30, 151n12
machismo, xviii, 58–59, 62, 83–117, 118–19, 155n18
Mack, Connie, 78
Madison, James, 156–57n1
Madrid, 9. *See also* Spain
Madrigal, Father, 28
Mafia, 40
mambises/as, 89, 104, 154n16
Mandela, Nelson, 131
Manifest Destiny, 120–21
Manifesto (Martí), 102
Manzanillo, Cuba, 28
Manzano, Juan Francisco, 155–56n24
Mariel boat lift, 36, 39, 57–60, 63–65, 93, 95, 124–26, 147n9, 149–50n8
Martell, Lazarito, 13

Martí, José, vii, xv, 12, 16, 22, 30, 72–73, 81, 83, 89, 101–4, 107–8, 115, 121–22, 144n36, 152–53n1
Martínez, Eugenio, 41
Martínez Campos, Arsenio, 88
Marxism, 20–21, 23, 27–29, 35, 37, 42, 53, 61–62, 66, 69, 71, 91, 95, 123, 132, 134, 149–50n8, 150n9, 157–58n4
Mas Canosa, Jorge, 44–45, 77, 90–91, 95
Mas Canosa family, 35
Mas Santos, Jorge, 5, 133
Masvidal, Raúl, 147n16
Matanzas, Cuba, 156n25
Matino (island), 153n8
Maya, 90
McDuffie, Arthur, 60–61
McGovern, George, 41
McKinley, William, 156–57n1
Medellín, Colombia, 27
Mercury orbit, 40
mestizaje, 16, 87, 106–7
mestizo Christianity, 16. *See also* Hispanic theology
Mexican American, 18, 35–36
Mexico, 9, 16, 18, 27, 43, 53, 62, 94, 98, 120–21, 128, 139, 144n39, 144–45n41, 156–57n1
Miami, Florida, xvi–xvii, 7, 11, 14, 18, 20–22, 25, 29–30, 34–39, 44–48, 56–60, 64, 69, 71–72, 75–76, 90–91, 114, 116–17, 124, 126–27, 130–36, 137, 139, 141n1, 148n21, 149–50n8, 153n7, 159n18. *See also* Calle Ocho; Little Havana
Miami, Port of, 45, 132
Miami Arena, 133–34
Miami Beach, Florida, 49, 60, 131, 151n12
Miami Chamber of Commerce, 19
Miami City Commission, 45, 131, 135
Miami Cubans. *See* Exilic Cubans; Post-exilic Cubans
Miami Dade Community College, 11
Miami Dolphins, 149–50n8
Miami Herald, 4, 19, 65, 133, 149–50n8
Miami River, 55
Middle Passage, 111, 144n40, 155n20
Midrash, 4
Milián, Emilio, 14
Military Units for Assistance to Production (UMAP), 133, 153n6
Miyares, Gustavo, 5
Moab, 152n29

modernismo, 144n36
Monroe, James, 120
Montejo, Esteban, 101, 109
monteros, 116. See also *guajiros*
Moors, 154n12
Moreno, Darío, 134
Morris, Charles, 120
Morúa Delgado, Martín, 105, 108
Moses, 9–10
Mothers Against Repression, 11
Mother's Day, 5
Movimiento de Orientación e Integración
    Nacional (Movement of National
    Orientation and Integration), 106
mujerista theology, 30
mulato (biracial), 16–17, 64, 99–100, 102–3,
    106, 109–10, 115, 144n38, 154n13
mulato Christianity, 16. *See also* Hispanic
    theology
Mundo, El (newspaper), 91
Muñíz Varela, Carlos, 13, 43–44, 49
Museum of the Ministry of the Interior,
    40
Myrdal, Gunnar, 109

Napoleon Bonaparte, 156–57n1;
    Napoleonic Code, 153n3
National Association for the Advancement
    of Colored People (NAACP), 59
National Council of Evangelical Churches,
    28
Nebuchadnezzar, 151n11. *See also* Babylo-
    nian captivity
Negrín, Luciano, 13, 49
Nehemiah (prophet), 70–71, 151n13
New Jersey, 31
New Orleans, Louisiana, 72, 156–57n1
New York City, xv, 20, 25, 31, 64, 72, 101,
    158n12
New York Times, 44, 147n17
New York Yankees, 150n9
Nicaragua, 44, 125, 149–50n8
Nicaro (mining company), 52
Niño, El (drought), 74
nongroup, 149–50n8
Noriega, Manuel, 72
North Korea, 74–75
Nuevo Herald, 4
Núñez de Valboa, Vasco, 99

Oboler, Suzanne, 36
Ochún, 1. *See also* Santería

O'Laughlin, Jeanne, 7
Omega Siete (Omega Seven), 43
Operation Bingo, 40
Operation Dirty Tricks, 40
Operation Free Ride, 40
Operation Good Times, 40
Operation Mongoose, 40
Operation True Blue, 40
Oriente, Cuba, 100, 105
orisha, 8. *See also* Santería
Ortega, Daniel, 72
Ortiz, Fernando, 16, 103–4, 108–9, 112,
    143n35, 144nn36,38, 144–45n41, 153n5
Ortiz, Tomás, 98
Ostend Manifesto, 156–57n1
Oswald, Lee Harvey, 45
Our Cuban Colony (book), 120
Our Island Empire (book), 120
Our Lady of Charity Shrine, 3, 5–6, 12–13

Pacino, Al, 65
Pacto de Zanjón (Treaty of Zanjón), 88
Padrón, Orlando, 49
Pagden, Anthony, 153–54n10
Pais, Frank and Josué, 27
Palma, Estrada, 154n17, 157n2
Panama, 44, 72
panopticon, 42, 46–47, 49, 51, 57, 74
Park Avenue (New York), 124
Partido Independiente de Color (Indepen-
    dent Party of Color), 104
Passover, 70. *See also* Judaism
Patio, El (restaurant), 31
patria. See under Cuba
patria potestad, 84–85, 153n3
Paz, Octavio, 94
Pedraja, Luis G., 145n43
Pedro Pan (Peter Pan) flights, 11
Pelaez, Concepción, 12
Peñalver, Rafael, 71
Penelas, Alex, 130
peninsulares, 116
Pennsylvania, 158n12
Pentateuchal, 152n29
Pérez, Lisandro, 71, 138
Pérez Castellón, Ninoska, 136
Pérez-Franco, Juan, 51
Pérez Serantes, Archbishop, 28–29
periodiquitos (tabloids), 48–49, 51, 91,
    148n21
Persia, 77, 79
Peru, 155n21

Peruyero, José, 14
Philippines, 144–45n41
Phoenicians, 144–45n41
Pierce, Franklin, 156–57n1
Pinochet, Augusto, 41
Platt Amendment, 92, 122–23, 157n3
Playa Girón, 29, 41, 50–51, 58, 62, 147n8;
    memorial, 5, 30
Plymouth Rock, Massachusetts, 119
Poland, 45
Polk, James, 156–57n1
Ponce de Leon, Juan, 119
Portes, Alejandro, 130, 138
Portugal, 144–45n41
Posada Carriles, Luis, 44–45, 147n17
positivism, 144n39
postcolonialism, 22–23
Postexilic Cubans, xviii, 55, 136–39
postmodernism, 22–23, 31, 146n45
Prida, Dolores, 49
Prío, Carlos, 151n12
Pritzker, Jay, 78
prostitution. *See* sexism
Protestants, 7, 10–11, 27–29, 154n11
Psalm 137, xvii, 54–55, 70–71
Puerto Rico, 13, 18, 20, 31, 35–36, 43, 128

Quitman, John A., 156–57n1

Rabbinical Association of Greater Miami,
    10
race riots and wars, 60–61, 100, 105, 110,
    116, 148n2, 156n25
racism, xvii–xviii, 15, 17–18, 25, 35, 61,
    64–65, 81, 84, 86, 88–89, 94–118,
    143n35, 144n39, 152–53n1, 153n6,
    157–58n4
Radio Mambí, 154n16
Radio Martí, 11
Radio Rebelde, 94
Radio Swan, 41
rafters. See *balseros*
raza negra, La (book), 103
Reagan, Ronald, 43–45, 77–78, 94, 139
Reciprocity Treaty, 52
Regalado, Tomás, 135–36
Registry of Expropriated Properties in
    Cuba, 78
Remirez de Estenoz, Fernando, 75
Reno, Janet, 29, 66, 150n9
Republicans, 19, 30, 118, 135, 145n42,
    147n16
Republic National Bank, 149–50n8
Resident Cubans, 3, 13, 31, 22, 57–58, 91, 97,
    113–14, 135, 141n1, 145–46n44, 151n16;
    contrast with Exilic Cubans, xv–xvii,
    7, 30, 53, 57–58, 62–63, 70, 72–76,
    79–81, 95, 97, 110, 114, 126, 133,
    145–46n44, 152–53n1; dissidents,
    14–15, 75–76, 159n18
Revolución (newspaper), 94
revolution theology, 145–46n44
Rice University, 139
Rieff, David, 22
Río Cristal (restaurant), 31
Risech, Flavio, 92
Riviera Hotel, 114
Roa Kouri, Raúl, 43
Roca, Blas, 14
Roca, Vladimiro, 14, 159n18
Rodriguez, Ana, 5
Rodriguez, Maria, 4
Roman, Agustin, 8
Roman Empire, 70, 102, 144–45n41
Romero, Juan Carlos, 150n9
Rondon, Mirta, 10
Roosevelt, Theodore, 121
Roper Organization, 65
Roque, Marta Beatriz, 14
Ros-Lehtinen, Ileana, 74, 131
Rousseau, Jean-Jacques, 23
Royal Caribbean Cruise Line, 78
Ruiz, Sonia, 129
Ruiz Suárez, Bernardo, 105
Rumbaut, Rubén, 68, 130, 138
Russia. *See* Soviet Union
Ruth (biblical book), 152n29

sagüesera, 56. *See also* Miami, Florida
Saigon. *See* Asia
Salabarria, Manuel, 7
Salman, Carlos, 147n16
Sánchez, Elizardo, 14, 159n18
Sánchez, Roberto, 9
Sánchez, Tomas, 14
sancocho Christianity, 144n37
Sandinista, 72, 149–50n8. *See also*
    Nicaragua
Sandoval, Arturo, 10
San Francisco Bay, 120
Sanguily, Manuel, 106–7
San Juan, Puerto Rico, 43
Santana, Father Francisco, 3–4, 6, 9, 13
Santería, 1, 7–8, 10, 143n34

Santiago, Cuba, 27, 120, 146n1
Santo Domingo. *See* Dominican Republic
Sardiñas, Father Guillermo, 28
Satan, xv, 29–30, 42, 66, 103, 129
Scarface (movie), 65
Schiff, Rabbi Solomon, 10
Seattle, Washington, 3
Segovia, Fernando, 145n43
Sepúlveda, Ginés de, 98
Serra, Rafael, 101
Seville. *See* Spain
sexism, xvii–xviii, 15, 18, 81, 84–97, 98, 109,
    113–14, 117–18, 153nn2,6
slavery, 89–90, 99–102, 106–7, 109, 112,
    115–17, 144n40, 154n12, 155–56n24
social power structures, xv–xviii, 1–2, 18,
    31, 42–43, 46–47, 51, 55–59, 60, 69,
    80–117, 123, 127–28, 131, 152–53n1
sodomy. *See* heterosexism
solá (barrio), 124–26
Soler, Juan Masimi, 45
South America. *See* Latin America
Southern Air Transport, 41
Soviet Union, 9–10, 27–28, 40, 43, 62, 66,
    82, 114, 123, 148n21, 148–49n4, 152n26,
    157–58n4
Spain, 16, 30, 82–84, 88–90, 92, 95, 98–101,
    104, 107–8, 111, 113, 116, 120–21,
    143n35, 144nn36,40, 144–45n41,
    153nn3,4,8, 154nn12,14,16, 156–57n1
Spanish American League against Discrim-
    ination (SALAD), 19
Spanish American War. *See* Cuban Wars
    for Independence
Spanish Civil Code, 153n3
Spanish Civil War, 27, 29
Spanish Council at Amoy, 111–12
Spanish Harlem, 124
Stalinism, 23
St. Augustine, Florida, 120
St. Juan Bosco Church, 12
St. Louis (cruise ship), 10
St. Patrick's Church, 131
Straits of Florida. *See* Caribbean
Strong, Josiah, 121
St. Thomas University's Center for Cuban
    Studies, 133
Suárez, Diego, 133–34
Suárez de Peralta, Juan, 98
Suchlicki, Jaime, 129
Sudan, 74
sugar, 52–53, 63, 100–104, 107, 112, 115,

122–23, 144n40, 144–45n41, 151n16,
    155–56n24, 157–58n4
Swatow. *See* China
Szapocznik, José M., 65

Taíno. *See* Amerindians
Tallahassee, Florida, 145n42
Talmud, 10
Tampa, Florida, 72
Taylor, Zachary, 156–57n1
Telemundo (TV network), 35
Temple, 68, 70, 150–51n10. *See also*
    Judaism
Ten Years' War. *See* Cuban Wars for In-
    dependence
terrorism, 13–14
Texas, 120, 151n16, 156–57n1
Thanksgiving Day, 1, 3, 5
Thomas, Hugh, 113
Three Kings Day Parade, 4
tobacco, 53, 63, 103, 153n5
Torricelli bill, 149–50n8
TotalBank, 5
tourism, 114, 157–58n4
Trans World Airlines (TWA), 43
Trinidad, 111

UMAP. *See* Military Units for Assistance
    to Production
Unidos en Casa Elián (United in Elián
    House), 118
Union City, New Jersey, 13, 64
United Nations, 43, 78, 80
United Nations World Food Program, 74
United Press International, 43
United States, 8, 10, 74, 89, 113, 120–23,
    143n35; and Exilic Cubans, xvi–xvii,
    1–2, 13, 18–19, 33–35, 53–55, 59, 61–62,
    65–66, 68, 70–71, 78, 80, 92–93, 97,
    124–28, 130, 135–37, 150–51n10,
    152–53n1, 159n18; relationship with
    Cuba xviii, 11, 13, 17, 28, 30, 33, 52–53,
    58–59, 62, 69, 71, 74–77, 81–83, 90, 92,
    113–14, 119–23, 135–36, 145–46n44,
    146–47n6, 148–49n4, 152–53n1,
    156–57n1, 157n3, 157–58n4, 159n18; rela-
    tionship with Latin America, 144n39,
    145–46n44
University of Miami, 40, 129–30
University of Miami's Research Institute
    for Cuban Studies, 78
U.S. Census Bureau, 18, 128

U.S. Coast Guard, 45
U.S. Congress, 9, 72–74, 130
U.S. Department of Commerce, 33
U.S. Department of Justice, 41, 45
U.S. House Select Committee on Assassi-
    nations, 45
U.S. Navy, 157n3
U.S. Neutrality Act, 41, 45
U.S. Senate Foreign Relations Committee,
    76
U.S. Senate Select Committee to Study
    Government Operations with Re-
    spect to Intelligence Operations, 40
U.S. Small Business Administration, 38
U.S. State Department, 69, 74

Vanidades (magazine), 153n7
Varadero Beach, Cuba, 34
Varela Project, 32
Vasconcelos, José, 17, 144n39
Vatican II, 27, 29
Veblen, Thorstein, 113
Venezuela, 43, 45
Vento, Charles, 10
Verdes, Ramon, 132
Verra, Lisset, 12
Versailles (restaurant), 56
Vietnam, 75, 144–45n41

Virgen de Guadalupe, 5, 20. *See also* Virgin
    Mary
Virgen de la Caridad (Virgin of Charity).
    See Caridad del Cobre
Virgin Mary, 1, 5, 7
Visigoths, 144–45n41

Waldrop and Company, 111
Washington, D.C., 10–11, 41, 61, 73, 75, 90,
    158n12, 159n18
Watergate, 41
West, Alan, 26
Whipple, Henry Benjamin, 121
Wieland, William, 69
Wood, Leonard, 52, 122
Woodland Park Cemetery, 151n12
World Trade Organization, 3

Yoruba. *See* Africa
Young Upwardly Mobile Cuban Ameri-
    cans (YUCA), 71, 151n14
Yucatán Peninsula. *See* Mexico

Zadokite priestly party, 79
Zenith Technology Services. *See*
    JM/WAVE
Zerubbabel, 150–51n10
Zion. *See* Judaism

Compositor:	Binghamton Valley Composition, LLC
Text:	10/13 Galliard
Display:	Galliard
Printer and Binder:	Malloy Lithographing, Inc.